KERALA'S NAXALBARI

Ajitha: Memoirs of a young revolutionary

KERALA'S NAXALBARI

Ajitha: Memoirs of a young revolutionary

Translated by
Sanju Ramachandran

Srishti
PUBLISHERS & DISTRIBUTORS

To the memory of Kunnikkal and Mandakini Narayanan and Comrade Varghese

Srishti Publishers & Distributors
Registered Office: N-16, C.R. Park
New Delhi – 110 019
Corporate Office: 212A, Peacock Lane
Shahpur Jat, New Delhi – 110 049
editorial@srishtipublishers.com

First published by Srishti Publishers & Distributors in 2008

ISBN 9788188575633

Typeset in AGaramond 11pt. by Suresh Kumar Sharma at Srishti

Foreword by the translator

On the night of November 24, 1968, a group of sixty determined to change the world, ran over a police station in the forests of Western Ghats. One of them was a girl, young enough to be a senior secondary student. The group hacked to death a wireless operator, fatally wounded an inspector and then went on to distribute the hoarded wealth of the feudal lords who had made slaves of tribal women and men, trading them in village fairs and binding them in perpetual debt. They were declared murderous dacoits by the media, the young woman's photograph was splashed everywhere as a warning and also to help law-abiding citizens to hand her over to the police. Soon the people for whom they had launched the revolution got hold of a few of them including the woman. Policemen, raining blows on her, forced her to shed her sari and her woolen pullover. In the courtyard of the local police station, on a raised platform where the policemen hoist the national flag and salute it on special occasions, they paraded the teenager in her blouse and trousers, which she was wearing under her sari. They called out to the huge crowd, "This is how she roamed around the forests with her men," thus, pronouncing her a whore. Journalists clicked away in great haste. With policemen all around her laughing, abusing and egging on the crowd to debase them, she stood next to the flagstaff, helpless, trembling, yet undefeated. She glared at the horizon from where her sun failed to rise. Thus was born, the poster woman of Kerala's Naxal movement.

Sacrifice is a tough notion to understand, particularly in the market place, that is life today. One wonders why some leave a normal life, home, relatives and the secure environs of a middle class existence to launch themselves into the unknown to deliver justice to a people with whom their only link is the human form. Perhaps justice, other than that which is prodded by expensive lawyers, has today become even more incomprehensible as an idea. My attempt in translating the memoirs of Ajitha was to make out why a young person from the city would go into the forests to fight people whom she had never seen, for people whom she had never seen. Of course, this was not an accidental 'drama in real life', but the result of a choice made out of ideological convictions, an analysis of forces that shape history and the result of a great deal of thought and planning, however flawed they be. This young person became a revolutionary and took part in an armed revolt when she was just 18. Sure, her father and mother were her senior comrades in the movement that was launched to get the villages to encircle the towns and bring in armed revolution in India. Ideology, no doubt, was the fuel. But what burned was a life. When Ajitha was released in 1977 from jail, she was only 27, but had spent almost nine years in jail, much more than the capital, many of our freedom fighters had accumulated to be pawned for positions of power.

Mandakini and Kunnikkal Narayanan were parents so different that, Ajitha's destiny was probably decided by her genes and the home she grew up than anything else. Narayanan, a Malayali and Mandakini, a Gujarati were comrades who as members of the undivided Communist Party of India, left their well-paying jobs in Mumbai and sought out revolution. Their journey continued from the CPI to CPI (Marxist) to CPI (Marxist-Leninist). Yet, Ajitha was an individual in every right and the choice was hers, because when the family plunged itself into the revolt, she was the only one who proceeded to the forest to attack a Malabar Special Police camp at Pulpally, while her father chose to lead the action in Thalassery town and Mandakini kept herself away from both.

The thunder of spring that struck Naxalbari in June 1967, was soon to echo in the forests of Kerala in November 1968 under the leadership of a man who had everything to lose and probably only others' happiness to gain by doing what he did. Varghese is no doctor like Che Guevara, nor a motorcyclist, definitely not handsome enough to have his mug on T-shirts, but he is the closest Kerala has in terms of the myth of the immortal revolutionary felled by the cruel system. He was the office secretary of the Kannur district office of the Communist Party of India (Marxist), that is, one of the key players in the citadel of the party from where apparatchiks rise to become Marxist chief ministers and party secretaries to manage huge amounts of party wealth and real estate. Had he been 'wiser', he could have been one of them. But he chose to be the *adiyorude peruman*, the headman of the oppressed, as the tribals still call him. He was from a family, which went from the plains to settle down and prosper in the mountain tracts of Wayanad. But instead of the peasant's thirst for land and urge to prosper, Varghese had an indomitable will to have justice for fellow farmers and the most miserable people of Kerala, the tribals. Plays and novels have been written about this man. But Ajitha's memoirs offer us unique glimpses of Varghese as a leader, a comrade and a man full of kindness. The Naxalites of Kerala had always alleged that Varghese was tortured, eyes gouged out and brutally murdered by the Central Reserve Police Force on February 18, 1970 under orders from the State Government. Recently, a former CRPF constable owned up the murder saying that he could not carry the guilt of having killed a great leader any longer. The self-proclaimed murderer wrote recently that Varghese wanted to know exactly when he was to be shot. The constable opened his lips to let out a 'shoo' sound before firing straight into Varghese' heart. "Viplavam jayikkatte" (long live the revolution), the constable recalls Varghese's thunderous shout that rose above the gunshot. Naivete? The question pops up. Why did these people give away so much? For what? The system continues to be what it was. Have they all suffered in vain?

To come back to Ajitha, the girl of eighteen was beaten up, molested and even threatened with rape in custody. She was almost a mental wreck in solitary confinement. Yet, she shunned all offers of freedom, insisting on an unconditional release, wanting to be true to what she believed. And when that finally happened she wrote one of the finest political memoirs in Malayalam in 1979 for a periodical, insisting all throughout that she might have got defeated but not proved wrong. We still have no answers as to why certain people, honest and ordinary people, often middle class, give up everything for others and suffer unspeakable horrors and still remain proud of all that they had endured. Instead, these memoirs details graphically the lives of a few people who did that, a group that included Ajitha, another teenager Sukumaran, who was just a year older to her, and the elderly Kissan Thomman.

The fascinating story of Ajitha is also that of the first wave of Naxalites in Kerala. Curiously, she spends a lot of time explaining the cruelty of society towards women. In fact, the latter chapters are about her life in jail, which reveal the miserable conditions of Indian jails and also the misery in the women's ward. Unconsciously, she was undergoing a transformation. In the preface to the second edition of her book in 1993, Ajitha declared that she was no longer a member of the Naxalbari movement and that she is a confirmed feminist, a Marxian feminist. Even the short 1993 preface had a scathing feminist critique of the Naxalite movement: "Even while in the movement, I used to get upset by the denial of opportunities on the basis of gender. There were occasions when the attitude towards women in the revolutionary movement was condemnable. At one level the 'men comrades' had a protective attitude towards 'women comrades' and at another level instead of being regarded as comrades, women were looked at as sex objects."

Ajitha had changed completely. Her husband, Yakoob also a former-Naxalite is in business, they have a daughter and a son. The poster woman of Kerala's failed and now frayed revolutionary dreams, was fading away from public memory. That was when she shook the conscience of Kerala by exposing sex rackets and how the powerful and the mighty make play things of adolescent girls. "Anweshi", her non governmental organization investigated and brought charges against a minister in the United Democratic Front government P.K. Kunjalikutty of having sex with a minor. The minister had to resign, while fighting Ajitha's charges, some of which went up to the Supreme Court. He was acquitted and exonerated by the courts, but not in the public eye. Ajitha's saga continues; if she is not leading marches brandishing brooms, she could be holding "people's trials" against the rape and murder of a poor tribal girl in Attapady or exposing huge tracts of ganja plantations in the virgin forests of Western Ghats. Some of her old colleagues may allege that she is sold out to apolitical funding agencies. But Ajitha has merely reinvented herself to fight within the system, but fight she does all the time.

My attempt is to render in English and to a wider audience the story of a young revolutionary and that of a young revolution that got nipped in the bud. It has been quite a long wait since the first appearance of the memoirs in a Malayalam periodical in 1979 and in the form of a book in 1982. I sincerely hope that Ajitha's memoirs and her version of the Naxal movement of Kerala would add to the efforts of understanding the Left radical movements in India. I dedicate my efforts to another inspiring woman, Radha R. Nayar, who though abhors violence of the strong and the meek alike, believes in sacrifice, justice and compassion.

January 2008 Sanju Ramachandran

Delhi

To the memory of Kunnikkal and Mandakini Narayanan and Comrade Varghese

Contents

1

THE FIRST STEP

"Ajitha, stand up!" Headmistress Annamma George thundered.

I stood up.

"Didn't you have anything to eat today?" The headmistress arched her brows.

"No, ma'am!"

Her anger flamed up; she gave me a tongue-lashing as the rest of the students looked on helplessly. She didn't spare them either.

"If you want to attend class tomorrow, each one of you should bring me a letter of apology from your parents." With this solemn order she left the classroom which had become almost a court.

About 100-150 girls were paraded as culprits there. Hearing the sentence, they gathered around me crying.

"If our parents come to know they would beat us to death. Ajitha, we did as you told us. Now what should we do?" They smothered me with their queries. Though I didn't know what to do, I got away promising them a solution.

Now, about the events that led to all this: In 1964, the government of Kerala cut down the quantity of ration through the public distribution system to six ounce of rice per person. This decision drew flak from various quarters. The student community too responded strongly. The students of Achuthan Girls' Government High School in Kozhikode actively participated in a protest march organized by the students' wing of the Communist Party. I was the head girl of the school then. The leaders of the Communist Party's Students' Federation had approached me seeking our participation in the strike. My parents, though not active members at that point of time, were sympathizers of the Communist Party all through their lives. It was precisely because of this background that I felt honoured when Student's Federation leaders came to me with the request. Also, I was aware of the injustice of slashing down the quota of rice. The government's decision was a severe blow for those families who depended solely on PDS rice and they formed the majority in the state. It was also quite clear that the Government resolution had only helped the black marketeers. The same rice was sold for double the price in the black market. It was terribly unfair to cut down the ration quota of rice, the staple food of the poverty stricken hard working people of Kerala, ironically blessed with nature's bounty. Each one of us had a right to protest against this injustice. Of course, I deliberated a lot on the argument that students should stay out of strikes. But, there were hundreds of students from poor families and how could they study on an empty stomach?

My school had no history of participating in a strike. In fact, the only time the students boycotted classes was when they were encouraged by their teachers to be part of the right wing "liberation movement" of 1959 against the first elected Communist Government. I decided to give it a try. I asked my parents' opinion. "You can do as you wish, we aren't against strikes," they said. Then I began instigating the girls and when the D-day arrived, many of them left their classes and joined me. Girls and boys from the neighbouring Government School walked out of their classes and reached our school. Seeing them I grew bold.

With a few friends I ran into the classrooms and exhorted the girls to join us and some 100-150 girls followed us. We shouted slogans and marched through the town to another girls' school. Chaos ensued. Though we tried till 11.30 none of the girls came out with us. Then we marched back and shouting slogans gathered at the District Collector's office. We spent half an hour in the scorching sun before we heard that the Collector wanted to see the students' representatives. Five of us went into the Collector's room and were asked the reason for our protest. The boys said something and we saw them handing over a memorandum. That was all, the strike was over and we returned home.

I had described earlier the trial that followed the day after. I was sure that the headmistress' verdict would prove harmful to some of the girls. That evening I discussed the issue with my parents and asked my father to write a letter of warning to the headmistress. We had protested for a genuine cause and I was angry at the headmistress' attempt to malign us. It would be better to confront her bravely than meekly giving in with an apology, I decided. My father wrote a letter: "I came to know that you scolded my daughter for protesting against injustice, it would be good for you not to repeat it." I gave this to her the next day. Expecting an apology she began reading the letter, but soon turned pale and started sweating profusely. She sat still for a while and then ordered, "Umm. Go to your class." She didn't dare ask any other student for an apology.

Though it took me three more years to plunge headlong into active politics, the success of this protest was my first humble step in politics.

I was down with jaundice during my class X board exams in March and could take them only in September, which meant a long holiday from September 1965 to June 1966, till the next academic session began. As I was fond of reading, my father used to get me books that he thought would help me in college. That was how I happened to read the autobiography of Charlie Chaplin. I had heard from my parents about his film, The Great Dictator, which lampooned the Nazi leader Hitler, who terrorized even the most powerful capitalist nations during the Second World War. In that movie Chaplin told the world in his inimitable style that actually Hitler was just a paper tiger when confronted by the Allied Forces. The whole of Europe doubled up with laughter at Chaplin's caricature of Hitler. I had heard a lot about this one and some of his other movies, and had earlier watched two-three of his silent movies. But, I didn't understand them then. I was drawn towards Communism when I read in his own words how the Government of America forced him to leave the country for being a sympathizer of Communist Russia, and for criticizing the Capitalist regime fearlessly.

It was very well known that America had sent its forces to South Vietnam in 1965 and committed massacres and atrocities that would put Hitler to shame. That was a time when all progressive people despised America. China and Russia protested against America in various ways. Through them, the world came to know about American atrocities against the peace loving people of South Vietnam, a place not bigger than the small state of Kerala. I used to listen to these bits of information with interest. Any one who had to face the ill will of such a savage government could only be a good soul, I concluded.

It was around this time that I read *China: The Surprising Country* by the Australian writer Maira Roper. She had set out with lots of apprehensions and preconceived notions about China and had decided to scrutinize anything a Chinese said closely before believing it. However, the real China caught her by surprise. One of the chapters is titled 'No Women on the Streets'. Shanghai was infamous for being world's second largest prostitution centre. This chapter described how the Communist Party destroyed the city's whore houses, bringing about a change in the inmates' attitudes, giving them vocational training so that they could sustain themselves, thus preparing the ground for a social set up that would help those women lead a normal family life. Several organizations under the guidance of the Communist Party made sincere efforts to change the attitude of society to these women. I read all this and it made an impact.

In fact, it read like a description of some ethereal world. Could heaven exist on earth? If it could, I wished it would come true for our women too. Still, I couldn't believe all that I read. In India, we only know what Manu said: 'A woman should obey her parents in her childhood, her husband in her youth, and her sons when old.' I never believed in our tradition, which made women playthings for men. I used to argue that women are not born to serve men.

Another book that influenced me was *The Other Side of the River* written by Edgar Snow the celebrated writer who also wrote *The Red Star Over China*. He wrote this book after his visit to China in 1960-61. In it he compared the old miserable China to the new liberated one. The old China was a picture of present-day India. Gradually I began to feel that there was some greatness to this neighbour of ours.

Thus, days passed and I continued my studies and went on reading more books. Then something else happened.

The Government of India had declared an emergency during the Indo-Pak war in 1965 and arrested and imprisoned many political rivals. Almost all the Marxist leaders were in jail. This was just after the split in the party. Elsewhere, heated debates were going on between Russian and Chinese Communist parties. Gradually, it dawned on my father that Russia had changed its stance after Stalin and that the Soviet Communist Party had let down the working classes and the ideals that had led to the Revolution. It occurred to him that the Republic of China led by Mao Tse Tung was one nation rooted in Communist ideology. As father's political interests grew, he started caring less for his business. At last, in 1964, he decided to dedicate all his time to the party. His business was handed over to one of his nephews.

As all party documents were in English, most activists were unaware of the international debates on Communism. It was declared that the Marxist Communist Party had been supporting the Chinese stand, but none of these arguments was translated or published in Malayalam. My father and the other comrades of Kozhikode Municipality's 27th division believed that this had happened because all our leaders were in jail. They thought that these debates should be made available to the public and party members so that they could be aware of the correct ideological line. They decided to translate the recently published English pamphlets of Communist Party of China such as the *Civil Line* and *About the Stalin Argument*. They approached the State committee led by E.M.S Namputhiripad for permission, but got a negative reply. These comrades just wanted fellow party members to know certain basic facts about the international debate on Communism, but the leadership didn't like the idea. However, they were not disheartened. They were ready to face all odds for the sake of their ideology and went on to publish each of these pamphlets.

A bookstore, named Marxist Publications, was opened at Kallai Road in Kozhikode to distribute these pamphlets. The comrades of the 27th division had to suffer at the hands of the leadership each time a pamphlet was translated and published. But each such attack left them stronger. Gradually, they began to translate and publish Mao's works. In fact, this hit the leadership where it hurt the most.

In June 1966, I joined college. I was not quite interested in father's politics. Though I was aware of the changes in his ideology, it was not enough to inspire me to take up his path. Also, my extended family was hostile to his politics. Of course, I was convinced that father was working for the greater good.

In 1967 the Marxist party called a Kerala *bandh*. Father was arrested on the eve of the *bandh*, though he was not supporting it actively. It was a severe blow to me. I hated the Government for this injustice. I couldn't forget it, nor could I forgive those responsible for it. Father spent five days in jail. I went to see him there with my uncle and other comrades. I was totally unaware of the different hues of politics and the mean world out there and couldn't bear to see my father behind the bars. I came to understand that some of my family members were indeed happy to see him in jail. That was a rude shock to me. I asked myself: Should I join politics? I discussed this with my mother. Let's think it over, she advised. I found myself thinking about it all the time.

I felt relieved once he came home. He said that only two or three others were arrested on the pretext of the *bandh* and that they were set free the very next day. The Party was not willing to get him out on bail, so, he had to be in jail for five days. It was after this incident, that is, by the end of January 1967 that he was expelled from the Party. A campaign to paint him a CIA agent began in earnest at the national level. But I was happy that father was back from jail. For the time being, I forgot all about joining politics...

2

THE DECISION

I was not bad at studies. Still, as I grew older I began to wonder about the futility of it all.

I considered a doctor's profession the most respectable and useful to society. Science and Mathematics were my favourite subjects and even while at school I had decided to be a doctor.

But in college I got a clearer picture of our educational system. It took seven or eight years for an outstanding student to become a doctor. Others would have to toil for ten or more years. You should have a sound financial background to support you all these years. There was no use dreaming of higher education without money. And what if one spent this much money and finally became a doctor? Each person would only be worried about returns on investment. The so called motive to "serve the society" would long be forgotten. The only aim would be to see that the society served them well. Helping the poor becomes a non-issue.

Right from class 1 we follow a system that helps us to deal with the sly arrow called examinations. Issues of creativity and knowledge don't count here. And, higher education is just a matter of reading books. It just helps to turn students into bookworms. Theory papers are given more importance that practical lessons. Basic lessons of science and knowledge that theory and practice should go hand in hand to impart real wisdom are overlooked everywhere. No one sees anything amiss in the system, as this is the only type of education we are familiar with. If we try to evaluate the practical knowledge of a student who has spent many years in schools and universities, we would realize that he/she is absolutely worthless to society.

But what do we aim by this educational system? It encourages the student to strive for one's own benefit — to get a government job, or an even better one in the private sector— and to brighten the scope of his selfish need of a luxurious life. He finds it humiliating to do physical labour. He learns to degrade the menial workers and their labour. What does the contemporary educational system do to instill in the students the awareness that it's only labour that helped man to achieve the heights that he has reached today and that everything essential for his existence is made by hard work? How does today's educational system help a student to raise his voice against the inequalities and exploitations in society and try to curb it in his own way? It does nothing of that sort; instead it arouses in the student a feeling of detachment and indifference and teaches him to mind his own business. As a result, he doesn't mind joining the club of exploiters when an opportunity comes his way.

These thoughts grew within me. Probably, it was an outcome of my reading of Mao's works and listening to programmes on the Chinese Cultural Revolution on the radio. It was a time when winds of revolutionary changes were blowing in the world of education in China. What Mao said about the old education system was an eye-opener for me.

It was during the vacation after my first year pre-degree (class XI and XII were part of university education and were part of pre-degree courses held in college campuses) exam that I happened to read the

Four Ideological Works of Mao. It explained in simple terms, the fundamental ideals about Marxian outlook of the world; even I who had no basic grounding in politics could understand it well. I felt as if a door to a fresh new world was opened for me leaving behind the world of falsehood, betrayal, exploitation and torture. That book played an important role in shaping my life.

As my interest in politics increased, there were undercurrents of opposition against father's politics within our own family. My father worked along with the comrades of the 27th division to expose the true nature of the Marxist leadership. But their activities were limited to publishing the translated versions of some important Chinese pamphlets.

The allegation that father was a C.I.A agent gathered momentum. Some family members became instruments of Marxist leadership in perpetuating this. Provocations against father led to increased tensions. Thus, the hatred that had been dormant all the while came to a head and a split in the family became inevitable.

This split affected me considerably. I saw for myself the true shades of some people, whom I had considered my well-wishers. I opened my eyes towards the harsh realities of life; people who I thought loved me sincerely were in fact trying to lead me astray, away from my parents.

I began to feel that I had to break away from this meaningless life that was limited to my own self, that made me a slave of decadent values. As each day passed by, I felt more and more suffocated with the urge to break away from my mundane everyday life.

When the college re-opened, I started my second year pre-degree course. But deep within me, the revolutionary spirit that had struck roots in my conscience, refused to give me respite. I spoke against each and every instance of corruption in college.

The attitude of the educational system towards the poor was clear from the way it reacted to the students from affluent families. I went to Providence Women's College, Kozhikode, a Catholic institution. One of my classmates was the daughter of a senior officer in Mavoor Gwalior Rayons factory and she stayed in the hostel. She would entertain herself either by reading novels in class or bunk them and retire to the hostel. I don't remember her scoring more than 20 marks in any of the examinations. There was another girl from a very poor family who used to work very hard and get pass marks in all papers. But the college authorities looked down on her as she had availed of fee concession. Those days, the college authorities and not the university conducted the first year exams. So, they could tamper with the results as they wished. That year the Gwalior Rayons girl was in the list of successful students, but my poor classmate failed. What surprised me more than her failure was the Rayons girl's victory. It was clear that she passed because she had money. My poor classmate's failure meant more money to the management since the rule was that if a poor student failed she had to pay the full amount of fees to continue studies.

There was another farce called moral science class. But the nuns who preached, "truth shall prevail" showed clear duplicity while dealing with the poor. I couldn't stand it once they started screening movies and documentaries justifying the Americans who were engaged in an unjust war against the Vietnamese. I couldn't keep mum listening to their barbed remarks like "Indians are a lazy lot", "Countries like Britain and France should be our models", and "Capitalism is the best system". I questioned some of these ideas openly. I could no longer bear the oppressive atmosphere in college.

Thus, in the second year I attended class for just 15 days. I decided to fight for what I believed to be true and dedicate my life for the cause, which shed a new light on my inner self. The college principal tried her very best to get me back to college tempting me with a fee waiver and so on. But I refused to return to that despised life again...

My parents were surprised at my decision. But they found me adamant, and didn't persuade me much. I wouldn't have listened to them even if they had.

From then on, I too joined the Marxist publications. Every evening the comrades of the 27th division gathered together to read out and discuss the translated works of Mao. On most occasions these meetings were held at our house. I took part in these discussions once I quit studies. We also used to listen to Radio Peking regularly.

I left college in June 1967. It was around this time that the Naxalbari event happened. The newspapers weren't forthcoming with details about the incident. But we could gather that the peasants belonging to the vast territory of Naxalbari, Kharibari, and Fancideva of West Bengal on the Indo-Nepal border had resorted to weapons and taken to the red flag with the help of certain revolutionaries; that the Marxist government had fired at these peasants who demanded land and that they had not spared even women and children. In Kerala, a United Front Government led by Chief Minister EMS Namboodiripad was in power. There was discontent among the cadre against the dubious stand of the Marxist leadership that was conveniently ready to forsake its glorious Communist ideologies for the throne of power. Indira Gandhi's Central Government in Delhi and Kerala's Marxist leadership wept in chorus decrying the menace of terrorism in the West Bengal.

On July 5, 1967 Radio Peking broadcast an editorial of the People's Daily called 'The thunder of spring on the Indian horizon.' Though we couldn't understand the whole significance of it then, it was like a ray of light in our world of darkness. It praised the Naxalbari event and declared it the real remedy for India's problem, which is primarily agrarian. It said that the true liberation for India lay in solving its agricultural problems since the majority of India's population lived in villages. It explained how big capitalist countries like America and

Russia, exploited the Indian farmer. The Indian Government, which called itself democratic was actually serving foreign interests and brutally suppressing the governed majority. The Parliamentary way, ahimsa etc., were mere illusions to lead the Indian people astray and the leadership of the Left Front had turned revisionist by accepting the Parliamentary path.

We grouped together to set up a cell or 'samiti' in aid of Naxalbari peasant revolution, and also to prepare notices and wall posters to celebrate the Naxalbari incident. We also decided to translate the Radio Peking editorial as soon as we got the English version and if it could not be printed we made plans to make copies by hand and distribute it among the network that we had created by publishing pamphlets. Soon we got involved in printing the notices and making posters. Notices were supplied in public places. Comrades pasted the wall posters on all major centres of the town.

It was around this time, probably in August 1967, that we read in the newspapers that P. Sundarayya, the general secretary of the Marxist Party was visiting Kozhikode. It was a golden opportunity to protest against the deception of the Marxist leadership that had no qualms in putting down the Naxalbari peasant revolt with a bloody hand. We busied ourselves preparing more placards and red flags.

The comrades met a day prior to Sundarayya's arrival and decided as to who all were to participate in the protest. Some comrades were against my involvement. They argued that a public protest was unlike other normal activities that I had participated in so far. But I countered that I too had the right to participate in the strike, as I had chosen these very activities as my mission. The comrades had to give in at last. I mention this to point out the society's narrow outlook towards women's role in public life that was reflected even amongst my comrades who were supposed to be above such shameful gender discriminations.

The next morning around 20 of us walked through the heart of the town carrying placards and flags. We reached the town hall where Sundarayya was supposed to arrive. Standing on both sides of the gate we shouted slogans. Another group of people too had reached with notices to mark their protest against Sundarayya. He was supposed to reach there at 10 o' clock. He must have gathered what was going on; he didn't turn up at the appointed hour. The Marxist leaders who had already reached the town hall were in a fix. Later we came to know that they even thought of removing us by force. The news of our protest spread like wild fire across the town. People started gathering around. Sorne workers of the nearby Commonwealth factory stood around us not attending to their work. It was obvious that this bold new form of protest in favour of Naxalbari had some influence on them. Even among the Marxist representatives from the three neighbouring districts who had gathered in the town hall were sympathizers who subscribed to our cause. Probably this prevented the Marxist leadership from using force on us.

After a while it started to rain. But could that dampen our spirits? Our slogans rose above the sound of lashing rain. Some of the onlookers who had gathered there opened their umbrellas to shield us. Even after 12 o'clock there was no trace of Sundarayya. He might have been hoping that the rain would compel us to retreat. But that was not to be and by 12.30 his car arrived. The moment it reached the gate we showed the placards and shouted slogans against the betrayal of the Naxalbari uprising. The door of the car didn't open for five minutes; he probably feared a physical attack. Then, a few men with big moustaches came out from the hall, stood as if to cover Sundarayya, and opened the door. Sundarayya's face was pale as he stepped out of the car and he was led inside through another door. We had achieved our aim. Victoriously, we marched back, shouting slogans. Lots of people had gathered along the roadside shops with joyful faces to see our demonstration.

We returned to our homes, content that we could successfully utilize the first opportunity to display our new-found ideas. Our hearts overflowed with enthusiasm sensing the favourable response of the people. None of us even sneezed despite getting drenched in the downpour for two whole hours.

Obviously, my life after June 1967 was not that of an ordinary girl. This change, or this revolution that first happened in my mind and then in my relation to the outside world, was not an easy one because I was no different from any other middle class girl. I was very interested in stories, novels, magazines, and so on. I was a movie-buff as well. But our magazines and publications are all controlled by those who want to safe-guard their interests by exploiting the easily swayed sentimentality of young minds. They drag these youngsters away from the world of reality turning them into hazy eyed dreamers. The products, which today's retailers of culture bring into the market, serve only the interests of the exploiters.

Is it easy to extricate oneself from these influences? As the fable of *Naranathu Bhranthan* goes, it would be impossible to roll a rock up to the hilltop even if one toiled one's whole life. But it would take just a moment to push it down the hill. I understood that only if I decided to take a path filled with stones and thorns would I be able to dedicate myself for a greater cause leaving behind a beastly lowly life of utter selfishness.

Herein lies the impact of Mao's works on my life. It was the time of Cultural Revolution in China, a time when severe ideological struggles were taking place. I used to listen to Mao on Radio Peking and his words proved to be helpful in solving the combat of ideas in my mind. The battle Mao unleashed was aimed at promoting a fresh youthful outlook towards the world in every Chinese and to instill in him or her an awareness to contribute to the liberation of the exploited class. This was based on a great principle that every man should work for the betterment of society, which would eventually lead to the progress of mankind. This helped me to free myself step by step from the decadent influences of my life. For instance, I was a movie fan. But gradually I began hating movies. I stopped reading novels and stories altogether. I began to feel that all these would lead me to a shameful way of living. I was in Bombay with my mother's relatives in April-May 1967. There I saw the English movie, Dr. Zhivago. This American movie contained many vulgar scenes and insulted the Russian Revolution and Lenin. Considering all this my interest in movies died out. I used to love jewellery earlier and all kinds of adornments like silk saris and bright clothes. But as the influence of the new world perception grew within me I began to feel that all these embellishments were meaningless. I understood that women projected themselves as commodities by showing off their beauty this way.

Three valuable articles that helped me achieve this were "Serve the people", "In memory of Norman Bethune", and "The foolish old man who shifted mountains". The first is the story about a soldier who lost his life while serving the people and the interests of the Revolution. The second is about the death of Norman Bethune, a Canadian doctor who served selflessly in a Communist camp in China, neglecting his own health. The third is the story of a foolish old man who shifted mountains. The old man was determined to dig out two mountains. Another clever old man advised him that he would never succeed, but the foolish old man went on digging with a determined heart along with his sons. God saw his strong will and sent two angels who flew away carrying the mountains on their shoulders. The old man became successful in his attempt. Through this fable, Mao tried to tell us three things: "Be determined to achieve victory, be brave in the face of sacrifice, overcome all troubles." Thus he explained the three essential qualities a good communist ought to possess. These words of Mao became my weapon. These ideas gave me strength to uproot the nasty influences in my mind and to overcome every difficulty.

I mention this to prove that I was not unique. People believe that I had some special powers, a different sort of courage. These changes wouldn't have been possible if I had not comprehended Mao's ideas. As I went further along the difficult path that I chose for myself, I had the support of his words to lean on.

3

THE CAMPAIGN

I became brave enough to work in public after the Sundarayya episode. Every Sunday our comrades used to spend two hours at crowded centres of the town to promote the pamphlets that we had printed. Our tools included a folding table, a banner that said "Learn and promote Mao's thoughts" in big red letters and a red flag. We would spread our pamphlets on the table and urge all those who came by to understand the truth in these pamphlets. If some elections were round the corner we would circulate notices, which said "to hell with elections" explaining our stance on all major issues of the time.

I began to take part in book distribution. Most of our products were in the form of pamphlets that were priced very low. Once we took our positions, people would begin to gather around us. There would be all sorts of people in the crowd. Some of them would be curious to know what Mao and C.P.C said and would engage us in friendly discussions. They would buy the pamphlets too. But certain others came with the intention of picking up a fight. There were times when people looked straight into our face with utmost hatred and accused us of being CIA agents. Still others called us traitors: "You are Chinese spies. You don't have any nationalistic feelings. You can get away with it here, because ours is a democratic nation. Would you be able to do any such thing in China?" We would return to the book shop after spending two hours dealing with favourable and unfavourable responses and tackling all ploys to provoke us into a brawl. Invariably, we would have sold more than 120 pamphlets in two hours' time. The book that sold the most was *Quotations of Chairman Mao*. We had published *Quotations* in pamphlets and book forms. With added vigour we would move to a new destination the next week.

We used to write to the Chinese Embassy for new books. After a while, they began to send us photographs as well through the New China News Agency in Paris. The photographs presented a world in transition — the advance of the Cultural Revolution in China, the long marches of the Red guards, Mao and other leaders welcoming them warmly, production increasing manifold due to the new enthusiasm Cultural Revolution evoked among workers, peasants and other sections of society, the new advances of the people of Laos and Vietnam against the American invasion. We also came to know of various protests of exploited people all over the world against America and Russia interfering with their rule and their own respective governments reduced to mere puppets. When we began to receive these photographs without fail, we planned another thing. We knew that it was not enough for us to see these photos. We adorned the bookshop with these so that all those who came to our shop saw them. Our shop was located at a place that caught everyone's eye. A red flag flew high all the time. We made our shop so attractive that the passersby couldn't but peer at it. As days passed, the number of visitors to our shop increased.

Our pamphlets began to be circulated widely all over Kerala. People from different sections of society wrote asking for books. Similar publishing houses were started in Palakkad and Thiruvananthapuram. These were initiated by comrades who had fallen out with the Marxist Party and its youth wing over the leadership's revisionist stance. These comrades believed in the path of Naxalbari. We cooperated with them in all their endeavours. We used to circulate handwritten copies of certain pamphlets that we thought were not possible to print. The network now being wider, comrades supplied the handwritten copies and cyclostyled copies of these pamphlets all over Kerala. *The Thunder of Spring on Indian Horizon* was one such pamphlet. Later, comrades from another region got it printed.

Gradually, our study group expanded. After the Sundarayya episode some factory workers started coming to our study classes daily. They used to join us with exuberance in supplying books, pasting wall posters and distributing notices.

Yet, with each step many comrades on the front line of the movement backed out. This phenomenon was apparent from the very beginning. When father was expelled from the Marxist Party, all the comrades of the 27th division had resigned as a mark of protest against the leadership. Still, two-three persons who were with them all the time took back their resignations within 24 hours. The decision of the comrades to translate and publish Chairman Mao's Quotations petrified a teacher who was popular among the comrades for his fire spewing revolutionary speeches. "If it continues this way, I will end up on the streets," he concluded. Such people were there even at advanced stages of the movement. It was difficult for me to understand this dropout phenomenon then. Later I realized that such people leaving the movement should be considered a sign of progress. Sure, we committed mistakes. It was natural for an active worker to make mistakes due to inexperience, lack of understanding of the ideology, decadent influences of the society that he lived in and the basic nature of the class that he or she belonged to. But these errors could be rectified through constructive criticism and an in-depth study of ideology on the face of problems.

It was during this time, when our activities were gaining momentum fast that we came to know about the decision of the Marxist Party to hold its Central Committee meeting in Kozhikode in October 1967. We were delighted; this was the golden opportunity to expose the Marxist leadership and protest against its anti-Naxalbari attitude. This time we decided to register our protest in a novel way.

We planned to put up the photographs we had collected, just opposite the venue of the Central Committee meeting and supply books all through the time of the meeting. We had acquired a fresh confidence and new spirit after the protest against Sundarayya.

Our enthusiasm overflowed as the D-day arrived. After the Sundarayya episode, Marxist leadership could guess that we would not keep quiet. But we never gave them even a hint as to what our mode of protest would be. Chief minister EMS handled home ministry too. They must have apprehended that some major conspiracy was being hatched at our house. On the previous day, an inspector from the crime branch came to our doorstep and peeped in while the meeting was on. His suspicious manners gave him away and we didn't allow him to enter the house.

That night we gathered together to decide who all were to participate in the protest. The comrades explained that the Marxist leadership was quite flustered with our protest against Sundarayya and now they would try their best to put down any of our attempts to upset this meeting that would converge all its power and strength. So it was unwise to expose all our members to them. It was decided that only ten comrades, ready to face any odds should take part in the actual protest and the rest should remain on the scene unnoticed. Thus ten comrades came forward to be part of this suicidal mission. I was one of them.

The next morning, around 10.30 ten of us started out with a determination to face anything in the world for the sake of the truth that we believed in, proud and confident that the demonstration that we were about to carry out was part of the heroic fight being pursued by people all over the world. The person at the front held a red flag high on a bamboo pole. Behind that, six persons carried three photo panels on their shoulders. Another comrade held a placard with Mao's quotations. The next person took our folding table and the last comrade carried the pamphlets and books. Slowly, we walked along the town. People on either side of the road stared at us with curiosity. We moved on silently, not uttering a word. We reached the spot opposite the building where the Central Committee meeting was being held. There was a huge ground opposite it. We arranged the photo panels in such a way that they would attract the attention of the people. The placard with Mao's quotation was placed near it. The bamboo pole was fixed on the ground with the red flag flying high. A little ahead of all this, we set up our folding table to spread out our pamphlets and books. The Marxist leaders were confused. It was an occasion when numerous people from all over Kerala came to see the senior leaders. Obviously, they couldn't meet them when they were holed up inside the building. But our photographs were visible to all, and people gathered to see them. Some people bought the pamphlets. They scrutinized each photo closely and read the captions. Many of them had political debates with us. Some journalists too took interest in our new way of protest. Things were moving in an amicable way. By nightfall, one or two volunteer captains of the Marxist Party came to us with their leaders' response. They informed us that all the leaders were upset and the red volunteers and the local leaders were putting their heads together to find a way out to tackle our protest, which was proving to be a nuisance. The Central Committee meeting would go on for two more days. On Sunday there was to be a public rally. The leaders were determined that we shouldn't be around that day. They didn't know how we were going to go about our demonstration and so the first day passed peacefully. But the people who were mostly party workers and sympathizers encouraged us with an eagerness to know more and were happy that they could see the pictures of protest of progressive forces all over the world. This made us greet the coming days with more enthusiasm and resolution.

The next day too we took our position around the same time. Lots of people crowded around us. But we could see a marked difference this time. Some of them started accusing us: "You are American spies. Where else could you get these photographs from?" We did answer them promptly, but at times we had to restrain ourselves from getting into a fight. There were people who supported us too. Refusing to get into the trap they had laid for us, we focused our attention on the photos and pamphlets. We understood with that day's experience that the Marxist leadership was all out to suppress us. They had sent these people to provoke us. But we decided to face whatever that came our way. We were clear that we would not start a fight.

On Sunday morning, we reached the place again. Groups of people approached us and tried to engage us in provoking debates. Their accusations became bitterer. Our comrades tried their best to ward off attempts to draw us into a fight. Some people in the crowd were ready to guard us if a physical assault took place. By noon, the provocateurs began to retreat when we failed to respond to their taunts. A Marxist volunteer informed us later that around 50 reserve police were put on alert in the nearby police station and they had been ordered to teach us a lesson and arrest us at the slightest hint of a skirmish.

In the evening, we spread our weapons on the pavement opposite the front gate of Manachira ground where the public meeting was to be held. The moment we reached there, people began to gather around us in large numbers. Lots of people bought our books and pamphlets. We explained to them about the photos and hadn't a minute's respite from selling books. Special crime branch officers from the centre and state stood at a distance watching us all the time.

The huge public rally began. We saw senior leaders like Sundarayya, EMS, Jyoti Basu and Ranadive mounted on a truck waving to people on both sides. When they reached the spot where we stood, they turned their heads the other way. Like an ostrich, they must have thought that we would cease to exist if they pretended not to see us. The demonstration lasted for hours. When the public rally began, Red volunteers came to see our exhibition and buy our pamphlets. The quotations priced at Rs.5 were all sold out and we received orders for more. We were running out of stock of pamphlets too. Still, people were thronging around.

Seeing this, an announcement was made repeatedly: "Our official bookstore is not in the front, it is at the back of the stage. All comrades should come to the back of the stage to buy books." But people ignored this announcement and kept coming to us like iron filings to a magnet. The leaders were giving magnificent speeches. We could hear them sneering at the Naxalbari incident. But still these leaders couldn't stop Mao's and CPC's words from reaching out to the thousands of comrades who worked for the party with revolutionary spirit. Our pamphlets were sold out before the rally was over. That day we made Rs 300 from our books and pamphlets. Except *Quotations* none of the pamphlets was priced more that 50 paise.

We went back joyous having achieved our modest mission. More than anything else we were surprised at the eagerness of the people to know more about revolutionary ideas. This increased our enthusiasm manifold. The leadership would not have spared us if we didn't have the direct as well as indirect support of the public. This backing gave us courage and spring in each step forward. It gave us the strength to sacrifice something for the cause.

We came across an amusing piece of news a few days after the rally. Comrade Sivkumar Misra, a central committee member from Uttar Pradesh was expelled from the committee at the Kozhikode meeting.

A major allegation against him was that he tried to brew trouble in the U.P students' movement in association with Kunnikkal Narayanan, a C.I.A agent. This comrade met father only months after he was expelled from the party.

4

COMRADE T.V APPU

I had attempted sketching the activities of Marxist Publications and Rebel Publications in the last chapter. But this would not be complete without the story of an unforgettable man. All through the turbulent times, Comrade T.V. Appu kept his belief alive till his last breath. We called him Appu Maash, or Appu master. Today there's no one to narrate the story of his sacrifice, to collect funds for his helpless family, to write poems about him or to build memorials and pay tribute to his mortal remains. He never tried to become an M.L.A or M.P broadcasting his revolutionary tradition. He never cashed in on his fame to acquire a prominent post in the party. And he died of hypertension brought on by imprisonment at an advanced age. Comrade Appu, a tailor was among the first to join the Communist party from our neighbourhood in 1935-39, when the legendary comrade Krishna Pillai was organizing the party in the underground. Another person called Unni who repaired watches too joined the party along with him. His house was a stone's throw from ours.

Comrade T.V Appu worked for the party in the underground. The party asked him to join the army in 1941 during World War II. It was a time when the party thought it its duty to help the British

Government in its war against fascism. He served the army for four years. He returned home to open a tailoring shop, without much success. He couldn't earn a decent living or provide for his wife and children. Even while battling a life of poverty he was committed to his ideology and preserved his objective of revolution. Years rolled on, making no difference in Appu Maash's life.

After getting disillusioned with the party, it was when despair was threatening to smother Appu Maash that he set out to fight for the words of Mao and CPC. This gave him a fresh lease of life. Thus, he got involved in all our activities and at times, he came forward to shoulder the responsibility of running Marxist publications and Rebel publications single-handedly. He was involved in the Thalassery police station attack of 1968 and was incarcerated. But he never regretted his decision. He was released in 1971, after three years in jail. By then he was seriously ill. This real disciple of Marx succumbed to his illness just 18 months after his release. He earned his place among the millions of martyrs who laid down their lives for the liberation of mankind.

Only a true Communist could sacrifice his life for the ideas he believed in. Appu Maash gave away his effervescent youth for the party and held on to his convictions even while his life passed through difficult phases. His life is a brilliant example for the masses. When I write this, the memory of another historic man comes alive in my mind.

He is none else, but Karl Marx who fought all through his life and died a premature death. The German biographer, Franz Mehring, who told Marx's life story with great poignancy, was a Lasallian. The bitter debates of Marx and Lasalle are well known. But Mehring had to accept the greatness of Karl Marx and his book *Karl Marx The Story of His Life* is a hymn of praise. Marx had many scientific inventions to his credit. He could make a mark in all fields he handled. One such invention was enough for this man to lead a life of luxury and peace. But Marx was not a man to be satisfied easily.

England gave Marx shelter when he was driven away from Europe. But there his family was sucked into a whirlpool of illness and poverty. Newspapers never paid him promptly for his articles. He would be paid only for those articles, which went under his byline. There were numerous instances when editors stole Marx's articles. Marx could take it no more when one by one his children succumbed to death and he applied for a job with the British Railways. But when he got the appointment letter, his wife, brave as she was, took one look at it and told him: "Finish what you are doing now. Forget about this job!"

Around that time Marx was writing his magnum opus *Das Capital*. Hearing his wife, he set aside forever his wish to take up a job. If he had taken a different decision then, there wouldn't have been Communism. That great man, who sacrificed two of his children for the greater cause of Communism didn't betray us, the future generations. I remember him with heartfelt gratitude and bow my head to the memory of the harshness of his sacrifice. I believe that today's youth should be inspired by the lessons from the life of this pious soul.

Today's social set up doesn't permit any comfort in a true communist's life. When he is alive he is crucified every moment. When he is dead, the same people who made his life miserable pose as his true disciples and distort and destroy the ideology for which he lived and suffered all his life. Look at what happened to the great iconoclast Jesus Christ. He raised his voice against injustice and was crucified by the leaders of the unjust society. When he was dead, he was made a god, an incarnation with supernatural powers. Atrocities are still committed in his name and the essence of his life stifled for all times. The lives of Marx, Lenin, and Mao Tse Tung prove nothing different. How easy it is to pay tributes to the mortal remains once the person is dead! And his successors are put in jail or wiped away from the face of earth.

This, then, is the road to Communism. It has been a difficult thorny path forever. But is there another way for the onward journey of history? No. History has always moved ahead in this trail of acid tests and it will be so in future too. This is what the lives of Karl Marx and his true disciple TV Appu confirm.

5

A PROBLEM CALLED CHINA

As days passed by, the popularity of comrade TV Appu's Marxist Publications and the 'Naxalbari Peasant Revolt Aid Samiti' associated with it crossed the borders of Kerala to spread all over India. The main reason behind its success was that it was directly encouraged by China.

We used to send copies of each of our translated published pamphlet to the Chinese Embassy in New Delhi. We were obliged to do this, as these were the Malayalam translations of the articles published in English by the Foreign Language Publishers in China. A few months before we gharaoed Sundarayya, Radio Peking had reported about Marxist publications in Kozhikode and had even named 12 of our published works. Certain Malayali comrades in Calcutta wrote to us hearing this. After the Sundarayya episode, comrade Shushital Ray Choudhury, a leader of the Calcutta Naxalbari Peasant Revolt Aid Samiti wrote to us. He told us that this incident had deeply moved the comrades in Calcutta and that he was interested in meeting us. He said that they wanted to keep in contact with such samitis all over India and was aspiring to set up an All India Co-ordination Committee with their co-operation. The Sundarayya event happened months after the Naxalbari revolt when its leader Charu Majumdar and other comrades were still negotiating with the Marxist leadership. This small incident, which revealed the grit to challenge the leadership had a great impact on the comrades in Calcutta. The news made headlines in their mouthpiece *Desabhruthi*. We received a letter from comrade Shushital Ray Choudhury a few days before the Marxist party's Central Committee meeting at Kozhikode. It said that he and another comrade had set out to South India to have an initial round of talks with comrades all over India to set up a co-ordination committee and had decided to meet us too. This was a thrilling bit of news for us. It was quite inspiring that a comrade who played an important role in the Naxalbari struggle albeit an indirect one, was coming to meet us from the land of Naxalbari with an intention to involve us in an all India organization. I too eagerly waited for that precious day. We received another letter from Bangalore after three-four days that they were starting for Kerala via Madras. Their date of arrival too was mentioned. We waited, impatiently. But then we got a telegram from Coimbatore that the comrades had postponed their visit and that they were returning. We were surprised and disappointed. What would have prompted them to change their decision, we wondered.

But we didn't allow these matters to interfere with our activities. We fervently displayed our protest at the Central Committee meeting. Immediately after that, we again got a letter from comrade Shushital Ray Choudhury inviting father and comrade NC Shekhar for the first meeting of the Co-Ordination Committee.

Comrade NC Shekhar was a leading figure among the early communists of Kerala and had worked with comrade Krishna Pillai. There was no one in the communist movement who had not heard of him. This comrade used to visit our home regularly and have political debates with my father. NC was a communist activist even when my uncle Kunnikkal Madhavan was alive. My uncle was a thorough Congressman. His party activities had landed him in jail too. But all this apart, our house served as a resting place in Kozhikode whenever comrades Krishna Pillai and NC Shekhar came that way. My father too maintained the same relations. I too had great respect for NC. Whenever he came home he would talk to all of us in the didactic tone of a senior member of the family. I must say that I was not always very happy with him raising the voice of authority.

Whenever NC came home, he used to register his protest against the revisionist stance of the Marxist leadership and reiterated that he considered the path of Naxalbari and the Chinese party right. Maybe that was why he too was invited to Calcutta along with father. But he didn't take much interest in the invitation. "I am involved in solving the riddle of my life," he said. But this very same NC who was engrossed in just his own life's troubles later wrote a long letter to comrade Sushital Ray Chowdhary against my father. As comrade NC excused himself, my father took Philip M Prasad with him to Calcutta. He used to work in association with us from Thiruvanathapuram.

We came to know the real reason behind comrade Shushital Ray postponing his visit only when father returned from Calcutta. A comrade in Coimbatore had warned them that father was a C.I.A agent and that they shouldn't get involved with him. My father learnt that the comrade who accompanied Shushital Ray Choudhury was against the latter's decision to return without meeting father. Comrade Choudhury's decision met with stiff criticism from comrades in Calcutta and that was when he decided to invite father for the Co-Ordination Committee meeting. Father had to strive hard to extract this much information from comrade Chowdhary as he was trying to steer clear of father all the time.

The comrades of the 27th division including my father had protested against the Marxist leadership collectively. They had all accepted the path shown by the Chinese party and Mao, based purely on ideology. But the Marxist leadership singled out my father both within and outside the party for the simple reason that the struggle he led was gaining popularity amongst the party workers, and they couldn't take him on politically. We were pained by the conduct of the comrades who had led the Naxalbari struggle against the same Marxist leadership.

We were encouraged and supported by the Chinese party all the while and therefore, we couldn't turn ourselves to be mere cronies of the party leadership. As we grasped Mao's words more and more, we gained strength to analyse everything in our capacity and support what we felt was right. This was the lesson of Cultural Revolution. We followed its essence that people should always be wary about their leaders. The Cultural Revolution urged the people to stick posters criticizing their leaders and voice their protest in public if they found them going astray. This was the only way to ensure that the revolution and the party remained incorruptible. But certain comrades who held high positions in the party buttressing its erroneous ways could not accept us.

Anyway, we didn't take this setback seriously. We sincerely believed that such misunderstandings would fade away once they get to know of our activities. The very fact that we were invited for the co-ordination meeting was a vindication of our efforts; we consoled ourselves.

We had received the declaration of the first co-ordination committee. It exhorted the party workers to protest against the revisionist attitude of the Marxist leadership and its stance against armed revolts and to organize more peasant revolts on the lines of Naxalbari. This exhortation made a deep impact on my mind. But I was not aware then, that this would give my life a whole new direction.

The backing we received from China proved to be a much longed-for weapon for those who used to call us spies, and antisocial elements. Incidentally among these very people who called us names where those who were earlier stamped as Russian, Chinese spies by their political rivals. We are mere political offshoots of these old Russian and Chinese spies, yet they use the same old tar brush to malign us without shame!

6

THE BACKGROUND OF THALASSERY-PULPALLY

Gradually, our pamphlets began to get distributed all over Kerala. Many people wrote to us demanding these pamphlets that were creating a major transformation among party workers. We also had bookstores in Kannur, Palakkad, Thrissur, Ernakulam, Idukki, Alappuzha, Kottayam, Kollam and Thiruvananthapuram. The comrades in these districts re-published what we had printed earlier and also those major pamphlets, which we thought were not printable. Lots of comrades who resigned and others who were expelled from the Communist Party of India or the Communist Party of India (Marxist) joined the Naxalbari Peasant Revolt Aid Samiti. The words of Mao and CPC gave them a new life.

According to instructions from Calcutta, we attempted to organize a Kerala Co-ordination committee, bringing together all our comrades in Kerala. A meeting was held at Thiruvananthapuram. We discussed the issue of coordination one whole night but didn't reach a consensus. Later, a meeting was organized at Ernakulam. The group had people from all walks of life —students, teachers, trade union leaders... The meeting welcomed the declaration of the all India Co-ordination Committee which had come out in pamphlet form, and resolved to act accordingly. It was decided to agree upon a statement suitable to Kerala and publish a magazine from Ernakulam for the promotion of our cause. The magazine was called "Left Front." The comrades took a pledge to organize struggles on the Naxalbari model.

Following this, we invited around hundred comrades for a meeting in an attempt to organize a local co-ordination committee at Kozhikode. We had invited Ambady Sankaran Kutty Menon who was expelled from the Thrissur District Committee of the Marxist party to preside over the function. He gave a brilliant speech but didn't have anything to say about Naxalbari, or the teachings of Mao or Chinese party or their battles based on ideology. He said in an emotional voice that EMS had grown jealous of the growing popularity of comrade Krishnapillai and that comrade Krishnapillai didn't die of snake bite but EMS had hatched a plot to kill him and so on. We suspected this was an attempt to sabotage the meeting. We had wanted him to expose the revisionist attitude of the Marxist leadership and not indulge in character assassination of any leader. Ambady's ranting made the meeting meaningless. After this we never attempted another meeting of this sort.

Meanwhile, "Left Front" became functional. But only two or three volumes came out. By then, father and Philip were invited for the second All India Co-ordination Committee meeting.

It was decided that comrades should now get into the realm of action and go into villages determined to sacrifice all. They should organize peasant revolts all over the country. The comrades who came back from the meeting informed us that there were differences of opinion among the representatives of the All India Co-ordination Committee, especially the comrades from Kerala who criticized whatever fault they found did not go down well with some leaders. When the discussions were on, the comrades would admit their mistakes and promised to correct them, but they would make them over and over again.

For instance, the declaration of the Kerala Co-ordination Committee, approved months earlier was not published in the All India Co-ordination Committee's newspaper 'Liberation'. When this issue came up during the discussion no one could give a convincing explanation. Comrade Charu Majumdar said that though he subscribed to the declaration personally, some comrades in the editorial team were against it. Later, when it came out in Baba Gurumukh Singh's English magazine "People's Path", they hurriedly published an edited version in "Liberation" too. There were also other instances when words and action didn't match.

We decided to respond to the call of these two co-ordination committee meetings. By now we were certain that joining up with people hungry for power would only hinder our activities. So we didn't call another meeting and instead, the comrades who returned from Calcutta went visiting the members of the Kerala co-ordination committee and briefed them about the Committee's resolutions. On the basis of this, it was decided that our plans should be altered a little and comrades, ready to go into the villages, should start preparing themselves. We stopped publishing 'Left Front' as the magazine no longer served our purpose.

Again, we got busy publishing pamphlets. Several comrades from all over Kerala who were involved in distributing our books and pamphlets reached out to us. We held discussions with them on our future plans and to facilitate this, the comrades became active in villages. I was thrilled to know that there were comrades involved in our kind of activities in every nook and corner of Kerala, even in remote hilly hamlets. It boosted our morale that there were people, workers, peasants, teachers and students who were willing to follow the path of Naxalbari. We could feel the revival of a common public spirit everywhere. The idea of a heroic revolution could move people all over the state into a potent power that would uproot the foundations of a feudal society. There was a steady flow of letters from Kerala to the Chinese Embassy. They sent us English versions of the selected works of Mao, Quotations and other works, as demanded. They also sent us badges, which featured the smiling radiant face of Mao. Our enthusiasm knew no bounds when we went out for book distribution campaigns wearing these badges.

These changes were felt in Kannur district too, which was a Marxist bastion. Denouncing the leadership's diktats, comrades wrote to us and visited our bookstores. A group of comrades had already opened a bookstore there. The first blast of dissent took place in the Youth federation of Kannur. A large group of comrades walked out of a meeting protesting against the Marxist leadership. KP Narayanan master was one among them. An independent bookstore was opened in Kannur after this incident.

It was around the same time that a lockout at the Ganesh *beedi* factory plunged thousands of families into poverty. With this, the concept of a fresh revolution exploded like a volcano. Suppressed revolutionary emotions broke free. There was a mass movement within the party against the Marxist leadership. These comrades, in turn, accepted the path of Naxalbari. Study classes of Mao Tse Tung's thoughts came up everywhere, like mushrooms sprouting in fresh rains. Kannur did uphold its revolutionary tradition.

With this, our activities were raised to a different plane.

One day, the postman brought us an envelope with a strange address on it. It said, 'Kunnikkal Narayanan, Town Hall, Kozhikode.' This letter, which read like a dissertation on oppression and poverty reached us by sheer luck. It was from a poor peasant who lived in the Pulpally Devaswom (temple management) owned forestland of Pulpally in South Wayanad. Pulpally Devaswom owned around 27,000 acres of forestland. These forests were homes to thousands of families who were displaced from Meenachal Taluk of Kottayam district. They were settlers who had lost their ancestral small farmholdings and homes to various irrigation and rubber development projects. They were lured away to Wayanad by agents who promised them farmlands for a nominal price.

But when they reached Pulpally they could see only forests. These agents took money from the farmers promising them to get the rights to the land and urged them to clear the forests. The devaswom board and the forest department were nowhere on the scene then. The farmers cleared the forest and planted bananas, spices and paddy before the Devaswom made an appearance with threats to call the police if they didn't vacate the place. They knew very well that the farmers would not leave the land since they had already started farming. The farmers pleaded for possession of the land and were ready to offer whatever money they had. The Devaswom representative took the money and left assuring them that they would think over the matter. Then came forest officials with an even greater threat. They slapped criminal cases against the farmers for felling of trees and this led to an increased animosity between the farmers and Devaswom management. Farmers were distraught that their labour would be lost. The Devaswom management too grew impatient. Both the parties approached the Government. The government agreed to set up an M.S.P (Malabar Special Police) camp with the sole intention of evacuating these farmers as demanded by the Devaswom and showed no concern to the farmers' plea. A police station was already there. But the Devaswom management argued that this was not enough to contain the farmers and so, the M.S.P camp and a wireless station were set up.

The historic Sitadevi temple at Karimam was in the possession of the Pulpally Devaswom. The priest, a namboothiri, did his daily puja after an early morning bath. And the infamous M.S.P camp was stationed in the *oottupura* (dining hall) of this temple where the policemen made free with wine and women. The namboothiri priest turned a blind eye, and continued to pray clinking his bell. With the establishment of this camp, the police became the administrators of the land. If a farmer was caught in a case, however petty, the treatment he would get was inhuman. The farmers spent days and nights in fear of the police. They were better off with wild beasts and poisonous reptiles. They endured death and illness, spilt sweat and blood to turn the forests into farmlands. But these people who were driven away from their homes to forests could not bear these bestial men in uniform. The farmer's letter sketched the pathetic picture of the sons of soil who turn mud to gold.

They had approached almost all the political parties to save them from this distress. They had sent memoranda to scores of ministers. No one did anything to help them. The Marxist party took up their issue during the assembly elections of 1967. They promised the farmers land deeds if they came to power. In Pulpally, this became a major factor in the campaign for votes. They formed a farmers' organization. With great enthusiasm and hope, the farmers voted the seven party coalition front led by the Marxist party to power. EMS was sworn in as the Chief Minister of the coalition government, but the forest officials and police continued to hound the farmers. The farmers went all the way to Thiruvanathapuram to submit petitions after petitions and even resorted to satyagraha and picketing of the Secretariat. The police atrocities only grew despite EMS holding the home portfolio that controlled the police.

This was what the letter said. The farmer had thrown a challenge towards the end of his story: "You go on and on about Naxalbari, peasant revolt and armed revolution. Are you prepared to put an end to your verbosity and practice what you preach? Here is the field of action for you. This is a challenge that will put you to test. Accept it if you have the guts!"

That evening the comrades gathered together to discuss the letter. Conventional approaches had failed in this case and only the path of Naxalbari remained now. This was precisely the advice we had got from the all India leadership. We decided to go deep into the matter, but had to wait for some more time since the address of the sender was not clear from the letter.

After a few months, yet another blow shook the Marxist leadership from within. The majority of the comrades of the Mananthavady party committee revolted against the leadership and resigned from the party. These comrades led by comrade Varghese scoffed at the misleading attitude of the leadership and were ready to accept the path of Naxalbari. This found an echo in the Kannur district committee as well. Four district committee members including the district commander of the red volunteers brought out a notice defying the leadership.

In those times, political parties all over India had their own volunteers — rashtriya seva dal for congress, R.S.S and Shiv sena for Jansangh and the red volunteers for the Marxist party. Others called them Gopalsena, after the Marxist leader AK Gopalan who was the chief organizer of the Marxist party. The leadership of each party used its volunteers as storm troopers, as a means to demonstrate their strength to achieve their political agenda. But those who joined the Gopalsena were different. These red volunteers joined the troop dreaming of an imminent revolution, with a passion to launch an armed struggle. It was then in the interest of the Marxist leaders to keep this rebellious zeal burning in them. But after the Thalassery-Pulapally events the Marxist leaders abandoned these martial activities altogether.

The majority of the comrades who came forward to accept the message of Naxalbari were members of the Red volunteers. The concept of the armed struggle spread like wild fire in hill tracts like that of Wayanad. When those who still called themselves revolutionaries were engaged in hollow verbal duels, the comrades of this region with an unmatched zeal marched to the battlefront to realize their ideals.

The activists who went by the all India Corodination Committee's exhortation to organize local protests modeled on Naxalbari and the comrades who resigned from the Mananthavady area committee decided to put their efforts together. Three comrades — Varghese, Thettamala Krishnankutty and my father — came forward to accept the challenge from Pulpally. They chose to have first hand experience on problems of the peasants.

The moment they reached Pulpally, they met the farmer who wrote the letter and held many meetings with the peasants. That was when they understood the real gravity of the issue. The farmers retold their tale of terror. The number of settlers in the area had gone up in the recent times forcing tribals to move deeper into the national parks which in turn made them vulnerable to the threats and torture of the forest department. Above all was the persecution from the M.S.P camp. The officers of the MSP camp ruled like kings. One of the sub-inspectors was particularly cruel. Once the evening set in, he would go for a walk waving a baton. No hut was supposed to have a lighted lamp at this time. During the day, he was even more virile. If he happened to get hold of a peasant, he would beat him up without any show of emotion or strain, as if he were an automated torture machine. The conflict between the peasants and the M.S.P camp aggravated day by day. The forest department had charged around 500 peasants with various criminal offences. That meant a loss of Rs 100 for bail per person. This would upset the families' budgets for years if not months. The accused had to be present at the Sultan Bathery court once in two weeks, which meant a long walk of over 17 miles. The farmers were so scared that they rarely ventured out of their homes.

The Marxist farmers' union made the peasants go through the ritual of fund collection, picketing and memoranda. Farmers were disgusted with this sham. Everyone was convinced that something definite had to be done now though none knew what it ought to be. They asked our comrades the same question. So the comrades put forward their proposition — "You have tried all conventional modes of protest, but they have all proved to be futile. The Devaswom and the police still operate as unquestioned forces. The Marxist government, your last ray of hope, has done nothing to lighten your burden. Instead, its attitude has only helped to strengthen those who torture you. Doesn't your salvation lie in fighting against the callousness of the governing class? Don't these people deny you the fundamental freedom? Isn't it a life and death issue to establish this fundamental right? Your predicament is naturally the predicament of this whole village. Do you think your problems could be solved within the existing system of laws? Think about it."

The farmers accepted what the comrades said. They were impatient to break the chains that had shackled them for centuries. The idea of a revolution started boiling over. They promised the comrades to spill their blood in return for liberation.

A thorough groundwork was essential to deal with such serious issues. So the comrades returned to plan a long-term strategy with the promise to meet again as fast as they could. This news sent waves of excitement across our group in Kozhikode. The experience of the comrades who returned from Pulpally moved everyone. As the time for the acid test drew near, many comrades retracted and many others joined in with greater enthusiasm. The comrades who had gone into the villages had no words to describe how they were welcomed by the farmers, and about the excitement among the peasants and workers.

I was raring to go into the field of action. When would my time come to meet these comrades brimming with revolutionary fervour, to see those villagers and to urge them on about the truth that I believed in? But the comrades wanted me to wait for some more time. I felt depressed and disappointed that I was pulled back because I was a woman. I was fully aware of what tales people would tell about girls who freely moved around with men. I hated this inequity and was determined to fight it.

To talk about Kannur — most of the workforce were beedi workers and handloom weavers. There were thousands of families who earned a living just making beedis. Their life was so pathetically on the verge of starvation that even children were driven into beedi rolling. These children worked in the neigbourhood beedi factories breathing in the poisonous air filled with the smell and dust of beedi leaves and tobacco. There were a lot of families who made beedis at home, filling them with pollution. A bus journey through Kannur would bring more clarity to the picture. In the buildings on either side of the road one could see rows of workers. But these companies just meant a place where workers gathered for work. None of the customary labour laws were followed here. The workers were given a nominal amount for all their hard work. Even little children came to the factories either to learn the job or to help out their elders who sat there breaking their backs from morning till midnight. For generations the poor of Kannur rolled beedis, which left them with respiratory tract diseases, retarded growth, finally reducing them to skin and bones.

Weaving was another traditional occupation of the people of Kannur. The industry survived on exports. Wages were far higher in western countries to which the textile products were exported. In fact, with the onslaught of synthetic cloth, demand for handloom had gone down in our country over the years. War and wartime clothing requirements were those rare occasions when the local handloom industry could talk about some business. But that is a temporary relief. This industry behaved like an asthma patient with its dependence on exports for money and the power loom sector for yarn. When there was work, there was no time to blink. But once it was over, nothing could be predicted. The woven cloth was priced low. The industry didn't abide by labour laws. Workers were taken on contract, and didn't get any benefits. Poverty and illness kept them company. Most of the weavers died of tuberculosis while young.

Beedi workers and weavers were only too aware of their misery and craved for a change. That their political awareness was quite high was evident from the fact that they closely followed political developments and participated in debates and discussions. Beedi workers had another peculiarity. Newspaper reading was a daily routine for them. There was no clatter of machinery, nor was there any noise when experienced hands rolled the tobacco leaf and filled it up with tobacco powder and tied it with a string. All of them wouldn't get time to read the paper, so they took turns to read newspapers every day. Others would divide the reader's work among themselves. The beedi workers and weavers had a legacy of revolutionary struggles and they never thought twice before plunging into revolt. They had fought on the forefront in every struggle that cropped up in North Malabar and contributed numerous martyrs for their land. The consecutive governments in the State and the Centre had done nothing to alleviate the miseries of these people who form a major workforce. With every passing day they sank deeper into the abyss of poverty and hunger. The words of Marx "there is nothing for a worker to lose, just his shackles and a whole new world to gain," were literally true with regard to the beedi workers and weavers. They were aware that only a revolution that would turn the social hierarchy upside down would liberate them from this hell.

Ganesh and Bharat beedi issues cropped up after EMS assumed power. In a bid to appease the workers, the government brought the beedi-cigar workers within the ambit of the Minimum Wages Law. But this led to more confusion. The owners of Ganesh and Bharat beedi companies in Mangalore, Karnataka saw that this would make their Kerala operations less profitable. They could make beedis in Mangalore at a cheaper rate where they did not have to pay minimum wages. One fine morning, these companies closed down their branches all over Kannur without notice and left for Mangalore. They didn't feel accountable to the workers who were on contract. The workers' job depended on factories giving them tobacco leaves. If they didn't, there was no work, and no pay. Even the new beedi-cigar laws didn't add much to making a beedi-worker's life secure. That was why the company owners could have their way leaving EMS' government aghast.

One morning, the 20,000 strong work force found their companies closed. Even with their jobs they could hardly sustain their families and now they were tossed into a sea of deprivation and starvation. More than one lakh lives were dependent on these 20,000 people. They approached all political parties and the Marxist Government, which they believed to be theirs. Fund collection, picketing, satyagraha and protest marches followed as usual. But the Government didn't react. Even if they had wanted, they couldn't have done anything to solve the problem since the Centre favoured industrialists. The economy of Kannur was on the verge of a collapse. The workers were forced to look for jobs in paddy fields and farms for half the normal wages. This, in turn, affected the agricultural labourers. Surplus labour was more than what the landlords had ever asked for. Murder and dacoity increased in villages and this had an impact on those who were well off. The weavers too found the going tough. But even after months, the Government did nothing to salvage the situation.

At the peak of summer, a tiny spark can reduce a whole shrivelled forest to ashes. This is exactly what happens when parched lives chance upon fiery revolutionary ideas.

Comrades in Thalassery got drawn into this issue. As the problem came to a head, more and more activists resigned from the Marxist party. Literature of revolution was being read by all and sundry. But after a while, literature became irrelevant and practical solutions were called for. It was during this time that some comrades reached Wayanad with the message of Pulpally. These comrades saw the notices brought out over the problems of the beedi workers and weavers and thought of linking it with the Pulaplly issue. To go into the heart of the matter, comrades organized meetings with workers who were out of job. The workers were briefed on the Pulpally issue and the activities the comrades had started there. Since the workers had been reading revolutionary literature for a while they were receptive to new ideas. All this led to a complete conviction that both the matters were closely linked and that one could be deciphered only with the help of the other. A police reprisal after a revolt had scared a few workers off initially, but the idea of a safe shelter in Wayanad egged them on. The beedi workers took up the mission — revolt, and march to Wayanad; then let loose a brave and heroic struggle rallying up with the peasants, farmhands and tribals.

Suddenly, the activities in Pulpally and Wayanad gathered momentum. Like a toddler trying to copy the grown-ups around him, we too began our humble attempt to walk down the magnificent path shown to us by Mao, and our own history...

What were the questions raised by Pulpally and Thalassery? And what were the answers to them? If one pondered over it, one would realize that these questions represent the basic issues troubling the working class all over India before and after independence. The problems of the peasant, the worker and the intellectual cannot be solved separately. These issues are interlinked. Among these, the peasant's problem is of greater significance.

Immediately after the Thalassery-Pulpally incident, the Government gave the peasants the right of ownership to the land they held. The government opened Dinesh Beedi Company to employ the jobless workers. This could be termed a solution all right. But did these measures really put an end to all the issues a farmer and worker faced? Even as the Government allotted land to the peasants they didn't forget to build a fortified police station in the vicinity. Before the Pulpally revolt, peasants had to walk over 17 miles to reach Sulatan Bathery. Now, there is a tarred road connecting Pulpally and a lot of buses ply to Sultan Bathery. Every care has been taken to ensure that the Pulpally incident does not repeat itself.

But cracking the issue of one beedi company doesn't mean anything. The iron clutch of foreign capitalism over our economy hasn't slackened one bit. If it was Commonwealth for a while after August 15, 1947 now it is World Bank, European Economic Commission and *Comicone.* Earlier there was only one exploiter, the British, now there are many – America, Russia, Japan and Germany. Could anyone find a remedy for the rancid ulcer that festers the entrails of our agriculture, which is still dependent on rains and the aid of the World Bank? These capitalist forces, which still bombard us with various subsidies haven't got their fill even after feeding on every drop of sweat and blood of our millions of workforce.

Still, it is considered a sin even to challenge the pyramid-like social hierarchy. The ancient Indian civilization is all about ahimsa and non-violence. But is it a sin to violate the tenets of ahimsa to sustain one's own life, to have a life with dignity? The oppressed have always stood up against their oppressors from the time the society was divided into classes. The War of Independence of 1857, the Malabar Peasant Revolt of 1921, the Naval Mutiny of 1946, the Telangana-Punnapra struggles and many other historical events bear testimony to this.

Man has always defended himself on the face of an attack. Victims tend to brace themselves up even if the assault is spear-headed by the government and its authorities. This was what had happened to the Tsar in Russia and Chiang kai Sheikh in China. Even to this day this is the story in South Africa, Palestine, Iran. Wherever there is oppression, there tends to be resistance. Only those who want to perpetrate the oppression would demand to stop this defiance. There is no leader who hasn't ruled us in the name of ahimsa. But do these people practise ahimsa? They greet the peaceful protests of labourers, peasants, students, and teachers with guns. The number of people who have fallen to police guns within these last 46 years is uncountable.

Violence against the powerless is what the authorities term peaceful and passive. This is ahimsa for them. When the oppressed rise in protest, it becomes violence and *himsa*. Our working class has been sold off to serve the interest of foreign countries and the ruling class, which is a minority of the population. The authorities resort to naked force to ensure a smooth sale. This is patriotism, ahimsa and non-violence for them.

I don't mean to say that I am a spokesperson of violence. On the contrary, I despise violence. I love to lead a peaceful life. But the world around me, and my life experiences taught me that no one can distance oneself from violence. It prevails in every realm of human life, in one form or the other. Even as one tries to avoid it, it makes itself felt like an omnipresent power. I realized that it could only be dealt with in the same coin. I decided never to be part of today's inhuman social set up. Being a woman, it would not be easy for me. But I refuse to give up.

7

MA

A few days before the Thalassery-Pulpally incidents, my mother resigned from the Gujarati school in Kozhikode, where she was headmistress. That put an end to our only means of livelihood. I will have to take you a little back in time to explain what led to this situation.

My mother, Mandakini Narayanan, is a Gujarati. Her parents were from Bhavnagar district. My grandfather used to work in Bombay and so my mother and her two brothers were raised there. They were orthodox Gujarati Brahmins.

Mom was a student during the Second World War when Bombay was the base of most of the Communist activities in the country. Communists all over the world, including India took immense pride in the spread of socialism in the Soviet Union under the leadership of Stalin. Communist ideas caught the imagination of the younger generation, particularly the students and Ma was no exception. She became active in the Student's Federation. She and her friends used to sell the party magazine "People's war" and she had interesting stories of Congressmen chasing them away.

Father reached Bombay around this time. He was a worker in garment factories and a Communist activist.

Ma landed a job soon after her studies on compassionate grounds because her father had recently died in harness. He had a good job in Bombay Secretariat and Ma was accommodated in the same department. India had just established diplomatic ties with the Soviet Union and Ma was a member of the group of Soviet Friends. But Communists in India were hunted down soon after the railway strike of 1948. Vijayalakshmi Pandit, the Prime Minister's high profile sister was the president of the Soviet Friends' group and it was a lawful organization. Yet, Morarji Desai, the then Home Minister of the Bombay Presidency, under whose department my mom worked, warned her not to get involved in it if she wished to keep her job. Ma didn't care much about her job and in a matter of few days she was fired.

Communist ideology had a great impact on Ma's personal life as well. She was never a practising Brahmin; she was so irreligious that God never figured in her life. Her brothers too had given up wearing their sacred threads long ago. She didn't mind losing her job for the sake of her convictions. Soon, with the Party's blessings and under its auspices she married my father. Despite her brother's support, Ma had to confront her extended family, which could not stomach the idea of an inter-caste marriage. But she was adamant, and gradually, her family gave in to her wishes.

There was a deep crisis in the party after the infamous Calcutta Thesis of Ranadive in 1948. Already, there was frustration within the party about the duplicity of stance over the Naval Mutiny and the armed revolt of Telangana peasants. The Calcutta thesis aggravated the situation. A few of the party workers raised their voice against the leadership. The Calcutta thesis went completely against whatever Lenin, Mao and Stalin taught about colonial-semi colonial countries. Ranadive argued that there were no different phases in the revolution in India as these masters had taught, but with independence a ruling class which resembled those in western countries had come into power, and that here, the phase of people's democratic revolution had merged with that of socialist revolution. Ranadive didn't lose any opportunity to run down the greatness of Mao. My father was among those workers who protested against this thesis and was promptly expelled from the party. After Independence, and especially after the Calcutta thesis and the aborted railway strike, communists were persecuted. Father had been in hiding those days. But now he lost the shelter of the party too. The party even asked Mom to divorce him! Later, the Calcutta thesis was withdrawn due to widespread resistance within the party. Father was taken back into the party after a period of six months. But by then the party in Bombay had gone to the dogs.

I was born a year after my parents' marriage. My father's brother died prematurely and he felt he should return to Kerala to help his family. With the permission of the party leadership we left Bombay for Kozhikode. Soon afterwards, Ma joined the Gujarat school in Kozhikode.

The Gujarati people in Kozhikode had come here for trade and later settled down. The Gujarati school was opened for the children of the community under a private management. It was an upper primary school to start with, and grew into a senior secondary school. Ma worked there for 18 years. She joined as a teacher, and later served as the headmistress for 10 years. Ma was a graduate and when it became essential, she did a one-year B.Ed course from Bombay. I was twelve or thirteen years old then. When she came back, she became the headmistress of the school.

My father and mother settled in Kozhikode in 1950 and were active in the party. Ma spent all her spare time after school in party activities. They set up a library near our home, the Kunnikkal Madhavan Memorial Library. Ma never confined herself to home. She grew up during a period when the whole world was in turmoil and the spirit of revolution prevailed in India. All these made her a valorous woman. Purged from the rotten influences of conventions, she never found it odd to work with men at any juncture of her life.

In 1956, there was an internal crisis in the global Communist Movement. The Communists all over the world were shocked at the public outbursts of Khrushchev against Stalin. The comrades who were ready to lay down their lives for the movement built up by Stalin in Soviet Union found this dubious stand of the Soviet leadership hard to digest. Comrade Stalin who led the anti-fascist movement during the Second World War successfully was the champion of the communists all over the world. Communists in the oppressed countries of Asia, Africa and Latin America particularly looked up to him. The communist movement was in ruins now. The workers felt orphaned.

My parents were among those millions of communists who grew up admiring Stalin. They found it agonizing to listen to Khrushchev abusing their idol. The party leadership in India supported Khrushchev, which made the whole affair unbearable. They couldn't compromise with Khrushchev's view or the Indian Party leadership's tepid stand. They along with all the comrades of the unit decided to resign from the party. But this only made matters worse, especially for my father. I could sense a growing tension between my parents. Away from the party, father got into many debauched friendships. He was a totally different man. He lost his soul when material desires replaced ideological dreams.

Gradually, I too grew away from my parents. I rarely saw them all day. Ma reached home only in the evening, and father came back late at night. I spent my time in school and afterwards with cousins. My father's family urged me to distance myself from my parents and their way of thinking. Many in his family disliked Ma's independent lifestyle and her job. They tried to instigate this hatred in me as well.

Despite all this ideological turmoil, the embers of revolutionary hope were not completely extinguished in father. When he had money, many leaders came to him for contributions. But now, when he was down in the gutters, no one could lift him out of it. Years later, in 1963, the Chinese party made public statements about the dubious stand of the Soviet leadership. Father's life underwent a sea change when he listened to Radio Peking about the ideological war the Chinese party under Mao was fighting against the Soviet leadership. The declaration of the Chinese party was the magical wand that transformed my parents' lives. Gradually, father left his unhealthy friendships and became active in the party once again. Towards the end of 1964, after the split in the Communist party, father joined the newly formed Communist Party of India (Marxist), which created an impression of proximity to the Chinese party.

Ma had to go through much travail when she drifted away from the party. My father had fallen into a despicable way of life and I too was slowly drifting away from her. But she stood like a rock through these testing times. Her association with kids in school was a great relief to her. Within the family, no one was sympathetic towards Ma. On several occasions, she had even decided to put an end to all this and leave for Bombay for good. But finally, father came back to his normal self and renewed his party activities. My mother supported him in all possible ways. In 1967 father was arrested which prompted me to join politics. Ma was happy that I was freeing myself of the corrupting influences of the convention-ridden society. She was not sure about my decision to quit studies, but she never imposed her opinions on me.

After we severed all ties with the rest of father's family, the three of us had just Ma's salary to live on. Our political opponents and enemies within the family were aware of this and there were attempts galore to get her sacked.

The Gujarati society was grateful to Ma for her sincere service to the school. She was always welcomed as a friend in Gujarati families across Kerala. They never doubted her teaching skills or morality.

During 1967-68 the Gujarati school management, the Government and even the Kerala Governor began to get anonymous letters about Ma. A copy of each of these letters was sent home too. "Guardians of students" signed them. But the management didn't take this seriously.

Our Naxalbari-triggered activities were getting feverish each day. Ma was an active participant in all the debates and meetings held at our house. We knew that we too would have to take a plunge into the field of action soon. She had had enough of threats and anonymous letters. The school management, pressured by the government, had begun to show signs of doubts. In June 1968, when the school reopened for the academic year, the management went back on its word about Ma's salary. She protested, but the management stood its ground. Ma realized that it was a tactic to fire her. She resigned in July and never regretted her decision once. We too felt we were free at last. Ma then became integral to the movement.

The bitter lessons of life during the troubled phase of the party and the Communist movement were a source of strength to my parents. The crisis in the Indian party following the Calcutta thesis of 1948 and the trouble the global communist movement underwent after the onslaught of Titoism in Europe were specific instances. In 1956, came the volte-face of Khrushchev and the disease called electoral politics that consumed the Communist party of India forever. My parents faced the impact of these crises bravely and as a result, their belief in the ultimate victory of communism got only strengthened. This gave them the ability to withstand all the troubles that brewed in India, and the international scene in China after Mao's death in 1976. And, their experiences show me the way today...

Ma with little Ajitha.

Ajitha, Kunnickal Narayanan and Mandakini with their comrades in police custody.

8

PREPARATION FOR PULPALLY

The months of September and October 1968 were decisive for us. The activities in Pulpally were fast gaining ground. The number of peasants attending our secret meetings had gone up. They were determined to make an attempt to break free from the age-old instruments of power that smothered them. Tribal comrades from Wayanad also attended these meetings. Comrade Kissan Thomman, a prominent leader of the Marxist Farmers Association was passionately involved in all these proceedings. The honorofic *kissan* was the result of his long involvement with the struggles for the rights of farmers. Even age did not deter him.

Meanwhile, we had informed the peasant comrades about the seriousness of the beedi workers' and weavers' issues in Kannur. The peasants of Wayanad were thrilled to learn that beedi workers and weavers of Kannur would also join them in their war for land and justice.

We in Kozhikode promptly received all the news from both these places. Efforts were made to garner support from comrades across the state. This was the time to put to test our devotion and courage. Around this time we translated and published the 'Quotations on people's war' by Mao. This book had some important portions that Mao compiled from wartime literature with a Marxist-Leninist perception based on the experiences of the Chinese revolution. This gave us fresh energy. We were ignorant of the basics of armed revolution, but were prompted on by the unadulterated belief in revolution and the fact that peasant-labour comrades had embraced the idea of revolution. It was a matter of life and death for them. If we had limited ourselves to mere ideological campaign, our fervour would have died down with time. Lack of experience never held us back in this onward journey.

Ma had by then resigned her job. Father was busy in Wayanad and Thalassery (a town in Kannur district where beedi workers were being organized). He would return to Kozhikode occasionally and then travel to other parts of Kerala to update comrades about the progress of the groundwork. They were being prepared for an imminent strike. Ma and I were supposed to go to Wayanad. We sold off our furniture. I sold off my radio, my last prized possession before leaving home to join the armed revolt that was to soon begin in Wayanad. We told the rest of the family that we were shifting to Bombay. There was no direct bus from Kozhikode to Pulpally, we had to get down at Mananthavady and then proceed to Pulpally. Our comrades who were working with local farmers in Mananthavady had a great influence over them. So, we decided to go to Mananthavady and join them.

This was in November 1968. Ma was not well. Even I couldn't bear the bitter cold in Wayanad. Reaching Wayanand was difficult; the bus service was almost non-functional. There were long stretches in the journey when we had to walk. Bred in the city, we were not used to hardships faced in the countryside, but the dream of revolution kept us going. We stayed in many houses in and around Mananthavady and got a first hand experience of the lives of farmers. We kept their revolutionary hopes high by holding meetings and reading out Mao's works and other revolutionary literature to them.

We went to a *paadi*, the long row of houses allotted by tea estates for their labour force. The estate workers' life was pathetic. These rows of sheds had cave like narrow rooms like prison cells, stuffed with people four times their capacity. In the bitter cold, children roamed around naked, with running noses and boils all over their bodies. A swarm of flies followed them around.

Profit from these estates went to foreign estate owners who sold tea in the global market. Two-thirds of the tea estates in Wayanad belonged to foreigners. They paid these workers a pittance. Any failure to report to work would mean a wage cut. There was no one to support them when they fell ill. Their children never went to school. Forget education they could barely survive on their wages.

All political parties were active among the estate workers, but the Marxist party was the most influential. The workers believed in the party because revolution regularly featured on its list of promises. The party and its leadership with their fire-spitting speeches kept them hooked. But gradually the truth dawned on the workers. When a majority of the party activists under comrade Varghese's leadership resigned from the Mananthavady Block committee, some other activists working among estate workers too gave up their party membership. Thettamala Gopi, K.C.Ayamutti and P.S Govindan were among them. They began to spread the message of Naxalbari among the workers and were able to convince them that only a revolution could end their wretched existence. Even women declared their willingness to go to war.

The advance of colonialism and centuries of brutal exploitation by local landlords, rich farmers and traders had forced tribals, the real owners of Wayanad, deep into the forest. They were the aboriginals of Wayanad; there existed within their community a sort of primitive communism, feudalism and even slavery. The British had realized that they could harvest gold from the fertile lands of Wayanad. The tribals did fight them, but they didn't succeed against the Empire's weapons.

Englishmen brought people from the plains over to Wayanad and cleared the forests, planted tea and coffee. The settlers cheated the tribals of their lands with the active support of the British estate owners. All this gradually left the majority of the tribals landless. The rich farmers and foreigners reduced them to slavery, and the situation worsened with every passing day. The control of these estates is still with the colonial forces. Even today, tribals are being hurled into the midst of wild beasts and wilderness; none of the parties that swear by parliamentarism could bring any change in their lives. Tribals will get their due only if they rise in protest like other marginalized sections of the society to wipe away the old social system. No political party with vested interests in the prevailing system would be ready to help them in this effort. For, tribals do not constitute a majority anywhere in Kerala and hence they do not become a constituency or vote bank for mainstream political parties.

We spent a few days amongst the forgotten people, inspiring them with the ideas of revolution. A lot of comrades were involved in the last stage of preparations in Pulpally and Thalassery. We were thrilled about this great event, but were naturally anxious about how it would shape out. Ma and I thought over our roles as women in the revolt.

That was when we got a lasting contribution to our efforts from Calcutta! The Mathrubhumi daily reported from Cochin that father has been expelled from the All India Coordination Committee led by Charu Majumdar. Ironically, we got this news in the forests of Pulpally when we were working round the clock to create naxalbaris all over our state, as directed by the first and second Coordination Committees.

But this bit of news didn't mean anything to us. We went on with firm steps...

As the time for the revolt drew closer, father concentrated more on

Thalassery. Some senior comrades who had taken up serious responsibilities there were developing cold feet. So, father decided to stay put in Thalassery. The victory of Pulpally was closely linked to that of Thalassery. The struggle that should follow was to be shaped on the large section of comrades who participated in the Thalassery revolt who would then go to Wayanad to take part in the Pulpally struggle. Therefore, more efforts had to go into making Thalassery attack a success.

Comrade Varghese was in charge of activities in Pulpally. Comrades Thettamala Krishnankutty and Philip M Prasad assisted him. Around 400 peasant volunteers including tribals were recruited in Pulpally alone. The comrades were aware that the cops would have informed about our preparations to attack the police, the Devaswom and the forest departments. The excitement was palpable. As the D-day approached most of the comrades were living in the forests or in huts near forests. If at all Thalassery revolt got postponed or didn't happen, the police could easily go on a hunting spree in Pulpally.

We heard about Philip M Prasad's reluctance when we reached Mananthavady. When the activities in Pulpally were at its highest pitch, Prasad said: "I can't go on now. I am going to Thalassery." But the rest of the comrades explained his mistake to him and brought him back.

There was no scope for hesitation for a team led by comrade Varghese. The comrade's ability to merge with the marginalized sections of the society was truly outstanding. He could go to any tribal hut and live with them, like them. He knew their lives like nobody else could, the atrocities committed against them, and the significance of their liberation. Comrade Varghese was a true revolutionary, he felt the tribals' agonies as his, hated their enemies as his, and would safeguard their interests as his own. He was born and brought up in a conventional Christian home, but could still become one with those people who were cursed to live an inhuman life with the animals in the jungle. Only a person who was truly devoted to the cause of revolution could display these unusual qualities. The revolt of Pulpally shone bright with his selfless sacrifice for the Naxalbari movement. There were many valorous peasants like Allungal Sreedharan and Kissan Thomman to support him.

It was not a smooth sail for us in Mananthavady. I did commit mistakes due to my inexperience, but instead of correcting me in good faith, a comrade who had promised to help us went around spreading rumours about me. We thought it could be due to some misunderstanding, but the fangs of his hostility were bared out, as the day of Pulpally revolt got nearer.

That day, my father was supposed to arrive from Thalassery to meet us to decide about our participation in the revolt. So, along with some other comrades, we waited for him at a pre-determined location. Father and comrade PS Govindan were supposed to come, but comrade PS said that father couldn't come. We asked him what father wanted us to do. He told us that father had asked Ma to go back to Bombay as she was not keeping well enough to undergo the strenuous struggle,. and that he wanted me to stay in Mananthavady.

That was a huge blow! For months, I had been looking forward to be a part of the Pulpally revolt. Mananthavady was just a stopover. Should I stay back after coming all this way, leaving everything behind? Weren't they trying to avoid me because I was a girl? I couldn't bear it any longer and burst into tears. The comrades were confused. But comrade PS remarked in a sarcastic tone: "We have seen enough of these crocodile tears." I couldn't control myself. I gave the comrades a piece of my mind. I told them in no uncertain terms that I was not staying back in Mananthavady. Whether they liked it or not I was going to Pulpally along with them. The comrades realized that they couldn't change my mind. Ma refused to go to Bombay and decided to stay back in Mananthavady. But we came to know the whole truth only much later. Father had actually assigned P.S to ask Ma and me to discuss the issue of our participation with the rest of the comrades and take a decision on our own.

The day after the meeting, I parted ways with Ma. I went along with two other comrades to meet up with another group. Thus, after a brief meeting, around 30 of us set out for Pulpally on foot. Earlier, another bigger group had gone to Thalassery. A few comrades were supposed to camp in Tirunelli forests to link the two group of comrades after the revolts. When we reached the stipulated place, the meeting was over. But the comrades greeted us warmly. I could see comrade Thettamala Krishnankutty, Sankaran master, Kunjiraman master, Ramankuttiyettan from Kattikkulam and Kunjaman, a kurichya tribal comrade. There were a few other peasant-worker comrades too whom I had already met in Mananthavady. These comrades were waiting for us and we set off immediately.

This unusual procession moved ahead in the darkness of the night. Excitement bubbled within. When the world was asleep, we went on crossing fields, hills, streams, bridges, and tarred roads in silence. The comrades had with them two-three country made guns. We were overwhelmed by the thoughts of the heroic revolution that was to take place. After walking for miles together, we sat down for a while. We resumed the journey soon, for we had to reach Pulpally by daybreak. The company of brave comrades who had left their families behind, for the sake of the armed revolution instilled courage within me. I was not used to walking long distances and my legs were swollen. But the happiness of having joined the war could overcome any discomfort. We reached a forest in the wee hours of the morning. There was a village path a jeep could ply through, but all around there were no signs of human settlement. We broke into small groups before daybreak. The comrades understood my plight. The non-stop walk for twenty miles without sleep had taken its toll on me. They took me to a near-by house and spoke to the family. They knew the comrades and welcomed us with love. They gave me some herbal ointment to rub on my legs. We rested for some time and started at noon after lunch. My heart was overflowing with gratitude. We lost our way and wandered for a while. We had to ask our way around and by evening, somehow reached Devargadda in Pulpally.

We met a local comrade there. He took us to an empty house where we could have some rest. I had by then tried various ointments on my legs, but they were still aching. Yet, I didn't regret my decision. That day, no one could persuade me to turn back. I told the comrades that they shouldn't worry about me. We had to meet up with the rest of our comrades. As we walked further into the forest, we were told that comrade Varghese and others were camping on the other side of a river. The comrade told us that another group would be going into the forest the next day and we were supposed to join them right away.

We reached a small shack. It had no walls, just four bamboo poles to support the roof of grass. A young peasant lived there, with his wife and baby. How could they be living here, in the middle of the forest, exposed to wild beasts and the chilly November wind, I wondered. How many more families would be suffering this fate! Our host was a member of our team for Pulpally. That night, his wife gave us food, and then we lay down wherever we could. The cold was unbearable, but I dozed with weariness. We got ready early in the morning. We were not supposed to talk during the night. So, I couldn't get introduced to any one.

The elderly comrade *Josephettan* (elder brother Joseph), a close associate of comrade Kissan Thomman, led us through the forest. It was quite a feat to find the way through that forest where wild climbers and shrubs intertwined. But I guess it wasn't all that difficult for someone who was familiar with the area. The twigs and thorns kept getting into my sari. My body was scratched all over. At time, I had to forcefully break strands of hair that got entangled with twigs.

Though it was morning, sunlight had not begun to seep into the thick forest. We walked for over five miles in the soft light of the dawn. Then we saw a small stream. There were people on the other side, busy cooking. They greeted us with joy. These comrades led us to where comrade Varghese and others were camping.

There were over 50 comrades gathered together and they welcomed us like long lost friends. Many of us were complete strangers, but the belief of one ideological goal bonded us. After exchange of greetings, we were introduced to each other.

Most of the comrades gathered in the Pulpally forest were youngsters. Among them the majority were peasants and farmhands. The intellectuals formed a minority. Comrades Allungal Sreedharan, C.S Chellappan, Gopalan, Sasimala Raman Nair, Kissan Thomman, Sukumaran, Josephettan, C. N Sreekantan Nair, tribal comrades Maran, Kaalan and two-three others — these were the comrades who had come from Pulpally. The comrades from Mananthvady included Sankaran Master, Kunjiraman master, Tailor Muhammed, Ramankuttiyettan, Kurichyan Kunjaman, and two-three other tribal comrades. Thettamala Gopi, who later turned approver in the Pulpally case, painted this particular incident in a different hue. He said in court that while introducing myself I had said that I was unmarried. But no one had asked me any personal detail, nor did the atmosphere solicit such trivial thoughts.

We reached our camp in Pulpally forest on the day the Thalassery attack was to have happened. We believed that the attack was over. Our anticipation was enormous because the Pulpally strike was planned within 48 hours of the Thalassery police station assault. Our sole source of news on the Thalassery attack was a radio. We had some food and rested for a while. Then we sat around and read pamphlets aloud: "The thunder of spring on the Indian horizon", "Indian masses learn their lessons from Telengana strikes" and Mao's quotations and also three articles that explain the communist world perception: Serve the people, In memory of Norman Bethune and The foolish old man who moved mountains. We lost ourselves in thoughts of the great event that was to happen and once more reiterated our commitment to the cause of the revolution for the sake of the oppressed multitudes. Though there were a few voices of dissent, resolve was etched on the faces of most comrades. The surging waves of excitement drowned these voices. The valour of the comrades from Pulpally was beyond words. Their revolutionary fervour was infectious. Comrades Kissan Thomman and Sukumaran stand out vividly in my memory.

Comrade Kissan Thomman was the senior-most among us. His face was always serene, his visage wise and mature. He didn't seem like a restless ocean, but was a volcano carrying deep within the potent embers of a fierce eruption. He was not a hollow man like many intellectuals who had not experienced life's tribulation. No whirlwind could uproot his commitment. Comrade Kissan Thomman resembled the old man in Mao's teachings. I have heard the elderly sit back and complain that they could do nothing now because they have grown old. Comrade Kissan Thomman proved with his life that those were mere excuses to shirk life's responsibilities. Defying his age he came forward to take part in the revolution against injustice and was always ready to help youngsters. Nothing dissuaded him from joining us, not his family, not his age. He was a beacon of inspiration for all youngsters in the group.

Comrade Sukumaran was the youngest. He was all of 18 or 19 years and is one of the lesser-known warriors of the Pulpally rebellion. His passion was like electricity, easily transmitted to others. He didn't know fear. He was firm in his belief that only an armed revolt could end the misery of peasants and labourers and he knew that Mao's way was the right one. Comrade Sukumaran went into hiding in Malabar after the Pulpally attack. He worked there as a farmhand and later joined mainstream politics, but was soon killed by his political opponents.

We shifted camp in the forest twice or thrice. The task didn't prove too difficult because our tribal comrades steered us through the forest. They knew the forest inside out. We did some shooting practice in the forest. Weapons were chiseled out of sturdy branches. The comrades had with them knives and daggers. Some others had made country bombs and dynamites. A few of the literate comrades wrote posters saying, "Armed peasants revolt Zindabad!" "Red Salute to Naxalbari!" "Long live Chairman Mao!" Other comrades went to buy food and seek information from nearby villages. They returned with the assurance that our presence in the forest was not noticed.

We planned our itinerary as we waited for news of Thalassery police station attack. A council of 17 members was formed to take important decisions. Varghese, Thettamala Krishnankutty, Kurichiyan Kunjaman, Kissan Thomman, Philip and I were part of the council.

Earlier, we had decided to attack the Pulpally M.S.P camp. Apart from some rich farmers and the temple management, the entire local population despised the camp. There was a palpable mounting tension between the people and the police. We knew that the people would stand by us; after all we were just doing what they have been dreaming. Another reason why we had planned this assault was that the M.S.P camp had a wireless instrument and a lot of guns. We had to destroy that instrument, so as to stop the police from immediately transmitting the news of the attack to the outside world. The police shouldn't get at us till we reached the Tirunelli forests. They never stocked ammunition in the local police station. But the M.S.P camp had some 12 guns, that many constables and ammunition. So there was no point in destroying the local police station without attacking the M.S.P camp. If we could secure the guns, it would prove to be a great asset for our further struggle. We had also decided to burn down the registrar's office, which kept the false records that denied land rights to the peasants.

Later we planned an attack on two landlords on the way to Tirunelli. These landlords of Chekadi village were terribly cruel. They used to make the tribals slog like slaves to fill up their granaries. They possessed two-three guns. They were lords and masters of the land who could at their whim kill or maim any tribal they chose. No one dared go to the police. A complaint would turn out to be a bonanza for the local policemen who served the landlords. The complainant would soon become the culprit and end up behind bars. So we decided to scare them, take their guns and then loot them. We would force open the granaries to the tribals who rightfully owned them. Thus we would torch the flame of armed revolt in Kerala challenging the police, the government's device of torture and shake its foundations of feudalism.

On November 22, the news of Thalassery police station attack was aired in the afternoon Malayalam news bulletin. On the previous day, a public meeting was held at Karimam junction to protest police atrocities. A notice, which was brought out a few days earlier, had stated clearly that the meeting was to be held by the S.S.P-Marxist parties. The notice said that if the police didn't stop its brutality against the peasants who were seeking their rights peacefully, they would be forced to resort to violent means. The leaders made the meeting spectacular. The Thalassery M.S.P camp was located next to the police station. In an attempt to add spice to their speeches, the leaders pointed to the M.S.P camp and proclaimed: "If you don't stop your unjustified violence, we would raze this camp to the ground." These mainstream political leaders always played to the gallery, later forgetting all about the expectations they had kindled in the masses. Even in their wildest dreams it never occurred to them that a group of youngsters were at that very moment hiding in the forests to put to practice what they have been merely preaching! The leaders went back homes for a good night's sleep, glad that they played with the masses' emotions. When the MSP camp was attacked the next day, the police obviously, went after Thomas Master and the other organizers, Kesavan and Kunjupanikker. Thomas master somehow managed to flee, but the police caught the other two. This was a major police goof up.

We heard the news and got ready to strike. But little did we know that the Thalassery attack didn't shape up as it was conceived. I still doubt whether Pulpally would have happened if we had known about the failure of the Thalassery attack. Anyway, charged with the traditional revolutionary fervour of the peasants of Wayanad, we set out.

I got rid of my sari and got into a pair of trousers. Sari was a nuisance; it slowed down my pace. I wore two blouses and a sweater but was still feeling cold. One of the comrades gave me a shirt too. But there was no time to bother about my increasingly swollen legs or the cold. We were readying ourselves for a life and death battle.

9

THE PULPALLY REVOLT

There were sixty of us huddled in the Chitalayam forest when we got the news of the attack on Thalassery police station over the radio. It was time for our final preparation. To boost our confidence, we re-read a few passages from Mao Tse Tung's works and CPC's pamphlets and had some weaponry practice as well. We were all excited. "After the Thalassery action, the comrades must have started for Wayanad now. We should not be late," we thought.

The Supreme Council had taken the final decision that the plan should be carried out by midnight the following day and this message was conveyed to the members of the council and all the comrades. There was no disagreement. The next day morning, two comrades were sent to Pulpally ahead of us for a last surveillance of the MSP camp. We approached our destination changing camps often and cooking our own food. We had rice with big wild gooseberries steamed in the hot starch water drained from cooked rice with salt and coconut oil added to them. The curry tasted heavenly. One such gooseberry could revitalize us when we were worn out after walking miles together. The forest was full of such small blessings!

As we continued walking the need to prove my commitment to the ideology I have chosen over my personal life grew stronger within me. I was living among sixty other comrades, all men. There were all sorts of them in our group — adolescents, youngsters, middle-aged and old men, and comrades from the tribal community who stood out with their distinct features even in a crowd… They were of different natures and hailed from various sections of society. Some were poor peasants, some farm workers, others intellectuals, but I was the lone woman among them. Lost in thoughts of the revolt we were .o begin, there was no place for such trivial gender differences in our minds. We were all one in our mission, emissaries of a new world, bound in pristine thoughts of emancipation. But later, political opponents used this fact to slander me and other comrades, and run down the significance of Thalassery-Pulpally revolts, but all rumours died down after a while. The greatness of Pulpally shone bright challenging all such disparaging barbs.

With soaring spirits and a will to challenge the heavens we left for Karimam on the 23rd night. Each one of us had a weapon in our hands; I got a wooden spear. The comrades who had gone to observe the MSP camp came back by 12.30 in the night. That was when we came to know that there were no MSP men in the wireless room and that a sub-inspector and about ten other policemen had gone to Sultan Bathtery carrying all the arms with them. The S.I who had accompanied them was the infamous Allappan, the king without a specter who ruled over the farmers. Everything was chartered out to the last detail and then the disappointing bit of news!

But we decided to stick to our plan. At least we should destroy that wireless machine and mark our protest against the malevolent reign of the police. We couldn't postpone this any further, no comrade had a different opinion. Another youngster, Ravindran from Sultan Battery, had come with two comrades to join us. He was just 18 or 19, and this last minute addition to our troop deepened our inspiration.

In the all-enveloping darkness of the night we inched forward in a single file in absolute silence. Stopping only to clear the path off tall wild grass, we walked over three miles to the Sita Devi temple at Pulpally. Just two or three furlongs more and we would reach the temple. Our group stopped again. A flight of stairs from the temple led down to the *oottupura*, which served as the MSP camp. We had to observe the scene before we moved further. Comrades Varghese, Krishnankutty, Sukumaran, and Kissan Thomman hid behind a bush near the camp to survey the area. The rest of us stood in a row near the path that went up to the temple.

Suddenly, we heard the sound of a truck. The silence of the night enhanced the sound and it seemed that the truck was just behind us. It only proved there were still some cowards amidst us. The moment they heard the sound, they cowered behind the bushes on either side of the road. "It's the police" they sent panic waves with this cry. The rest of us stood confused for a while, then hid behind the bushes. I too went behind some undergrowth and could see no one near me. The commotion that we created when we tried to hide would have been enough to alert the police. The comrades who had gone to observe the camp were nowhere to be seen. I sat for about two minutes and then stood up. I could see a few silhouettes and walked towards them and found that they were our comrades. The sound of the truck faded in the distance; it was going some other way. What had happened, no one knew for sure. Was this sort of reaction a common phenomenon even among comrades who had launched themselves into the battlefront thoroughly prepared? Around 400 comrades had been recruited for the Pulpally revolt. Only 60 turned up. Was this a common trend when one moves on from the plains of promise to the heights of action? We had no time to ponder over these disturbing questions.

A few of us decided to search for comrades Varghese and Krishnankutty. We moved on to the path leading to the Sita Devi temple. We must have taken five or six steps when we saw somebody walking towards us. It was comrade Sukumaran. He told us in an angry voice: "What have you done? Comrades Varghese and Krishanankutty are waiting for you behind the camp. Come on, comrades, let us march forward."

Suddenly, we heard the sound of a shot. The thought that one of our comrades might have been injured propelled us forwards. With shouts that shocked the whole of Pulpally village we ran to the camp crossing the courtyard of the temple. Some of the comrades who were still hiding came out to join us. "Who is it?" The temple priest asked in a terrified voice. "Shut up, or you will lose your head." We said loudly as we stomped down the stairs. The policemen and the sub inspector must have gathered what was going on. Frightened, they had hid somewhere. Some comrades went to the verandah and smashed the wireless set. The door of the wireless operator's room was locked. It was blown open with a hand grenade. When we entered the room we saw the wireless operator crouching under his bed. He pleaded pathetically for his life. But the fire of revenge, kept under control till then, flamed up in the farmers' heart. They hacked him to death. "This is our answer. This is the punishment for your arrogance that makes you commit sins of power." Someone from our group shouted.

Another group went into S.I Sankunni Menon's room. He was not there. We searched everywhere, but could not find him. There was a big cot in the room and underneath it were the sandal wood logs that he had collected. He was hiding behind them. We stepped out of the room when we could not find him. But he made the mistake of trying to run away, believing that we had gone. One of us saw this. We charged back into the room and attacked him. After a while, he became absolutely still. We came out of the room, piled up all the records and files in the courtyard and set them ablaze. We gathered in the courtyard, shouting slogans: "Red salute to Naxalbari, long live armed peasants revolution, long live Chairman Mao!" We scattered some of our pamphlets and books all over before leaving the place.

Then, we marched towards the police station. We had reached the junction leading to the station when we heard a loud blast. The shock paralysed us and we stood rooted to the spot. Was it the police, or was it some thing else? We looked at each other not knowing what to do. Then we saw comrade Gopalan, walking towards us, his palm blown off, with just the little finger dangling from it. He was bathed in blood. The comrade had with him a hand grenade, which could go off with a slight rub. He was a settler, skilful in handling these sorts of bombs since he used them often to deal with wild boars. He was trying to catch up with us when he fell into a pit and the grenade had blown off. His right palm was torn to pieces. We had wanted to follow up our successful attack of the camp with further assaults, but this came as a severe blow. Comrade Gopalan was a deprived peasant, who earned his bread toiling with his hands. This tragedy dampened our spirits. He couldn't accompany us in this condition. We handed over some money to a comrade and asked him to take comrade Gopalan to the Battery hospital. Two other comrades were sent with him.

After this incident we didn't feel like attacking the police station or the registrar's office. All of us felt that it would be wiser to leave the place at the earliest. We walked towards Chekadi slowly. We realized then that our number had come down. Some comrades who had hidden themselves on their way to the MSP camp had not joined us at all. But then, a large group was supposed to join us from Thalassery. There was nothing to worry.

We could see the dawn breaking in the horizon while we moved towards Chekadi village. The impact of the misfortune that had befallen comrade Gopalan started to fade away. Now we were about to attack the houses of two well-known landlords of Wayanad. The tribal comrades began to narrate in detail the atrocities of these landlords. The comrades reminded us how important our mission was. We commended each other for the role each of us played in the MSP camp attack. We appreciated those who displayed exemplary allegiance and criticized those who lagged behind in commitment. On our way we saw temporary sheds of tribals where they guarded their landlord's crops against wild beasts. The comrades went into two-three of them to ask if they had guns. But obviously, the landlords never entrusted a tribal with a gun, even if it were for self-defence.

We crossed hills, mounts and fields and walked for over six miles before reaching Chekadi. It was 7-7.30 by then. We met some local tribals on our way. We exhorted them to join us and told them that we had destroyed the MSP camp and that our next aim was to attack the houses of the landlords. Their faces lit up. The news of MSP camp attack filled them with happiness, a new way of liberation was now open before them. Some of the tribals asked us to go to their colony to get more people, but we were running out of time already.

Shouting slogans we rushed into Thimmappa Chetty's house. A group of comrades went upstairs and dragged down Thimmappa Chetty to the verandah. "Give us your guns. If we search them out, you will regret it. Do you see our gun? If you don't want us to train this on you, you better give us all your guns." We threatened him. Some comrades went to his room and forced open his treasure chest and recovered thousands of rupees and sovereigns of gold that he had secured from poor peasants as security for loans. We burned all records of land deals he had acquired fooling uneducated tribals. We distributed the grain in his granaries to the workers in his house and the tribals who had followed us. We too kept some. A few of the comrades took sack full of grains to the adivasi colonies. The women in the house were trembling with fear, but we never threatened them even once. Thimmappa Chetty had hid his gun somewhere. We couldn't get hold of it. We warned him of dire consequences if he ill treated his slaves anymore and told him that we would be back soon. We left the house in exuberance having successfully completed our operation. We took one of Thimmappa Chetty's sons along with us. Some people followed us to tell us that there was another landlord who lived near-by and he had made their lives miserable. To their joy, we told them that we were going there, to Dasappa Chetty's house.

I could never forget the affection the tribals poured on us once they were convinced that we practised what we preached. They were on the forefront, showing us the way, helping us with our loads.

On the way to Dasappa Chetty's house, by the bank of a paddy field there was a small tea-stall. Some comrades went in to get some bidi. One of the tribal youths told us that Thimmappa Chetty's elder son owned a much bigger shop which was not very far from there and we could get any number of bidis and cigarettes from the shop. As luck would have it, we had with us Thimmappa Chetty's eldest son himself. Soon, we stormed the shop. It was a relatively big shop in that hamlet. In the tea-stall next-door hot *puttu* and other snacks were being prepared. We went in there and supplied everything to the tribals. We took some for ourselves too. We were active since midnight and hence quite hungry. Whoever came for a cup of tea was sent back after a sumptuous breakfast. The little landlord looked on helplessly, frightened. Now, we proceeded towards Dasappa Chetty's house. The tribal comrades and others who were proficient in their language explained our purpose to all those following us.

The village must have found our procession in broad daylight devoid of any masquerades quite unique. We were followed by a huge number of tribals and we had in our hands all sorts of weapons. Dasappa Chetty was blissfully ignorant of what was going on. We entered his *padippura* and sprinted across the courtyard to his house, shouting slogans in full throat. In the verandah were three men – an elderly man with earrings, and two younger men. The older one was Dasappa Chetty and the other two were his children's tutors. We scared Dasappa Chetty right away. We told him in a menacing voice how we had attacked the MSP camp and Thimmappa Chetty's house. "We know how you treat these tribals. Will you do this again?" We asked him. "No, no, never." He shook with fear. Then we took him by force to his upstairs room. Thimmappa Chetty's son whispered something in his ears; he might have told him that we were dacoits.

We asked Dasappa Chetty to give us the key to his treasure chest. He gave it, terrified. He opened another big box and gave us all the gold in it. He had amassed all this at the expense of the poor. Though he gave away all his wealth, he didn't tell us where his gun was. He kept on repeating that he didn't possess one. One of the comrades pointed his gun towards him, and tried to scare him again: "We know you have a gun with you. How many tribals have you killed with it? Come on, tell us. You better get us that gun. Fast."

"Oh, God! No, don't kill me. Please spare me." He started crying. Another comrade got hold of his son and took his gun out. He continued to wail believing that we were going to kill him. He was completely out of his mind with fear. We locked him in the room and went downstairs. We supplied the grain in the granary to his slaves and others who had gathered there. Now it was almost 9o'clock.

We explained our stand to the teachers. "What India needs now is an armed revolt like that of Naxalbari. Elections are just an eye-wash. They won't solve any of the problems plaguing our society. We believe in armed revolt. And we want to put our belief to practice. There will be several attacks of this kind all over Wayanad. Our comrades have attacked Thalassery police station too. They will reach Thirunelli forests. We have to join them there. And then, we will decide on our next move."

The teachers were very excited about what we told them. They knew the atrocities of the police at the MSP camp. They congratulated us on destroying the camp. Did you manage to get S.I Allappan? No, we didn't. We will take care of him next time, we promised them. They accompanied us to the banks of Kabani river talking with us all the while. We gifted them some books.

Now we were on our way to Thirunelli forests. The river Kabani spanned one side of the Chekadi village and we had to cross it. My condition was getting worse every passing moment. Both my legs had swollen up. My feet and hands had marks of leech-bites. The wounds didn't heal fast. All the comrades bore such wounds on their legs. After the MSP camp attack, when we walked along the courtyard, a thorn had gone into my foot. I was limping all the way since then. But I was not worried about my foot. There was nothing that could be done, anyway. We didn't have any medicines with us. The wooden spear in my hand now became my walking stick. When we reached a difficult terrain, some elderly comrade would stop to support me. But I never once regretted my decision. This was a life or death battle for the sake of our ideology and I was happy to have joined these comrades. But sometimes I couldn't help feeling a bit desperate. Have I become a burden on my comrades? They never let me feel that way, though. On the contrary, they were always willing to help me. Once or twice I was reduced to tears, but they encouraged and motivated me to go on. "Comrade Aji, you should not cry. You are never a burden, but always a source of inspiration for us. We too have women in our homes. But none of them were willing to sacrifice their lives of comfort to join us. Your courage evokes wonder and determination in us. Stop crying. Instead, go on to inspire us." Hearing such words, I would wipe my tears and brace myself again.

I was acutely aware of my disability while crossing the river.

The Kabani river with its eight tributaries was a mind boggling sight. Through the pearl-like pristine clear water we could see huge rocks underneath. We had to use these rocks as steppingstones to cross the river. Each tributary was as wide as a river and separated from each other by just five to six steps. It was winter and water level was low. So the vast deep river appeared in eight streams. During monsoons, all these would join to form a big expansive river. Then you could not even imagine walking across it. Though the water level was low, the currents were strong. Even a physically fit person would have to use all his might to steady his foot, or else the current would sweep him away. How would I, with my swollen lame foot, cross this river?

Comrade Krishnankutty came to my help and tried to lead me holding my hand. The tribals were enthusiastically helping us with our luggage and loads. They forcefully took the vessels and the bag of rice from the comrades and carried them ashore. I could see all the comrades struggling to get a foothold on the slippery rocks. Comrade Krishnankutty would first try to set one foot on the rock and then he would fix his other foot too, and then slowly help me climb the rock holding one of my arms. All this while I supported myself on the wooden spear with my other hand. Thus we crossed two streams. By the time we reached the third one, comrade Krishnankutty himself was tired out. Worse, he was bearing my weight too. I feared that both of us would get washed away in the current. I was putting another comrade's life to danger. I couldn't bear it any longer. I burst into tears. Suddenly, a tribal comrade supported me by my shoulder. He must have noticed our misery. "Why are you crying? Don't be scared. I will help you cross the river. Don't be frightened!" he said. Though I was dressed in trousers and shirt, I had left my hair open and so, anyone could make out that I was a woman. Still, he treated me with utmost respect. The devotion these tribals displayed was unimaginable. They cried with each other to help us in all possible ways. All this taught us new lessons in love, which was hitherto unknown to intellectuals like us. The majority of the so-called intellectuals would only try to save their skin in moments of crises. But the dedication of these tribals was entirely devoid of any such opportunism.

This exploited class, which bears the cross of slavery never used to mingle with other people. Whoever had settled in Wayanad, had only done them harm, betraying their trust and exploiting them in all possible ways to build up their own lives. The best among the settlers became landlords. Those who were not smart enough became middleclass farmers, traders and poor farm workers. But all of them have in one way or the other contributed to the degradation of the tribal folk. For this very reason, the tribals never trust those in a white *mundu*, the settlers. Experience had taught them that after all the sweet promises the settlers make, comes the final betrayal.

But they trusted us since they had heard about the MSP camp attack and had seen for themselves what we did at their landlords' houses. They were convinced that we had come to fight for their rights and liberation, and to let out their own suppressed sentiments of hatred and revenge.

That day I crossed the river with the help of comrade Krishnankutty and the tribal youth. We were the last to reach the shore. Others were waiting for us. It was time to take leave of our tribal friends. I thanked the tribal comrade who had helped me. "No, you don't have to thank me. But would you people come again? You are our only hope." He said. We promised them that we would be back soon, to take on other cruel landlords on their behalf, but now we had to go. They stood there, the progenies of the forests, looking on, till we slowly walked away from their sight into the darkness of the forest.

10

COMRADE KISSAN THOMMAN'S MARTYDOM

It was in a celebratory mood that we entered the forest; we had achieved what we had set out for. More than that, the tribals' love and their repeated pleas to visit them again had touched our hearts. But, then, we had to reach Thirunelli as soon as possible. Our tribal comrades led the way. We climbed hills and trudged jungles to reach a small stream. We sat down by it, on the rocks. Some of us began cooking gruel. The comrades of the Supreme council after a brief meeting among themselves asked all of us to get all that we had taken from the landlords' houses. A *mundu* was spread on the ground and all the money and gold were collected on it. We found, to our surprise, that we had with us thousands of rupees and a lot of gold ornaments. These landlords were so stingy that they had locked all this up without spending it even on themselves. They were literally worshipping money! "After all, this proves that whatever we did was right", said a comrade.

All money and gold was handed over right away to the senior comrades of the Supreme council. It was decided that we would spend it for our common use. The issue of ornaments was to be settled later. Our immediate aim was to join the comrades from Thalassery. When the gruel was ready, we made plates out of all kinds of leaves and poured out the gruel into them. After resting a while we started again.

We passed hills, valleys and thick jungles. After walking for miles together, we would sit somewhere when we felt tired. After a 15-20 minute rest it would be time to walk. The senior comrades had warned us not to talk too much and our pace was somewhat fast. At dusk, the group reached an open space with some undergrowth. Maybe, we had transgressed into some village. Comrades Kunjaman and Varghese went ahead asking us to wait behind a huge tree. We switched on the radio. The local news bulletin reported that around 200 people had attacked the Pulpally Wireless station. It was clear from the news that our brave assault against the government's fortified authority had shocked the central and state governments alike and that it had created an anxious atmosphere in general. This would be an acid test for the seven-party coalition government of E.M.S, when it would need to renounce its revolutionary slogans.

"Did these Marxist leaders ever have anything to do with Marxism? Let us see how far their revolution takes them!" somebody said with contempt.

The news bulletin filled us with a new vigour. The Thalassery comrades too would have heard the news. They too would be excited. We sat in utter darkness and talked under our breath. Comrade Kissan Thomman and others had warned the rest against even lighting a beedi since it could attract someone's attention. After an hour or two, comrades Varghese and Kunjaman returned. Dinner was arranged for us in a *kuruchiya* hut. We proceeded towards that place. It was a small tribal hut, four bamboo poles on four sides supporting it. All of us sat down and helped ourselves. The comrades told us that this dinner was arranged much in advance.

After dinner, we climbed up the mountain again. It was pitch dark and we could move forward only with the help of a torch. We were not supposed to point the torch upwards. We climbed a steep hill and reached a meadow. The chilly wind of November was biting. I felt I would freeze if I remained there any longer. In spite of the woollens, all of us were shivering. But we walked on, as if to take on the chill. When we looked around we could see the silhouettes of tall mountains all around touching the sky. Comrades familiar with the place described each mountain in detail. Somebody pointed out a mountain called 'The fort of Banasura'.

"This is the tallest mountain here. Beyond that are mountains filled with the thickest forest. You should see this sight in daylight. The scenic beauty of this place would captivate all. Now you can only see the shadows." He continued.

"These forests are homes to leopard, tiger, bear and elephant. There's one good thing about these beasts. They would retract if they find the ashes of log-fire or get the smell of man. They won't come near fire or human settlement. But beware of a lone tusker. He would have got lost from his herd. He could launch an attack on us."

We walked and walked, but didn't reach the forest. We decided to rest for a while and sat down on the meadow. It was two in the morning. We lay down, some spreading the *mundu* they had with them on the ground and still some on the bare rocks by the ridge of the cliff. Now we began to feel the bite of the cold. When we walked, we hadn't felt it so much. I sat cowering in a small nook amidst boulders, shivering. How could I sleep in this freezing chill? I feared that soon I would turn into a rock. Then, one of the comrades called me to where the Supreme Council was holding a meeting.

We were nearing the Thirunelli forests. We were at Trissilery, a place next to Thirunelli, the comrades said. Next day we would enter the forests. But still, there was no sign of comrades from Thalassery. We could not see any trace of light anywhere in the forest. We were informed that around 300 comrades would be reaching Wayanad. We had learned on the radio that some comrades had been arrested. We would get conclusive reports once we reached Thirunelli, we hoped. We knew that the police were everywhere, hunting for us. But it was quite improbable that they would capture us here.

That night I couldn't get a wink of sleep. The cold was so intense that it froze my very bones. I tried to sit up and then to lie down. But the biting cold was overwhelming. It was an open space with just grass and rocks all around with no trees for firewood. We spent the night by the inclined plane of the mountain. Next morning, by 5.30 we resumed our journey.

That day, we covered a long distance and by the end of it reached a dense forest. There were big tall trees all around, competing with each other to kiss the heavens. We sat down by a small stream to prepare food. I felt strangely happy when I sat looking at the small round pebbles under the crystal clear water. We were back on foot as soon as we finished our food. We slowly made our way amidst the closely lined trees, their canopy so thick that not much sunlight seeped in. By night, we reached Thirunelli. We decided to stay put in the junction of four mountains, behind the Thirunelli temple. Let us not travel anymore this night, we thought. It was time for rest, discussions and analyses. This camp too was on the side of a stream. Some comrades were busy making gruel. The rest of us sat together for a discussion. It was then that we found out that some comrades were nurturing second thoughts. "What we did was not right, we should have stayed within our limits." They said. The majority of the comrades realized that this was a dangerous trend, and they countered them.

"Your fear is making you speak this way. Didn't you see the response of the tribals of Chekadi, how happy they were? That is the greatest testimony. This is the way of Naxalbari…"

The arguments were strong, so the cowards were pacified temporarily. Comrades Varghese, Kissan Thomman, Sukumaran and Krishnankutty tried to speak to everyone in an attempt to reinforce their resolve.

That night the supreme council met again. We had a serious discussion about the lack of courage that had sprung up in some comrades' minds. And, there was still no news from the comrades from Thalassery. What could have happened to them? At least a few of them should turn up. Some comrades had been sent ahead of us to Thirunelli to work among the tribal folk, to prepare them for our arrival and to continue the revolt by themselves later. We should contact them tomorrow. We would also send two comrades familiar with the route to the countryside. It was decided to station two comrades each on top of the four hills to try and spot the Thalassery comrades and to find out if the police had reached this place. We had to stay here, till the comrades who would go to Thirunelli come back. We had enough food to sustain ourselves for two or three days. Since we had money with us, we could also venture out into the village and buy whatever we wanted. Finding out about the Thalassery comrades was the key issue now. How long could we survive in the forest? If they didn't turn up, we would have to go into the midst of the tribals and with their support take on the police and the landlords. The senior comrades told us that those who were educated among us should read out the pamphlets to others and motivate them. This was the time to turn to Mao's works.

After dinner, we made our beds around log-fire. It was cold, still the warmth of the fire and the comfort of the plains put us to deep sleep.

The next morning after a proper briefing two comrades were sent to Thirunelli with some money. The comrades who were to keep vigil on the mountains were chosen and each pair was given a gun. Then, grouping together all the other comrades we started reading. First we read "the three essays that are to be read often." It dealt with the three essential traits a communist should possess. Then we read out 'Quotations' and 'Thunder'. This led to animated discussions. It was clear that the traces of cowardice have not ebbed out at all. The comrades of the Supreme Council tried to oppose them with the teachings of Mao. The police and the other enemies were hunting us and we were forever trying to escape them, and in such circumstances these developments would only make the forward path more difficult, they said. Some raised the question of the Thalassery comrades as well.

"We don't know anything for sure. We are still trying to find out." The senior comrades tried to explain. "We hope that at least a few of them would turn up eventually. But even if they don't, we would continue our revolt. We would gather the remaining comrades from Wayanad and step into the heart of Thirunelli. To our best of knowledge, the tribals of Thirunelli will support us." They advised us not to lose hope and to be like the foolish old man who moved mountains.

But still, I could see that many were not convinced and they looked downcast. The missing comrades from Thalassery must be the major depressing factor, I assumed. Also, all of us were dead tired. We had walked long distances without anything proper to eat. For the last three-four days we had had just gruel and starch water. We didn't have time to search if the forest had anything better to offer. Added to this physical strain was the nuisance of leeches. But all this would vanish once the comrades from Thalassery joined us. Whatever in the world had happened to them?

As the discussions went on, we heard a loud blast. We froze in shock. It came from somewhere near us. We couldn't see beyond a short distance, as it was dark in the forest. What was it? The comrades who sat near the sound of the blast were showered with splinters. Was it the police? In a split second, we all took cover behind trees. Could the police have already found out our camp? We remained silent, catching our breath expecting the police. About 5-10 minutes passed, but nothing happened. There was absolute silence all around.

That was when one of the comrades remembered: Comrade Kissan Thomman had taken the bag of bombs and grenades and had gone over somewhere. Could something have happened to the comrade then? Comrades Varghese and Krishnankutty came out of their hiding places. "We will go and see what happened. The rest of you remain here."

We sat in the camp, anxious and nervous. No one spoke.

After a while the comrades came back. Their faces were dark with grief.

"Comrades, comrade Kissan Thomman's whole body is torn apart and he is bleeding profusely. There are splinters all over his chest. He has broken the lower bone of one of his legs. When he saw us, he said: 'Comrades, I won't live now. But you must continue the struggle. You should never give up. Don't bother to take me to a hospital. Just do one thing for me. Please shoot me. I can't bear the pain.' He said with great difficulty, writhing in pain."

We listened silently, as if struck by lightning.

Comrade Varghese said: "Comrades, be brave! We can't take the comrade to a hospital. He will die on the way. I think it would be better to help him die and thus relieve him of this agony. But who will do that?" How could we shoot our dear comrade? We couldn't even think of it. Initially, no one could agree to what comrade Varghese said. The comrades who kept guard on the mountains had come to the camp, hearing the blast. But none of them, even those who were on the forefront leading the attacks on the wireless station and the houses of the landlords, came forward to take up this job.

Comrade Varghese said with visible anger: "So, you want comrade Kissan Thomman to endure the pain? Aren't we supposed to do whatever we could to end his suffering? He wouldn't survive even if we take him to a hospital. If he would, nothing, even the police, could stop us from doing that. But no one could save his life now. So, wouldn't it be better to end his misery and do what he wants?"

Slowly, we began to realize that he was right. At last, comrade

Sasimala Raman Nair, a farmer, came forward to take on the task, with a fluttering heart. He was a man with extraordinary courage. He went to where comrade Kissan Thomman lay along with comrade Varghese. We listened. After a while, we heard a shot. "It's all over!" Somebody exclaimed in deep distress. Comrade Varghese had barred us from going near comrade Kissan Thomman.

After sometime both the comrades returned. We were still in a daze; the impact of the unexpected tragedy left us numb. What had happened? How did the bombs explode? What was the comrade doing with the bag of bombs? The hurtling splinters had injured some of us. Comrade Neelakantan's back was pierced with tiny bits of glass. But we weren't worried about ourselves. We felt ashamed to even think about our injury. What was it compared to the agony comrade Kissan Thomman suffered?

When comrade Varghese came back all of us gathered round him.

"Comrades, our dear comrade Kissan Thomman has left us all. He was a source of strength to all of us. From the day he comprehended the idea of armed revolt he was working to make it a reality despite his age or failing health. He had taken the bag of bombs to check whether they had gone cold. He was good at making bombs and grenades. He had made these ones too. He had hung the bag on a branch and was trying to sit down when the branch broke with the weight of the bag. The bag fell and the bombs exploded. But he had kept the bag facing the opposite side of our camp and therefore, when they burst the splinters had flown off in the opposite direction. He was that cautious!" Comrade Varghese said.

We just listened to all that he said, looking on stunned.

After a brief moment of silence, comrade Varghese continued: "You have all heard the dying words of comrade Kissan Thomman — Comrades, carry on with the struggle, never turn back! We are duty-bound to remember these words all through our lives. We, his comrades in arms, should continue to fight for the cause for which he laid down his life. We should never retract, that is unbecoming of a brave martyr's comrades. Never forget this, my comrades, never ever!"

These words instilled courage in us. One of the comrades suddenly remembered one of Mao's essays, 'Serve the people'. He began to read it aloud. We listened to it with heavy but unswerving hearts.

'All men die. But death differs in its magnitude. Shuma Chein, the ancient Chinese writer had said, though death happens to all people, its impact could be either as grave as the Tai mountain or as light as a bird's feather. Dying for the sake of people is greater than the Tai mountain. But working for the Fascists and dying for the exploiting class is as insignificant as a feather.' The comrade stopped reading. He said aloud: "Comrades, comrade Kissan Thomman's death is as heavy as the Tai mountain because he died for the people." "Yes!" We said in chorus. He resumed his reading. Once he finished, we took a pledge that we would work to realize the departed comrade's dream and that his life would remain a model for us, the rest of our lives. There was determination in all the faces.

Now we had to bury the comrade. A few went ahead to dig the grave. They went along with Comrade Varghese to look for a suitable spot. A few comrades helped the injured ones pull out the splinters that had pierced their body. I too was hurt, but there was no medicine with us. Somebody asked me to rub a piece of lemon dipped in hot coconut oil on the wound. That would help to heal the wounds faster. Comrade Neelakantan's back was full of splinters. We could not take them out. It would be better to take him to a hospital. Comrade Varghese was sent for and he agreed that the comrade should be admitted. Comrade Neelakantan was sent back with some money.

We wished to see comrade Kissan Thomman's body. When the grave was ready we were taken to where his body lay. It was a pathetic sight. He was bathed in blood and his chest was riddled all over with splinters.

Some comrades slowly lifted up the body. We saw his leg dangling, the lower limb blown off. He must have gone through immense pain. Quietly we walked towards the grave. It was on the other side of the stream, a little away from our camp. The comrades lowered the body into the pit.

"Comrades, let's read the essay 'Serve the People' once more. Let's renew our pledge that we will never forget the last words of comrade Kissan Thomman." Comrade Varghese said. One of the comrades began to read the essay in a voice charged with emotion. I had read that essay several times and knew it almost by heart. But now when I heard it being read during the burial of a brave comrade who laid himself down for the mission of armed revolt, I realized it had a deeper meaning. It is easier to talk of revolution. But to renounce oneself for the sake of it, to nurture it with one's own flesh, blood and life is a difficult task. Last few days' experience had taught us this and it was reinforced by Kissan Thomman's martydom.

Comrade Kissan Thomman had a big family to look after. He had all those compulsions that a normal farmer had. But even on the face of unexpected death, he was worried about our country, our people. He was fully aware that he was dying, but still he said nothing about his family or his other obligations. "Comrades, continue the struggle, never turn back!" Even in moments of utter pain, even on the face of death, he had thought only of revolution. Kissan Thomman was the embodiment of the traditional revolutionary spirit of our farmers who could do any sacrifice once they realized the concept of armed revolution. Let opportunists hang their heads in shame before his exemplary courage! The day he sacrificed his life, Kissan Thomman elevated himself to the rank of an ideal revolutionary whom coming generations would forever remember with pride.

11

LIFE AT THIRUNELLI

Eyes fixed on the body of comrade Kissan Thomman and with clenched fists, we took a solemn pledge: "We will uphold the last call of Kissan Thomman and be its messengers for the rest of our lives and will try to live as ideal men as Mao envisaged." We remained silent for a while looking at our dead comrade's serene face.

After the burial, we went back to our camp. The intensity of the day's events had drained us out. We sat in the camp thinking of Kissan Thomman and sharing with each other fond memories of him. No one felt hunger or thirst. After a while, the Supreme Council met again without comrade Kissan Thomman. We feared that the signs of weakness certain comrades had displayed would have got augmented with the tragedy that befell comrade Kisssan Thomman. Each passing moment made us more aware of the awkward situation we were in. In this dense forest, we were away from any human settlement. The police were hunting us and we knew that they would close in on us any moment. In this desperate situation our only hope lay in contacting the Thalassery comrades. But where were they? The comrades who were sent to Thirunelli to gather information had not returned. We were uncertain whether the sound of the blast that killed the comrade had caught the enemy's attention. Around 10-12 grenades and dynamites had blown off simultaneously. For many reasons, it was not safe to remain in that camp any longer.

The Supreme Council reached the conclusion that we needn't wait for the comrades to return from Thirunelli. Get ready to shift the camp, the council told us. No one wanted to stay on in that camp after the comrade's death. We started off again, this time deeper into the forest. We climbed a mountain with huge trees. We could hear a wild brook gushing down the valley. It was mid noon; sunlight was just beginning to peep in. This was the place for our next camp. But the comrades who had gone to Thirunelli wouldn't know this place. Comrade Varghese sent two comrades back to the old camp to bring them to the new one. They were asked to come back if others didn't return by late evening. Once they were gone, we tried to tune into Radio Peking without success. We could only listen to the local news bulletin which reported that the police were employing extra forces to capture us and that they had already arrested a few of the comrades involved in the Thalassery station attack. We were relieved to find out that none of the senior comrades had been caught though we could realize that the situation was becoming increasingly grim. When it got dark, we made bonfires and gathered around them. After a long while, we saw the beam of a torch in the distance. It must be our comrades who had been sent to the old camp. Two or three comrades ran up to them. But they brought bad news. The comrades who had been sent to Thirunelli had not come back. And, there was no sign of the Thalassery comrades entering the forest. If they had, we would have met them long ago since they should have started for this forest two days earlier. We had achieved whatever we were supposed to do, quite gloriously, and we had reached this forest with an all-consuming passion to carry on with our protest, but had we been cheated? We found it difficult to believe. We were not ready to forego our trust in the

Thalassery comrades even when we were tossed about in the sea of seemingly endless perils.

The Supreme Council met again that night to discuss this grave issue. How could we find out what had happened to the Thalassery comrades? Why hadn't the comrades sent to Thirunelli for reconnaissance returned? Could they have fallen into the police net? We would have found a way out if only we could contact the comrades working amidst the tribals. But how could we get to them? We knew that some of the comrades had been arrested. But how could we confirm who they were? From the radio news it seemed that the key comrades involved in the Thalassery attack did not figure in the list of the arrested. We could have gathered some more comrades if we could get to Thettamala. We had considerable influence among the tea estate workers there. Anyway, we needed to go to a village and find out something about the state of affairs. Another urgent need was to buy some rice. We were running out of supplies. We had to send two comrades to buy some rice the next day. Two others should go to the village and find out the real situation. It would be better to buy rice from Thirunelli; one of our contacts could help us there. The comrades going to the village were supposed to come back within a day. They should start early morning and return by next day evening.

But now, we had to change our camp again. It was dangerous to remain in one place for long. We would leave a trail of signs to our new camp, so that it would not be difficult to locate the new place. The rest of us had to move deeper into the forest along the path the Thalassery comrades were supposed to take. We might come across them on the way. If only we could get to meet at least a few of them! Comrade Kissan Thomman's death had a lasting impact on us, and it had weakened many a comrade's resolve. We wouldn't be able to survive for long in this forest. We had to find a way out.

Comrade Krishnankutty told us that the next day he would go to

Mananthavady to get information and that he would gather as many comrades as he could and bring them to the forest. This came as a relief to all of us. Comrade Krishnankutty was a senior member of the Supreme Council. Though some comrades had shown signs of weakness, the comrades of the Supreme Council were not deterred from their determination to stand by the ideology of armed revolution. We were certain that comrade Krishnankutty would come back. The Supreme Council decided that the leadership should never waver from its resolve and that it should organize discussions and study classes to strengthen the spirits of the rest. But comrade Kunjaman wished to go home once. We let him go, though unwillingly. We couldn't have done otherwise. It was not proper to treat him as harshly as we did others, especially since, comrade Kunjaman belonged to the tribal folk. Moreover, it was wiser to send back those comrades who were unwilling to stay back. At least, the rest of the group would remain loyal and committed. We were passing through a severe crisis; and our future looked definitely bleak. In such a situation trying to retain the vacillating Hamlets would only do us more harm. They might prove to be a negative influence on those who were ready to fight it out to the last. So it was decided that anyone who wished to go home should be permitted to do so.

That night we lay down to sleep round the bonfire. After a while, we heard someone whimpering. Some of the comrades went to see what was wrong. When they came back, they told me that it was comrade Josephettan weeping. Comrade Kissan Thomman was a very close friend of comrade Josephettan. They were of the same age and were together all the time. Comrade Josephettan was familiar with the forest as a tribal was and all through our journey he was never seen weary. He too was good at making bombs. But comrade Kissan Thomman's death had taken its toll on him. We understood that it would be difficult for him to stay with us alone without comrade Kissan

Thomman. We would have to send him back the next day, we decided. The comrades tried to console comrade Josephettan and lay down to sleep. Few of us slept that night. The memories of the gory death of comrade Kissan Thomman and his face twitching in searing pain kept haunting me. He had placed the bombs facing the other side of the camp, or at least two three comrades would have been killed when the bombs exploded. He had been that cautious, his love for his comrades never allowed him to be flippant with his tasks. But we couldn't do anything to save his precious life. I was also in awe of comrade Raman Nair's courage. If he had not come forward ready to shoot comrade Kissan Thomman, his hours of agony would have been prolonged.

I was troubled that there was no news about the comrades from Thalassery. We were certain that they had attacked the police station. We had started for Pulpally after confirming the news from the radio. What had happened to them, then? Father too was supposed to come with them. I was hoping that at least father would somehow make it to the forest. I kept thinking this over and over again. It was severely cold and the woollens that I wore were inadequate. I was lying on an incline with my head at a lower level than my legs. I couldn't sleep. I spent the night watching the tall trees, the burning embers and the exhausted comrades lying around the fire. I kept on plucking out the leeches that crawled up my body and flinging them into the fire. My legs were even more puffed up now. There were scratches and cuts where thorns had gone in. I felt they were getting infected. I was aware that I couldn't continue this adventurous life for long. If this continued, I would collapse and die here, in this forest. The path that we were travelling was extremely hazardous. The comrades had told me that we were going deeper into the forest. There were more cliffs and steep mountains to be traversed. I was limping around with a stick; how would I survive? A pathway was made in advance to facilitate the Thalassery comrades' move through the forest. We were supposed to take that route now. I had started out with the comrades ready to face any odds. There should be no turning back. I shouldn't be weak. I told myself.

The next day morning, we made gruel with the rest of the rice we had. Comrades Varghese and Krishnankutty were talking to the comrades who were to go to the village to gather news, when Thettamala Gopi, who later became the approver for the Pulpally case and the police witness confronted comrade Krishnankutty: "I want to go back home. I came only because you wanted me to join you. I would never have come had I known what was in store..." It was decided the previous day that whosoever was unwilling to stay in the camp should be sent home. Comrade Josephettan and comrade Kunjaman had earlier expressed their wish to go home. These three comrades were sent back with adequate money. Two other comrades went to buy rice.

Now it was time for comrade Krishnankutty to go. Another comrade went with him to show him the way. He promised us that he would come back with as many comrades as he could gather and asked us not to worry. We had absolute trust in comrade Krishnankutty. We knew that he would return even if he could not meet the comrades from Thalassery. Then the rest of us would group together with the tribals and plan our next move. We bid him goodbye hoping for the best.

Then we sat in a circle and began to discuss our future plans. Some of the comrades started reading out from books and tried to instill courage in the rest of us. There were comrades who had been wrecked mentally and physically by the trials of the past few days, and there were a few others whose minds had not inched away from the path of revolution, like the farm workers from Pulpally. One of them, comrade Sukumaran, declared aloud with clenched fist that even if he had to perish he would never let go of his ideology. Some of the comrades cheered him and repeated this pledge after him. I felt that comrade Kissan Thomman's sacrifice had only heightened these comrades' committment to their mission. I began admiring these comrades when

I realized that nothing could dissipate the revolutionary zeal in them. They were actively involved with this revolt from the very beginning and now they were proud of being comrades of a brave martyr. Comrade Kissan Thomman's tragic death for the sake of a noble cause and the way he had bid us farewell without even a trace of self-interest had touched these comrades. The effervescent exuberance and determination of the comrades Allungal Sreedharan, Raman Nair, Chellappan and Sukumaran had an impact on others as well. The comrades who had displayed weakness were ashamed to give voice to their opportunistic excuses in the face of such robust enthusiasm. I could make out from their faces that they had become lifeless. It was obvious that they were shattered mentally. Though we had not succumbed to cowardice, it was a time when many of us found our initial zest dying slowly. In such a scenario, the revolutionary spirit of other comrades acted like a stimulus. These comrades had been telling the Supreme Council that even if we didn't find the Thalassery comrades we should put to practice in Thirunelli whatever we had planned.

We spent three four hours in discussion sitting around fire. We had nothing to eat. The comrades who had gone to Thirunelli came back with rice by the afternoon.

The comrades told us that the person whom they had approached for rice was scared out of his wits. It appeared the police had surrounded the hills of Wayanad. They had heard villagers discussing the event among themselves with great interest. We deliberated on these vague reports. The police were closing in on us. If they managed to catch any of the comrades who had left the camp that morning, it wouldn't be difficult for them to find out the camp. Our situation was becoming increasingly precarious. We must leave the camp as soon as we finish our meal. But the comrades who were sent to Mananthavady would be returning to this camp. Comrade Varghese detailed out the way to our new camp. Then, we started off.

The way we took now was even tougher. It was difficult even to clear the way. The tribal comrades chopped the entwining thorny climbers and wild branches with their knives and made way. We walked on to our new camp in silence. Darkness began to fall when we had covered some five six miles. We set up camp on a mountain slope amidst big trees. We had reached the north west side of Thirunelli. We listened to the radio that night too. But there was nothing more than what we had already known. After dinner, we lay down around fire. No one wanted any further discussions that night.

It was quite clear now that none of the Thalassery comrades had reached the forest. The Pulpally revolt was planned along with the Thalssery revolt relying on the strength of thousands of people who were supposed to come from Thalassery prepared for a great revolution. Pulpally was just an add on that would only supplement the intensity of the Thalassery assaults. Once the attack was carried out, we had to camp ourselves in the hilly expanses of Wayanad depending solely on the influence we had among the people in order to confront our enemies. That was the way Mao had pointed out — set up camps in the countryside, wake the farmers from the oppressive feudal slumber, use the villages to surround the towns, and at last capture the towns. These guerilla tactics that had proved successful in China, Vietnam and Cambodia left us in no doubt about seeking asylum in Wayanad. We were getting desperate wondering about the Thalassery comrades, not knowing where to go and what to do in that forest. When we set out to put the ideology of armed revolt to practice we had no experience of the trials we would have to undergo and the missing comrades only added to our agony. We had believed that Thalssery comrades would also do their duty with the same sincerity with which we had completed our task. But hadn't we too, at least to some extent, considered our mission as easy as leading a protest march, or a fast unto death at the Collectorate Gate, or stoning a few government-owned buses? Only when we marched to the front did we realize that it was a life or death struggle. But still, a few of us were unwilling to retreat.

Sacrificing our home and relations and all other social bonds was just the beginning. It was not only the success of our mission that encouraged us to stick to our path. More than that, it was the excited response of the farmers and the tribal folk, the underdogs of the society that made us realize that we were on the right path. To retract now was impossible. That was why we decided to go to Thirunelli village and plan our next strike with their help. But we had to wait till the comrades came back from Mananthavady. They were supposed to return by the evening or the next day.

The next day we just hung around the camp after breakfast. There were two three tribal comrades with us. They were getting tired and demanded that they be allowed to leave. These comrades were our navigators, extremely good at clearing paths in dense forests and sense the crucial turns we should take and to fix up places for camping. Sending them away would mean that we would be reduced to the plight of a set of blind people roaming around in the dark thick forest. But we had no other option. We couldn't inspire them any longer. Or else, we should fabricate a lie to hold them back. But we believed that there shouldn't be a trace of untruth in our relationships. That would be against our sacred ideology. Comrade Varghese requested them to stay on till those who went to Mananthavady returned. There was no news from them till noon. Were they not able to find our new camp? Two comrades were sent to the old camp. We spent some anxious four five hours waiting for their return. This was our last hope.

The comrades returned empty-handed. They could find nothing about those who had gone to Mannathavady or even comrade Krishnankutty. They waited in the old camp for some time, but no one came. We knew finally that all hopes had been shattered. All doors were being closed on us. We would not be able to gather more comrades nor would we be able to hold on to ourselves as a team any more. All plans had been defeated. Who should we wait for now?

Finally, 35 of us remained and we held a meeting. Supreme Council had long ceased to exist. Comrade Varghese addressed the troubled comrades with utmost pain, but in a voice still ringing with determination:

"I don't have to tell you that all ways have been closed before us. With each passing second the police is tightening their grip. We just have two three guns with us, nothing more. We lost all our bombs with comrade Kissan Thomman's death. Who all are still prepared to take this struggle forward, believing in armed revolution? We have a perilous path ahead of us. We should be prepared for the worst, even loss of life. How many comrades are ready for that? The tribal comrades have already expressed their wish to return. Who else would like to go back? Please be frank about this. Whosoever wants to go will be allowed to do so and will be sent back with enough money for travel and other expenses. Once this is decided, we will plan our next move. So, each comrade should frankly speak up his mind."

Around twenty comrades wanted to go home, though their hearts were heavy with guilt. Fifteen others decided to go on with the revolt and promised to stick to their ideology. It was decided that all those who wanted to go home should be sent away in the morning and the rest would plan the course of action after they had left. The comrades who had wanted to return home were too ashamed to look at us. But how could we blame them? Nothing had worked out according to our plan. They had come with us with great enthusiasm, but the consequences left them with little belief in armed revolution.

I used to read very often that the path of revolution is never straight and that it has more turns and twists than one would ever imagine. But I was not even vaguely aware of the horrifying experiences it had in store for me. It was nothing surprising that we, who had no prior practical experience, were crestfallen by the way events had turned out. Especially people like me, a petty bourgeoisie intellectual, perceived the world as a pendulum swaying between complete success and absolute failure. We could not easily grasp the working class' vision of the world that no success or failure is ever complete; there are traces of success in failures and failure in successes. Mao had addressed this issue a hundred thousand times. He had said that we might confront failure or taste success when we put to practice Marxian ideologies among the masses, that we should look at these experiences in the light of the ideology and only then would we be able to overcome the misery of fluctuating fortunes. But we couldn't recollect any of these. It wouldn't be long before the fifteen of us, who had decided to continue the revolt, would fall into the trap of despair and decide to break away.

12

IN POLICE CUSTODY

The next morning, fifteen of us remained. The quiet Allungal Sreedharan who perceived everything with absolute seriousness and was completely wedded to the cause of armed revolution; comrade Chellappan who did all his work with zest, pleasant even on the face of forsaking fortunes; comrade Sukumaran, the youngest among us who had a mature mind never failing to inspire us in times of trouble; comrade Raman Nair minimal in flaunting his revolutionary spirit but true to his ideals; comrade Varghese the valorous leader of our group till the end, who advised and motivated us at every critical moment; the middle-aged comrade Sankaran Master, a school teacher who never betrayed a trace of the vacillating will of a petty bourgeoisie intellectual even when the police boots fell on him with brutal force; comrade Ramankuttiyettan of Kattikkulam who fought along with us till the last moment defying the compulsions of his old age; tailor Muhammad of Thalappuzha, the young comrade who was with us all the while with exuberance and earnestness and Philip. M. Prasad, out of tune with the harmony of these brave comrades, pretending to be bold, good at fire spewing speeches but with a wavering heart, were all there among the fifteen who decided to carry on with the struggle till the very end.

We had to change our camp again. A few comrades, who had succumbed to stress, had just left this camp. For that very reason it was dangerous to continue there. But there was another problem that demanded equal attention. We were running out of our stock of rice. We had to buy more, or else we would be reduced to starvation in two days' time. We were on the forest path the Thalassery comrades were supposed to take. There were few villages in its vicinity. So two comrades were sent to get rice. We decided that we would walk all day and rest only after nightfall. During the day, we would stop only to cook and eat. We had to get out of the forest as early as possible. Our next move was to be decided only later.

We ate as soon as the comrades came back with rice, and then started our final, long journey.

We walked the whole day and moved further into the forest blindly following the path cleared out for the Thalassery comrades. As the tribal comrades had left us we could only guess the direction of our route. We didn't know where this path would ultimately lead us. When night fell, we camped by the bank of a stream.

After food, we assembled again, which turned out to be our last meeting. Our miserable mental makeup showed itself. Our dreams of a resurrection of farmers were dashed, though temporarily. Gradually, it dawned on us that the Thalassery comrades had betrayed the cause of Pulpally. We had planned the Pulpally revolt solely depending on Thalassery rebellion. But now, we had been reduced to the state of hunted beasts. From one camp to another, then to the next — we were on the run. It was impossible to continue the struggle in this way. The police were fast. Our small group was sure to get caught if we went to some village in Wayanad. And then, we would be wrecked in body and spirit. The betrayal of Thalassery comrades left us stunned, we were in no shape for an immediate strike. We still didn't know what had really happened in Thalassery. We hadn't the faintest clue as to what had gone wrong there. To the last we hoped that at least a few comrades would make it to the forest as planned earlier. We could already taste the bitterness of failure. We attempted to regain our will and go into the village to organize further attacks, but that too fell short.

No one had the energy to organize and execute another attack at that point of time. My condition was the worst. All of us were in need of a few days' rest. After that we would think about some means to renew our action. So our next aim should be to get to some village. We decided to split into different groups and seek out a hiding place for ourselves. After a month's break we could meet again somewhere outside Kerala. Each of us should try to earn a living, never forgetting that we were bound to our mission — to continue the armed revolt, to keep the promises that we had made to the tribals at Chekadi, to live up to the last dream of comrade Kissan Thomman. We had to closely re-read Mao and C.P.C and try to analyse in their light what had gone wrong with our plan.

We spent two-three hours sketching out our future plans before going to sleep. Next morning we continued our journey. The Thalassery comrades had made some markings on huge trees and so it wasn't difficult to find our way through the forest. We walked all day and stopped only in the evening to prepare food.

We had with us two three guns, some other weapons and a few bronze vessels used for cooking. We had decided to bury these somewhere in the forest and leave a mark so that we could retrieve them later when we came back. We walked again and spotted some marks on a few trees. The line of trees led to a waterway. Our path ended there. There were no more marks on trees on the other side of the stream.

On the third day of our journey we came across a place, which we found suitable to hide our weapons. We buried whatever we had with us there and walked on. Comrade Varghese thought it right to go to

Kottiyoor. We traversed mountains and meadows. From one such meadow, when we looked around we could see high mountains all around and jungles deep below. We had reached somewhere far above the plains of Wayanad. Next would be a walk down the mountains almost equal in measure to the steep climb we earlier had. On the third day we decided to go down the mountains. There was rice enough for just one more meal.

We started our down hill journey after some tea. We had made up our mind that we would make gruel only when we reached the plains. At seven in the morning we started going down a mountain with hardly any slope. It was so steep that once we started we could stop only when we reached the valley. The path was full of thorny bushes and if we wavered a little we could end up right in the crater. There were no mountain brooks to quench our thirst. My swollen legs were in a messy state and it was only the comrades' care and thoughtfulness that helped me survive that perilous trip down the mountain. The comrades came to my help putting their life in danger. If I slipped, I would have dragged along to the abyss my comrade who was helping me. Still, they took turns to hold my hand and help me down the mountain. By four in the evening we reached a valley amidst lofty trees. The comrades who had reached earlier were preparing food. But I was completely worn out. There were sharp stones on the plain and they pierced into my feet causing me immense pain. I collapsed there. Without some water I couldn't move, I told the comrades. A comrade guarded me while another went to fetch some watery gruel. I could lift up my head only after guzzling it down.

From there, we were entering a village. We didn't know what place it was. Comrade Varghese divided the rest of the money he had among five comrades. We were supposed to form five different groups and every group was to follow a comrade. We had some ornaments that we had secured from the houses of the landlords. It was decided that comrades Varghese and Sankaran would keep them for the time being and later it could be sold and that money could be used for our later ventures. We all agreed; we knew that these comrades would never misuse them. We had lived together all these days and all of us trusted comrade Varghese blindly. But, when these two came to know of our arrest, they threw the ornaments away to prevent them being used as evidence of dacoity against us. Later, the police recovered them.

After food, we started walking and reached a stream in a short while. We could hear the sound of axe on a tree, which meant that there was some human settlement. We sat for a while by the stream. I removed my shirt and wore a sari I had with me. Two comrades walked to the source of the sound. They returned to tell us that the village was Adakkathodu and that we had reached the private timberland of a landlord from Kozhikode. This was a colony of Christian settlers directly under the jurisdiction of the Church. The only town nearby was Peravoor, some five miles away. We had hoped to reach Kottiyoor, but were nowhere near it. Anyway, there was no other option now. We reached a narrow village road meant for trucks. We formed small groups of three and walked separately. I had comrades Raman Nair, Chellappan and Philip with me. We trailed behind, as I could not walk fast. We had to reach Adakkathodu, get into some bus and escape, that was our plan. As we walked on, we could see the workers resting by the road. When we reached near the habitation, one of the comrades who had gone ahead came back to tell us that we had already aroused some suspicion. The first batch of comrades who went into a tea-stall had enquired about the next bus. This question sparked off suspicion among the villagers because it was a lonely hamlet, where bus service was yet to start. Anyway, we mustered courage and walked on. One of the comrades stopped at a shop to buy beedi. I was standing next to the shop when a man with a red band around his head came out from the shop with a copy of that day's Malayala Manorama daily. It had one of my old photographs on it. He looked at it closely to confirm and then shouted:

"Yes, she is Ajitha. Look, here's her photograph." We had been caught, it was certain now. The Marxist with the red headband (I came to know this later from the villagers) came back with a gun and pointed it at me, yelling:

"I will shoot you right now."

"Go on, then." I said, not moving.

But the people who gathered there stopped him. He went berserk and stomped around like a drunkard. He spotted comrade Chellappan hiding somewhere and hit him on his head with a heavy knife. Then he and his minions dragged the comrade to where we stood. Amidst all this chaos, somebody fell unconscious behind me with a thud. It was Philip. After sometime, he sat up whimpering that the police would not spare us.

People were gathering around us in hordes. The church bells tolled nonstop. This was to bring out people from their homes to help capture all of us. Still some of them sneaked near us to whisper that they were sorry that we got caught in their village. The parish priest and the man with the red headband, quite clearly the leaders of the group, took us to a lodge. We explained to the people gathered there, our reason and motive behind the Pulpally attack. Some people howled, sneering at us, but some others asked them to keep quiet. We didn't stop and after a while the hooting died down. Somebody brought a nursing assistant to attend to comrade Chellappan's wound. We managed to give him an English copy of Mao's Quotations without anyone's notice. He took it quite happily. We discreetly gave away all the pamphlets we had with us before the police came. A middle aged farmer came, sat next to me and listened keenly to whatever we were saying. After sometime he said in a sincere tone:

"The dailies and the church had told us that you were dacoits. The farmers were specifically instructed to keep their eyes open for anyone who behaved suspiciously. They had told us that you people would destroy our crops. But now we understand the real story; you had done all this for us. I am sorry that you were caught like this, here in our village. Would you give me something for keepsake?"

We gave him one of the pamphlets. Four-five hours passed and then somebody said the police would be there soon. Meanwhile, we were given bananas and innumerable cups of tea. The sub inspector came with his battalion by midnight. They examined us from head to toe and asked us to move. They dumped us into the police jeep and started for Peravoor police station. The jeep was stopped en route at every police check post to show us to the policemen on duty. They assaulted us the whole way and showered abuses till we reached the Peravoor police station.

I came to know all about police offences with this arrest. We had dared to attack the MSP camp, kill the wireless operator and injure one of the inspectors severely. Our capture called for celebration.

The interrogation began the moment we reached the police station. Four or five policemen gathered around each comrade. They aimed severe blows at the comrade's back, stomach and chest with the clear intention of injuring the internal organs. One of them would hit with clenched fist, while another would use his elbow to strike. The next would kick him with his boots. When one policeman pushed him backwards hitting at his chest, another would thrust him forward punching his back. After 10-15 minutes of such torture the comrade would be a broken man, in body and spirit. I was shocked to see this horrifying action of the police. Till then, I had only heard about custodial torture. But that night I was stunned by the way my dear comrades were being kicked about like a football, or rather like mad dogs! In between they aimed some blows at my stomach and poked me with their lathis, but that was nothing compared to what they were doing to the other comrades. A policeman pressed down the pointed end of his lathi with both his hands on my big toe, as ordered by the inspector. I didn't cry out though the pain travelled from my toes to the top of my head. Some of them didn't miss the opportunity to molest me.

Each comrade was tortured and his statements noted down. Comrades Sankaran master and Kunjiraman master were captured and brought to the police station along with two or three other comrades. I could see them being flayed the very same way. We were thrown into the lock-up. But the half dead comrades were not given respite even in the lock-up. The tormentors asked them to jump up and down raising their arms above their head. If anyone stopped, they would come inside the lock-up and hit him. We could hear the comrades who were captured later being beaten up in the other room.

After a while D.Y.S.P Moideenkunji reached the station. Still, the torment didn't stop. The comrades who were hopping were asked to sit down and tea was brought for all of us. Then the police kicked the comrades, who were leaning on the wall and sipping tea and didn't forget to kick me on my stomach.

The police hadn't got hold of comrade Varghese. Their favourite pastime was to thrash us asking us about his hideout. We were sure that they would devour Varghese alive if they happen to lay their hands on him; their eagerness was so apparent.

Then, they caned us. Each comrade was made to stretch out his legs. One fat fellow with his booted feet would crush the knees of a comrade and another would flog the inside of the comrade's feet with a cane. Each blow made the comrades wince in pain and they were given 50 lashes each. At last they came to me. My swollen legs bothered them. The thorn lesions had got infected and if it got worse and started to bleed, that could become proof of torture in custody. They devised another method of torture for me. I was asked to stand up and each comrade was asked to give me five lashes, below the waist. If the blow was not hard enough they would be asked to repeat the whole exercise. And then, that comrade too would not be spared.

The next day morning we were taken to Mananthavady and the ordeal got worse through the journey. We were taken in a police truck. They hit us with bayonets and kicked us all the way. The comrades were asked to pull out hairs from the flowing beard of comrade Raman Nair. If they stopped even for a second, they were beaten mercilessly. Comrade Sankaran Master had an argument with the policemen. They didn't forget to reply in kind before we reached Mananthavady.

Behind us in a jeep, the Kannur D.S.P was following our truck. Soon, the young officer speaking Malayalam with an English accent took over the supervision of the torture session. A huge crowd had gathered at the Mananthavady station premises by the time we reached there. The previous day, Ma had been arrested from somewhere near Mananthavady. That too had attracted the attention of the people. Inside the station, I saw her in the lock-up. Her face was red, with the telltale mark of five fingers across her cheeks. The police had a great time grinding our lifeless comrades. The station was teeming with police officers and MSP men and none of them missed the opportunity to display his might. I could only look on helplessly.

I was in a sari. I was asked to take it off. Under it, I was wearing trousers. The officer allowed me to keep it on. I didn't understand his intent. They made me remove the woolen jacket too that I was wearing over the blouse. Then, I was asked to walk out of the station in trousers and blouse. Even as I walked they were hitting me on the back and stomach. They made me stand on the platform of the flagstaff in the police station courtyard and paraded me to thousands of people who had thronged around. I trembled with humiliation and helplessness. The police proclaimed to the people that I had moved around the forests in this attire with my comrades. Their zeal to portray me as a whore was blatant. Journalists without wasting a moment began clicking away. I saw Thimmappa Chetty there. "Isn't she the one who attacked your house?" the police asked him. "Yes, Yes!" he jumped with joy. I turned my face away in contempt.

I was taken to the nearby tourist bungalow from there. Locals followed us there, so the police didn't assault me this time. The D.S.P and another official from the Crime Branch began their interrogation. I could make out from the D.S.P's face that he could lynch a prisoner without batting an eyelid. I gave some vague replies to whatever he asked me. Some of his questions were too vulgar. Press photographers were invited to take my photos again.

As I was being displayed outside, the policemen were going on with their frolic, questioning the comrades. In the evening I was put in the lock-up. Even after the comrades were locked up, the policemen continued their cruel exercise. They asked the comrades to come near the iron door, and then aimed punches wherever they could. They broke three of Sankaran master's ribs. He lost a few of his teeth too. There were some tribals too in the lock–up with the comrades, whom the police had arrested from Mananthavady and neighbourhood.

That night the police caught comrade Ramankuttiyettan. They gave him the title 'Pulpally S.I' and beat him up to a pulp. Are these policemen human at all, I couldn't help wonder. We had killed one of them and injured a sub inspector. But how many lives did they ruin forever in their eagerness to avenge themselves? Pulpally rebellion was triggered off by heinous police atrocities on poor peasants. There is an old saying that violence breeds violence. The valorous peasants of Pulpally had comprehended the ideology of armed revolt and with the help of a few revolutionaries had risen up against the oppression the administration unleashed on them, but in the eyes of the administration, this was a major crime. Chief minister E.M.S.

Namputhiripad, the leading light of Marxian philosophy, was the home minister then. That didn't make any difference.

My mother was arrested from a farmer's house in Mananthavady. The moment she was caught, a policeman slapped her at least five times across the face. Jagada, the fifteen-year-old daughter of Gopalan Vaidyar was with her when she was arrested. The police tortured and made attempts to rape her claiming she was Ajitha. The only crime she committed was that she happened to be with my mother. They didn't stop even when they realized their mistake.

I lay in the lock-up thinking about all this. My thoughts were not coherent. I couldn't see the police in action but could hear them all through the night. They came to me several times in the night in obvious attempts to rape me. Somehow, they didn't want to open the lock-up, get inside and rape me. So, they kept calling me to the door, but I didn't go near the iron bars of the lock up. My heart was filled with aversion. I could gather from the way they treated us that the police were a depraved lot. There was no end to their stock of abuses. I couldn't even understand some of them. It taught me how gross their views on women were. Years later I was told that I was saved from rape in custody by Gauriamma, the then revenue minister, who called up the station officers to insist that it should not happen.

Long before all this happened, on the night of November 24, (the night of Pulpally attack) Comrade Gopalan, who was sent away to hospital with an injured hand, was caught. The middle-aged Kunjupanicker, a Marxist sympathizer who had organized a public meeting earlier on November 22 at Karimam junction, and Kesavan, a socialist were also arrested. What the police did to comrade Gopalan was unimaginable. They squashed with their boots what remained of the comrade's blown off hand. Dipping his good palm in the blood that gushed out of his wound, the police stamped the mark of his palm on the wall of Pulpally wireless station. Later they publicized the blood soaked hand on the wall as 'Ajitha's palm'. They did this to tell the world that I was a bloodthirsty witch. Comrade Gopalan's arm had to be amputated later. Kunjupanicker and Kesavan who were not linked to us at all were beaten up mercilessly for the simple reason that they had organized meetings to protest against police atrocities. The police had a great time breaking Kunjupanicker's fingers by pulling tips of his fingers backwards.

An atmosphere of a state of Emergency without fundamental rights prevailed in the whole of Wayanad those days. It was a godsend for the police to settle scores with all those who had dared to speak out against their atrocities. We came to know later that the police had arrested and tortured scores of farmers and tribals who were not even aware of the incident. They had gone into the huts of these poor people to molest and rape their women and to beat up the men. Those were the days when the police unleashed a reign of terror. But the landlords and their minions who adorned the chairs of power were ecstatic to say the least.

Didn't the then Chief Minister, the great Marxist teacher come to know of any of these incidents? They still claim that the police didn't torture anyone associated with Thalassery-Pulpally revolts proving again that they lie through their teeth to cling on to positions of power. These same people shed buckets of crocodile tears during the 1975 Emergency, when Rajan, the Kozhikode Regional Engineering College student was killed in police custody. While one group of politicians made a smoke screen out of the Shah Commission that was set up to enquire into the Emergency era atrocities, another group made money out of a series of sob stories termed 'Kakkayam (the police camp where Rajan was killed) tells its tale.' Their ability to change all tales of tragedies to votes is beyond comparison. They would argue openly that force should not be used against Naxalites and that we should be confronted and defeated politically and ideologically. Yet, away from the public gaze, they betray us to the police.

We spent the night in Mananthavady police station and were taken to Kalpatta on December 3. Half of comrade Raman Nair's beard was by then plucked out. But the police were still not satiated. All the way to the court, they trained punches on us. There was an ocean of anxious people at Kalpatta court premises. The magistrate was at home and so, we were taken from the court to his place. He remanded us to Vaithiri sub-jail. The jail superintendent flaunted all his skills of torture on the exhausted comrades before locking them up.

I turned into a lifeless mute. My misery was nothing compared to the brutality meted out to my comrades. That was what I found intolerable. I felt I could not bear this cruelty any longer.

The next day morning we were sent to Kozhikode special sub-jail because the police feared that our supporters would whisk us off from Vaithiri. That, for the time being, ended a chapter of police torture. I came to know about the police brutalities in Thalassery only much later.

Ajitha in police custody after her arrest.

Ajitha on public display outside the police station.

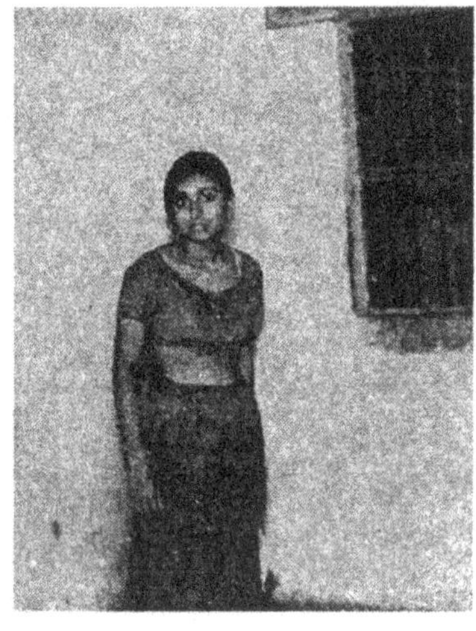

Policemen forcing her to pose for lensmen.

13

PRISON AND COURT

On December 5, we were taken to the Kozhikode jail. I parted with the rest of the comrades. I was sent to the women's ward, escorted by a woman constable.

I was totally exhausted. The Pulpally revolt, the tragic events, the ensuing stress-filled days and above all the harsh reality of custodial torture broke my very being. I lay unconscious for two three days in jail and was given penicillin injections for my swollen infected legs. Within a week, my legs became normal. Now, I looked around in alarm like a bird in flight suddenly caught unawares in a cage.

I was locked up all alone. Initially, I was confined to the cell, but later was allowed to walk around during the day. The cells next to mine overflowed with women. There was hardly any space for them to lie down. At first I didn't know what sort of women they were. Within a few days I came to know all about them from their conversations.

Most of the inmates were prostitutes whom the world held in utter contempt. These women had no homes but the streets where they made a living. They lived a life on the edge and were the leftovers of the society, brutalized by the police, the judiciary and the powerful. Periodically, the society would be 'cleaned up' with the police picking these women up from the streets and stuffing them in jail. Once they were set free they would go back to selling their flesh to sustain themselves. It is still a regular entertainment for the police to abuse these women and beat them up. Prisons for them, ironically, serve as a resting place.

I found the story of these trampled lives extremely poignant. These women are forced to take to the streets for various reasons, and once they reach the big cities there is a ready racket that waits to suck them into a vicious life. None of them ever leaves home to become a prostitute. Jilted by lovers, a majority of them are cast off by their families who would not let their unwed daughters bear children. Not knowing what to do and where to go, they roam the streets where they get raped or are forced into prostitution. Once they fall into this trap, they never escape. The society never reclaims someone who has been a prostitute. Even if they retract their steps and lead a saintly life later, they are stamped 'loose' for the rest of their lives. They too never hope to return to the society whose attitude they know only too well.

There is a striking difference in the society's approach towards men and women over sex. A man, even if he sleeps around with innumerable women, remains respectable. He is never looked down upon. On the contrary, it is dismissed as something very normal to a man. But, if a hapless young girl is betrayed by somebody and gets pregnant, her family simply disowns her. She will be forced to walk the streets or commit suicide. Society never gives her a second chance or helps her to put behind her a mistake she had committed either knowingly or unknowingly. I came to know from observing these women from close quarters that prostitution is the most venomous and naked form of crime against women.

These women are vulnerable to diseases as they are exposed to various kinds of physical stresses. Venereal diseases, tuberculosis and leprosy are their companions. Once their days of utility are over they are left to rot like garbage and die with no one to weep over them. Naturally these women spoke to each other about their pathetic lives. Still, with all my sympathy for their inhuman existence I couldn't bear to live amidst them initially. I was surprised at the amount of abuses a policeman could invent but I found these women's language even more intolerable. I was not exposed to a life like this till the police caught me. The atmosphere in the prison was suffocating. But I had to put up with it. I got some fresh air only when I was taken to the court once in every 14 days where I could meet my comrades.

Once, after ten days in jail, I was called to the office room. Lined up on the veranda were all the arrested comrades. I was taken to the superintendent's room. Many bigwigs were present there. Impichi Bawa, the honourable prison minister had come to lend an ear to our complaints. I learnt later that a reporter from the Blitz weekly was also with him. The minister asked me:

"I heard that the police beat you up. Is it true?"

"It's true." I said.

"Did you say this in court?" he asked.

"No. Would that have changed anything?"

"Didn't the magistrate ask you if you had anything to tell him? What was your reply then?" he asked again.

"We didn't say anything." I said.

"If you had told him about the police beating you could have got some respite." He stopped the conversation with this bit of advice.

It was when I was taken to the court for the first time that I came to know that more than 25 comrades had been arrested. There were 20 of us from Kozhikode. About seven-eight comrades were brought from Vaithiri sub-jail. Comrade Allunkal Sreedharan was among them. He was caught from somewhere around Iritti. Among the comrades from Kozhikode was comrade Thettamala Krishnankutty. When he came to know that all of us were caught, he took a room in a lodge and decided to meet us in the prison. But he was betrayed to the police by some acquaintance. The Kurichya comrade Kunjaman was also in police custody. I saw comrade Gopalan in the police van. They were all physically wrecked. Comrade Gopalan's rotting arm was cut off. The comrade told me that as police boots shattered his bone, the doctors had advised further amputation of his arm. Sankaran master was on treatment for his broken ribs. He had lost a few of his teeth too. Comrade Chellappan was admitted to the government hospital and was being treated for T.B.

It was then that I discovered the secret behind the 'blood-splattered palm'. Many had asked me about it, and I was perturbed. I understood from what comrade Gopalan disclosed that it was a police ploy to degrade our motives and me in particular. The comrades gave me a picture of the horrendous police atrocities going on in Pulpally, Mananthavady and the surrounding areas. It was painful to hear about the sufferings of the tribals of Chekadi.

There were thousands of eager people at the Kalpatta court. The crowd filled up the whole of court verandah and spilled over into the streets. There were many women among them and I saw a few familiar faces. There were many friendly faces that expressed their sympathy through simple gestures. It was obvious that our feat had indeed touched and swayed thousands in Wayanad. The public in many ways offered us sincere support as they came to know that we were not dacoits or murderers, that we had an ideology that motivated us to do these assaults. The crowds that thronged the Kalpatta courts proved this fact. We were presented at the Kalpatta court for over four months. Throughout our trial, thousands of people came to get a glimpse of us. The people's support was reflected in the letters too, which I received from all over the state. I got letters from young girls and women, and others who were politically inclined to our ideology. A little girl even sent me a money order for Re. 1. Baba Gurumukh Singh, the founder of Punjab's Gadar Party who had spent around 50 years in jail during the independence struggle sent me Rs.50 for our common use. Lots of people expressed their desire to meet me in jail, though the jail authorities never allowed anyone in. But these genial gestures helped us to overcome the despair and bitterness our temporary failure evoked in us.

There was another development within 14 days of our jail life. Two three days after our imprisonment the police and the crime branch came to Kozhikode jail and took away Philip, Sankaran Master and Chellappan with the permission of the court. They were taken to Mananthavady. Another gang of policemen took Sankaran master and Chellappan, handcuffed and chained around their waists, to the forest via Adakkathodu (where we got caught). Of course, they were beaten up throughout the journey. The police journey broke Sankaran master's fourth rib in the course of the journey. But, surprisingly, the police were cordial to Philip who was lodged at the Mananthavady sub-jail. Let alone torturing him, they didn't so much as tweak him and took special interest in his diet too. As soon as he came back Philip applied for a transfer to Thiruvananthapuram jail. The police took him there after a while in the pretext of some case. When he returned, he had a very high opinion about the police in general. As we weren't fortunate enough to enjoy the warmth of friendship of these poor good-natured policemen, none of us could subscribe to his view.

The plight of the Thalassery comrades was no different from ours. My friends and lawyers who used to visit me in jail told me about the horror stories of police atrocities in Thalassery. Whoever the police managed to apprehend was dealt with ruthlessly. The police used this golden opportunity to suppress whoever they thought were involved with us. Some of the ex-members and sympathizers of the Marxist party were also not spared. It was amusing to hear that Arayakkandi

Achuthan, (later a rabble-rouser of the Indira Congress) was put in jail and released on bail after a week. He was arrested from the bus stand near the Thalassery police station when he was about to attend the meeting of Revolutionary Communist Party, formed under the leadership of KPR Gopalan who had fallen out with the Marxist Party. The leaders of this party had condemned the Thalassery-Pulpally attacks in public, but the police wouldn't let go Arayakkandi whose very occupation was to spew revolutionary fire in public meetings. The police specifically aimed at those sections of the public who dared to challenge their authority, and terrorized the innumerable beedi workers and weavers. But even after successfully creating an atmosphere of terror, the police couldn't crush the revolutionary spirit of the working class and farmers. It was this same section of society of Kannur that gave shelter to comrade Varghese, extending all possible support to his activities. This just proves the amount of influence revolutionary ideas have on people. Kannur gave asylum to comrade Sukumaran too.

A few days after our arrest we heard that father had walked in to the Thrissur police station and gave himself up. The police didn't harm him, may be because of the increasing public resentment against police atrocities in Wayanad and Thalassery. All over India, the police were put on alert to search out father. A high official had questioned my uncles and grandmother in Bombay and had warned them against helping us. He had even threatened to arrest my grandmother. But she insisted that whatever be the consequence she would help her daughter. The police were taken aback when the man they were seeking so desperately came to them on his own. Within a few days KP Narayanan Master too was arrested. Now the police had in custody almost every one of those involved in the Thalassery case. While we were taken to the Kalpatta court, they were presented at the Thalassery court.

The status of the Pulpally case was quite hilarious. The First Information Report did not have any of our names, but socialist leaders

Thomas master, Kesavan and Marxist sympathizer Kunju Panikker along with comrade Gopalan figured in it. There was not even a mention of a woman's involvement in the case. This was because they did not have any clear information about us. There was no reference to my involvement in any of the statements given to the police by the landlords and their family members. The police were confused once they caught me, because according to the FIR, I was not in the picture at all. At last they got the FIR changed. This illegality was done through a quid pro quo between the police and the bench clerk in the Kalpatta court. He had asked for the release of about eight people who were arrested from Pulpally and were detained in the Vaithiri sub-jail. The police with the consent of the magistrate released these eight people and re-wrote the FIR, this time including a woman in the gang of attackers.

Many friends used to give us books to read while we were in jail. The Marxist led government insisted that they wouldn't allow Mao Tse Tung's works inside the jail. There was no restriction on other books. But we needed Mao's works desperately in order to survive the rotten atmosphere in the jail and to vigorously analyse our experiences and past events. The government turned down our repeated requests and we had to go on to a fast unto death. On January 26th father, mother, K.P and other comrades began their protest in Kannur jail. From the next day onwards we began our protest in Kozhikode prison. After three days the warden and superintendents, under orders from the minister tried to put down the protest using force. The comrades were beaten up, but they didn't go back on their demand. At last the government relented. This was one of the bitter experiences that helped to prove the Marxist leaders' loathing for Mao's works though in public they keep praising him as a great Marxist-Leninist. This fasting almost killed Ma. Scared, the jail authorities admitted her in Kozhikode medical college. They feared that she would die in custody and granted her bail soon after.

The government had a re-think about our case, particularly in order to get the case against my father strengthened. Initially, the government decided to try Thalassery and Pulpally cases separately. This decision put the government in a fix because nothing much had happened at Thalassery. So they knew that father, who was only implicated in the Thalassery case could not be punished. He could be punished only if they could connect him with the Pulpally incident. After months of scheming, they filed a conspiracy case in the Kozhikode District Magistrate's court linking Thalassery and Pulpally events. They framed charges stating that both these incidents were the result of a conspiracy hatched at our house and KP's tutorial college. Father was the prime accused, KP the second and Ma was listed third in this conspiracy case.

Many renowned advocates had by then extended their support to us. The CPI formed a defence committee of advocates to help us. But they had an ulterior motive. They wanted to exploit the overwhelming influence these events had on the common man and the rising indignation against police atrocities. They were a part of the Seven Party Coalition government that was ruling the state, but had their differences with the CPI (Marxist) better known as CPM, which led the coalition government. (Though the CPI split into CPI and CPM in 1964, within three years they came together to form a post-poll alliance of seven parties in Kerala led by chief minister EMS Namputhiripad). The CPI that had become a junior partner to the CPM wanted to use our cause as a weapon against the CPM. But we condemned their defence committee publicly and it soon got dissolved on its own. Interestingly, within months when conspiracy charges were framed against our comrades, CPI's supreme leader SA Dange publicly opposed that move. Shouldn't there be a limit to hypocrisy? Eminent advocates from Kozhikode Kunjirama Menon and Bhaskaran Nair extended their help on their own. Numerous advocates from Thalassery,

Ayyappan from Thrissur, Mayinkutty from Ernakulam and ASR Chari, a practising advocate in the Supreme Court pledged their support. Thus, public support ensured that we could fight the case without the patronage of any political party.

The many journeys from prisons to court brought in curious crowds.

14

THE THALASSERY FIASCO

I had recounted earlier the circumstances that led to Ma's release from jail on bail. She was alone in the hospital, with no by-standers or visitors. My father and I were in jail. Friends were scared of the police and kept away. The doctors and nurses were her only solace. They took good care of her and discharged her only after she recovered fully. But she was constantly ill. My repeated pleas bore fruit and the prisons I.G permitted me to visit her once in the hospital. I had seen my mother last at the Mananthavady police station. I hugged her and talked to her for a while. Once out of the hospital, she was asked to sign the register daily at the town police station and not to leave Kozhikode.

On April 2, 1969, a conspiracy case was charged in Kozhikode District Magistrate court linking Thalassery police station attack and the Pulpally attack. That stopped our journey to the Kalpatta court and that of the comrades of Kannur jail to Thalassery court. That day all of us were presented together at the Kozhikode court.

We greeted each other with the passion of bosom pals separated for years. Father and K.P hugged the Pulpally comrades tightly. My eyes became moist. This meeting should have happened in the Thirunelli forests from where the Pulapally and Thalassery comrades were jointly to pursue the armed revolution in Wayanad. But we were destined to meet each other in the enemy quarters, judged as criminals.

The District magistrate remanded all of us to Kannur central jail. We had regained our confidence after getting to read Mao's books in jail. The male comrades continued to live together and they could carry on with their study and discussions but I was far removed from them, confined to the female ward. This was a big setback for me. We requested the government to grant me permission to visit the comrades' ward during daytime. We warned them that we would wait for 14 days and then would go on a fast unto death. On the third day, about 80 wardens and superintendents stormed into the cell of the comrades and beat up all the fourteen comrades who had signed the petition. They singled out my father and K.P. Father was kicked on his chest and he fell down unconscious. When he woke up the next day, he learned that he was in a cell in the huge quarantine block, which was lying abandoned for a long time. K.P was locked up in the room meant to execute death sentences. Under special orders from higher echelons in the government, the officers, adept in torture, thrashed up the rest of the comrades and thus tried to put out the remaining flame of valour in us. Father's cardiac muscles were injured and he became a heart patient. Later, this illness restricted his movements, confining him perpetually to a room.

On April 16, I was released on bail on orders of the High Court, even before we got a reply from the authorities to our petition. I had to give two people's security of Rs 10,000 each and a personal guarantee of another Rs 10,000 and was instructed to sign at the Kasba police station in Kozhikode. I had to take special permission from the DSP to venture out of the jurisdiction of the police station.

I began to live with my mother in our house. The court gave orders to transfer father, K.P and the other 12 comrades to Kozhikode prison. The conversations I had with the comrades in prison and outside when

I was on bail, threw light on what really had happened in Thalassery.

One has to understand the real political background of the Thalassery strike to make an unbiased assessment of its failure. Earlier I had referred to the major crisis in the beedi and weaving industries of Kannur. This was the direct outcome of the many follies of the Marxist-led Kerala government and its eagerness to continue with the policies of the earlier Congress governments. About one lakh of poverty-stricken families in the coastal regions were hurled into the lap of bitter starvation due to this crisis. The pressure of this calamity was felt in the fields of agriculture and other industries, and an atmosphere of volatile insecurity prevailed in the villages around the small towns of Thalassery and Kannur. This area had a great tradition of revolutionary struggles. The CPI and CPM tried their best to solve the workers' issue through negotiations. Our comrades were not influential or capable of finding a solution to these issues. So, there were two options open to them. They could close their eyes to the workers' issue claiming that they were not prepared for it and continue with their activities in Pulpally or take it up bravely according to our perception based on Naxalbari principles and link it to the problems of Pulpally. They didn't have to think much to take the second option.

The first issue to be tackled was the place of action. Where should the workers congregate and begin their armed uprising? Should they all go to northern Wayanad, or should they gather at a point convenient to them, where they could amass some weapons? If the workers from Thalassery were to go to Mananthavady or Thirunelli (in Wayanad) and meet comrades who had already rebelled in Pulpally, the Thalassery group would have no weapons with them. In that case, those from Thalassery would just be an unarmed group joining those who had already begun an action. Then, it would have been absolutely foolish and dangerous to bring hundreds of comrades to such a place with sticks and stones as weapons. That would have only helped to forewarn the enemy. Therefore, it was decided to attack the Thalassery police station to grab weapons and to seize rice from wholesalers. This group of comrades would then march to Thirunelly to meet there those who have initiated the action in Pulpally. Thalassery is very close to Kannur, a military base and hence the comrades had taken all precautionary measures. It is one thing for those who have already participated in an action to join with rebellious farmers and quite another for comrades with no experience of a revolt joining them. It's only when they rebel that these comrades of the working class, already revolutionaries by disposition, gain the right to be called real revolutionaries. Thalassery police station was open and easily conquerable. KP's tutorial college was next to it and the comrades could assemble there. All this led the comrades to decide on Thalassery as the field of action. These decisions raised our activities to a militaristic plane, which were hitherto bound to the field of political struggles.

The proposed rebellions of Pulpally and Thalassery were closely linked to each other with the Thalassery revolt being the decisive one. The success of Thalassery was a pre-condition for the success of Pulpally. The comrades knew that our triumph would only be temporary if Pulpally rebellion succeeds and Thalassery strike fails. Therefore, all efforts were made to make Thalassery rebellion a success.

This brings forth moving memories of our declaration of Thalassery-Pulpally revolts. Those lines still stir the revolutionary in me. Let me quote a few lines from that spirited declaration titled "We have risen in revolt!"

We, the workers of Ganesh and Bharat beedi companies, weavers, estate labour, farm workers, students and teachers having lost all hope in peaceful protests have set out on a path of armed revolt against the beastly system of exploitation that exists today. We have declared a class war against the government propped up by forces of feudalism and big capital... Our people have a tradition of innumerable worker-peasant struggles. This is the land that turned red with the martyrdom of innumerable peasant comrades once again. We raise the glorious red banner made deep crimson by the warm blood of those comrades. This is not to repeat 1948, nor Telengana, nor Punnapra-Vayalar. Then, we set forth to learn the lessons of the defeats of those valiant struggles, and launch a long and tortuous 'people's war' under the leadership of the working class and through a peasant's revolution to demolish the imperial-feudal-comprador capitalist system and to replace that gradually with a new democratic system based on the alliance of workers and peasants... Worker comrades, peasant comrades, students, revolutionary intellectuals, small traders, toiling women, pick up a stick, an axe, sickle, hammer or whatever else, in your hands that you have for years used only to vote; march on for the last battle with the oppressive government; lie low and snatch the enemy's guns and all his other weapons. We have become an armed force now; a force that belongs to you, join up in thousands and ten thousands with this "people's army"! Let the flames of revolution spread all over! These flames will burn down the enemy to ashes.

Victory is only ours!

Despite such zeal and ardour why was Thalassery a miserable failure?

The one lapse that was evident from the outset in the Thalassery activities was the vacillation of some of the comrades in responsible positions. These comrades who had earlier adorned official posts in the Marxist party and trade unions, began to lose confidence as the time of action approached. Instead of effectively lining up worker comrades who were eagerly trooping to the front, these former bureaucrats of the Marxist party tried to enfeeble them. I will cite an example. The guerilla fighter of 1948 comrade Uchampalli used to give impressive revolutionary speeches, but when the time came for action he slipped out. The excuse was his wife's arthritis. This proposed revolt was a movement solely based on the Thalassery unit. Hence, father, K.P and other senior comrades could not take timely steps to weed out these wavering comrades and hand over the leadership to those steadfast in thought and action. And then, none of them had the slightest hint to believe that this fickleness of a few comrades would burst like a time bomb at a critical point of time. They hoped that their vacillation would be overcome by the flooding revolutionary ardour of the comrades from the working class and that their doubts would melt away in the flames of rebellion. Worse, the senior comrades lost in preparations didn't even take this problem seriously. They didn't have any experience in 'military preparations' nor were they aware as to how far the threat of revisionism had spread. They couldn't understand comrade Stalin's lesson correctly, that opportunists, that too in responsible position, within the fort are much more dangerous than the enemy knocking at the gates ready to strike.

Thus, on the D-day, not many comrades turned up. Only 315 comrades reached Thalassery on the night of November 20, when more than a thousand were expected. The attacks had to be scaled down and the Supreme Council called for a meeting. Two senior comrades had gone to observe the station. They returned with a frightening report. They told the supreme council that the police station was quite lively and seemed ready to tackle any emergency. Another comrade was sent to verify this report. By then, the other two had already spread alarm among the troops. They panicked as if the enemy would attack them the very next moment. They scampered around tearing down posters, hiding weapons and burying explosives in the nearby seashore. Things were slipping out of their hands, but father and K.P couldn't do anything to stop it. The comrade sent to re-check too brought dreadful reports. He said that there were lots of plainclothesmen around. Then, father decided to check out the facts and took another comrade with him. One thing was clear — there was not much basis in the reports they had received earlier. True, there were a few extra policemen in the station, two three additional lights, and a sentry holding a gun. The inspector went out in his jeep from time to time and it was easy to attack the station then. Father went back to argue in the Supreme Council that there were no big hurdles to carry out the attack that night itself. The earlier reports were merely expressions of fear in those comrades' minds. Some comrades kept quiet during the meeting. Some others were not willing to act that night. The discussion of the supreme council that started at 2.30 went on till 5 in the morning. They didn't come to a conclusion. The comrades who were camped in the tutorial college went to sleep tired of waiting. After a while they woke up to ask themselves what had happened. What should they do now? The worker comrades had forsaken everything and had come ready to be part of a grand revolution. They couldn't understand what was going on. The Supreme Council dissolved itself.

The worker comrades were angry and frustrated that none of the plans worked out. The leaders explained the situation to them and told them they would strike the next night. They were asked to go to the bus stand so that the police would notice them, and board different buses. But they were supposed to meet together again at night at a new place —Kunduchira, Ponniam. That place was chosen by one of the vacillating comrades of the Thalassery chapter. The police slackened their vigil a little when they saw the comrades leaving the tutorial thinking that everything was over. The policeman on duty at the bus stand reported that all the comrades had left for their homes. He was later suspended.

Instead of reliable guides, drunks and anti-revolutionaries greeted the comrades who reached Kundichira the next day to execute the previous night's failed plans. The wavering comrades in responsible positions had again succeeded in the attempt to sabotage the plans. Still, a few comrades managed to reach the Thalassery stadium from Kunduchira, but they too were discouraged at the last moment. Three senior comrades of the Supreme Council who had showed signs of wavering at the very outset didn't turn up at all. Another section tried to engage father and K.P in a discussion. But father saw through their ploy. He told them that he and K.P. were not ready to be drawn into another discussion till daybreak and that if no one was ready they would attack the station. Father and K.P knew that we would be waiting in Pulpally forest impatiently to hear the news of Thalassery attack and so it was inevitable that they carried out the attack that very night. When they started out, almost all the comrades marched forward with them. They were physically tired and emotionally drained, and these lifeless souls carrying weapons reached the station. Nothing happened there except a hand grenade being hurled into the compound. Even that didn't explode. The terror-filled roar of the sentry made them all vanish in different directions throwing away the weapons. Only father remained at the gate. Suddenly comrade Vellathooval Stephen charged in with another hand grenade and aimed it at the sentry who was standing rooted to the spot, shivering from head to toe. But the bomb fell by the roadside and was later found by the police. That too didn't explode. This brought the Thalassery rebellion to an end. Father walked back slowly. He was well within the range of the sentry's gun, yet he did not die. The sentry's gun had no bullets.

Later, the comrades analysed the reasons for their failure: "The rebellion was an attempt to heighten our political struggle to a militaristic level. The failure of the rebellion exposed our bankruptcy on the military plane. The police station attack and the amassing of weapons were not mere political activities they were higher militaristic action with a political intent. A military perception and mindset, soldierly discipline, strict vigil to keep secrets, a cohesive party organization capable of converting political ideals into military action are all essential for such a rebellion to succeed. These would come only with experiences of working class revolutions and revolutionary outlook.

Though we had tried to perceive things militarily, our attempts were totally inadequate. Our prime fault lay in our inefficiency to neutralize the destructive force called revisionism or worse opportunism. This opportunism displayed by those in responsible at crucial moments destroys the spirit of revolution rendering revolutionaries lifeless and subverting revolutionary plans from within. We were incompetent in identifying and removing these saboteurs. To an extent this failure was inevitable because we had depended a lot on the Thalassery unit. Yet, the total lack of anticipation of this great danger only exposes our inherent weaknesses. All this only high lighten our lack of experience and ignorance of Maoism..."

This was the gist of our analysis of the failure of Thalassery. Thus, it was no surprise that we failed despite the success of Pulpally. Though Thalassery revolt failed, the most important outcome of it was that we succeeded in an attempt to project that our plans were fully executed. Had the news of Thalassery strike not broadcast over the radio, the Pulpally revolt would have been abandoned. We in Pulpally would have been thoroughly demoralized. Our attempts to spread the Naxalbari message to every nook and corner of the state with the boom of a thunder and the power of lightning would have got aborted. There wouldn't have been a Thalassery-Pulpally incident with the message of armed revolt written into the annals of history with the blood and sweat of innumerable human lives!

If you ask me whether the Thalassery-Pulpally revolt was a failure my answer would be that it was not a conclusive disaster. In fact, this question reminds me of what Karl Marx said about another incomparable significant historical event. When the Paris commune was failing in 1871, Marx noted that, "...even if the commune is crushed the struggle could only be temporarily halted. The ideas of the commune are forever. They cannot be destroyed. They would keep recurring till the working class attains liberation." I would say the same about the Thalassery-Pulpally incident. It was a practical foray much more significant than hundreds of debates and political programmes. These heroic rebellions opened a new chapter in the history of revolutions in Kerala. Yes, it was only a beginning...

15

POLITICAL RESPONSES

It is worthwhile to record the responses to the Thalassery-Pulpally rebellions from various quarters within the state and the rest of the country. I got to know about most of these only after getting released on bail. All the parliamentary political parties of India opposed the rebellion, either openly or discreetly. For the ruling Congress Government at the Centre it was a dangerous forewarning. Hence, the Central Government promised all possible help to the Marxist led coalition government in Kerala. The Centre even pressed into service choppers from its Naval base at Cochin to assist the Kerala police in its combing operations to capture us, when we were wandering in the Thirunelli forests. Regressive parties like the Congress and the Jan Sangh termed us anti-national and anti-social. Congress used this opportunity to topple the Marxist-led Kerala government on allegations of aiding and abetting the Naxalites.

The political position of the parties, which claimed to be revolutionary and progressive, on our rebellion was not significantly different from that of the bourgeois parties. They applauded the revolutionary spirit of the youngsters involved in these rebellions and argued with righteous indignation that our motive should not be doubted. They proclaimed it their bounden duty to get the prodigals back to the fold. They unleashed a crusade of words against treating the young misled revolutionaries like ordinary criminals in jail. The C.P.I and Kerala Socialist Party were prominent among them. But they were absolutely sure that the path followed by the revolutionaries was wrong and that incidents like Naxalbari, which shook the very foundations of the parliamentary system, should be tackled. These proclamations of sympathy amounted to sweet nothings, yet they served two purposes for them: They hoped to drive the C.P.I. (Marxist) out of the seven-party united front. Second, they wanted comrades from our ranks to join their party in order to taken on the C.P.I (M). Their simple design was to convert the glory of Thalassery-Pulpally into votes.

But what was the response of the Marxist leadership, supposedly the most revolutionary party of them all?

The authoritative view of C.P.I. (M) was put on record by none other than its tallest leader, AK Gopalan on January 10, 1969 in the form of a short essay: 'Thalassery-Pulpally incidents — Other Parties and Us'. It says: "These attacks neither help the worker-peasant movement nor the non-Congress parties that work for workers and peasants nor the United Front government that has been their creation. The Palakkad meeting and the state committee have felt that these incidents would only help ruin the revolutionary movement and sustain and strengthen the bourgeoisie-capitalist system. The events that followed prove this right."

He wrote elsewhere: "The party doesn't believe in the display of physical power either at the level of the individual or as small groups. The Communist Party never took refuge in Gandhian non-violence to berate the use of force during worker-peasant struggles or nationalist movement in the days of the independence struggle. Yet, it had always opposed the use of force by individuals, which used to be termed as terrorism during those days. The communist-socialist movements had only praise for the use of violence against British imperialism and autocratic native princes. But they never approved individual acts of terror. The fact is that the groups that organized Thalassery-Pulpally attacks are but remnants of those terrorist groups that had been overrun by the achievement of the Communist-Socialist movements."

He marvelled at the armed struggles led by the Communist Party like the Morazha-Mattannoor incident in 1940, Kayyoor in 1941 and the violent uprising in Punnapra-Vayalar of 1946. Despite admitting the element of adventurism in these great struggles of yore, he attacked Thalassery-Pulpally: "These attacks were not organized as part of the growing worker-peasant movements nor the democratic struggle against the bourgeoisie-capitalist governments. On the contrary, these attacks were aimed at the ruling coalition government, which the people of Kerala had nurtured against the bourgeoisie-capitalist rule." He alleged that the organizers of the Thalassery-Pulpally revolts had actually helped the regressive political parties in their attempt to bring Kerala under the President's rule.

Kunnikkal Narayanan's (my father) surrender to the police was taken out of context and cited as proof of Thalassery-Pulpally attacks being isolated events with no links to the revolutionary movement. For A.K.G, the absence of any support from political parties was enough to condemn us as far removed from the people's revolutionary movements. Somewhere else he taunted the chief strategist Kunnikkal Narayanan for being cowardly, for having surrendered to the police.

It is not surprising that A.K.G suspected that at least some of the organizers of these attacks had acted as pawns of the Intelligence Bureau and the Congress government at the centre. He wanted these links to be closely scrutinized. A.K.G had seen the shadow of the dark hands of the US intelligence agency C.I.A over our activities much before the Thalassery-Pulpally revolt. Now, C.I.A has only become I.B.

Worse, his attitude towards Marxism-Leninism, armed revolt and the Chinese revolution under the leadership of Mao-Tse Tung was completely distorted and fallacious! He said somewhere: "It should be noted that the newspapers (especially Congress- Kerala Congress dailies like Malayala Manorama) supported the Central Government when it unleashed its terror on the Communist Party during 1964-66. These papers had argued that the C.P.I. (M) had adopted the Chinese model of armed revolution. Later this allegation was proved totally baseless." Towards the end of this essay, he says: "It was not Mao, but Lenin and Marx who catered to the view that aggression is inevitable in the transition from capitalism to socialism." He illustrates this point mentioning *State and Revolution* by Lenin. Even as he acknowledges this ideology in word he provides it with a loophole. "Neither Marx nor Lenin had prescribed armed revolt as panacea for all ills... Their advice was for a sudden attack on the enemy when the situation is conducive for such an attack or else to resort to other means. He went on to assert that Mao too was against indiscriminate violence. "Mao had led armed revolts only on inevitable occasions during the two decades of struggle between the Chinese communist party and Kuomintang. Under his leadership the Chinese Party did all to prevent the civil war that followed the last phase of this struggle. The ideologies that Mao formulated and which were used in the Chinese revolution were the practical forms of Marxism-Leninism. Mao had acknowledged the approach of Lenin and Marx that all peaceful ways and if need be, violent methods should be put in use for the success of the revolution."

What was that special situation that prevailed in India, which made the Marxist Party believe that armed revolt was unnecessary? "The mass movement of the workers and the peasants should be strengthened through legislatures and governments (as long as they exist) elected by the masses. Once such elections and governments become counter-productive to the vested interests, the ruling classes will try to demolish the Parliamentary system and bring in their autocratic rule. The Party should be prepared to deal with such a situation," wrote A.K.G.

Let me make it clear here that I was brought up in an atmosphere that led me to respect A.K.G. So, it was but natural that I was angry at his political position that went against the truisms of Marxism-Leninism. One thing that emerged out of his essay was his attempt to distort Lenin's *State and Revolution.* Misquoting Lenin, A.K.G desperately tried to establish that the Marxist government in Kerala was a creation of worker-peasant mass movements and that it was fundamentally different from the feudal-bourgeois led Central Government. He sought to remind the allies of the Marixist party that it was in the interest of the people of the state to sustain the Marxist-led government.

But look at what Lenin has to say in the same text about the all pervasive Parliamentary system: "The real essence of bourgeois parliamentarism is to decide once in every five years who among the ruling classes would repress and crush the people through parliament. And this is evident not just in parliaments of the Constitutional monarchies, but also in the most democratic of the republics."

If this was what Lenin had to say in 1917, should we gather from A.K.G that the essential features of parliamentarism had changed by 1969? The parliamentary system was established by Britain in India through the Congress Party founded by an Englishman A.O. Hume. He was after all worried about safety of his fellow colonizers and the prospects of an armed uprising against the British Government by the natives who had already taken to arms in 1857. Such a party created for dissent management and to blunt the people's wars against the British Empire was used to establish and sustain the parliamentary system in India. Even after 1947, this system is being perpetuated to churn out false dreams. A.K.G, instead of making his cadre alive to these political realities of our parliamentary system, was misleading his party and its workers. Even while terming the Indian State a bourgeois-capitalist one, AKG claims that ours is a democratic system.

I feel that his views on armed revolt too were tailor made to defend the reformist agenda of the Marxist Party. Let us see how far he has comprehended Marx's teaching that "violence is the mid-wife to any old society that is pregnant with a new one." Even as he says that violence is inevitable in the transition from capitalism to socialism he tells that there were traces of adventurism in Morazha-Mattoor, Kayyoor and Punnapra-Vayalar struggles. What does this mean? Is AKG critical of the Thalassery-Pulpally uprising, just to demean these great armed peasant revolts? Somewhere else he says that the communists didn't object to or rather cheered the use of force during the people's movement before independence. Talking of a Communist's duty Lenin had said, "The essence of the teachings of Marx and Engels is the need to impart to the masses, in depth and with discipline, the inevitability of a violent revolution." A.K.G's political life since 1952 proves that he had long forfeited his commitment to armed revolution. That year he became part of the Indian parliamentary system, which he clung to till the end of his life and was never apologetic about it. What Lenin had asked of a true Communist with regard to violent revolution never bothered him. His article shows how eager he was to seek lame excuses for not taking the path of armed revolt.

Let us see how far his reading of the Chinese Revolution is true. Whosoever has read the four volumes Mao's Selected Works can understand one thing effortlessly: Though Chinese party was established in 1921, armed revolt under Mao's leadership started only by 1927. The armed struggle that started on August 1, 1927 passed through various phases and ended on October 1, 1949 when the party seized power all over China. It is quite surprising that A.K.G could distort facts to such a large extent, considering that the guns never ever stopped booming in the 22 year long history of people's war in China involving three civil wars and one national defence war.

He argues that Thalassery-Pulpally revolts were not linked to the people's movements and that they were just isolated terrorist attacks. People's movements for him were merely trade unions created for the lawful struggles for the rights of the worker and the peasant. He has completely forgotten what the people's movement for an armed revolution is. This issue, which was central to his politics in his youth, was reduced to insignificance after the Communist Party's betrayal of the Telengana armed struggle in 1952. Once the goal of the Party shifted to winning seats in legislatures and parliament, the party leadership has manipulated all its organizations to that end.

Lastly, let me explain the circumstances that led to my father's surrender. After the failure of the Thalassery-Pulpally revolt, the C.P.M and the C.P.I exploited the mood of despair and confusion that engulfed the captured comrades fully. There was much to doubt the attitude of the leadership of the All India Committee of Revolutionaries towards my father. The C.P.I formed a defence committee to help the Thalassery-Pulpally accused. The comrades could have inadvertently walked into the trap laid by these Communist parties and the Thalassery-Pulpally incident would have lost all its political significance. Especially, when the Pulpally comrades had concluded even while in the forest that they were betrayed by the Thalassery comrades. It wouldn't have taken long for the Pulpally comrades who had achieved their goals to decide that the leadership and the very course of the Thalassery incident were treacherous. The Government had schemed to treat Thalassery and Pulpally as separate incidents so that the Pulpally comrades were kept totally in the dark about what had happened in Thalassery. That was when father realized that he should reach out to the comrades in prison to defeat the designs of the C.P.I and the C.P.M to mess up with the politics of the Thalassery-Pulpally incident. All the key comrades who participated in the Pulpally revolt, except comrade Varghese, were in police custody. Father knew that if he gave himself up, the government would get confused and would only try to keep him in jail as long as it could. It was after his surrender that the idea to link Thalassery and Pulpally occurred to the Government. There was no provision to punish father for more than six months if the Thalassery case were to be treated separately. Father had surrendered considering all these aspects, but the Marxist leadership was joyous to have a device to give the revolt a bad name. For the Marxists, father was till then an agent of the I.B and C.I.A, but now he became the anarchist who surrendered to the police with Rs 8 and 25 paise in his pocket. They had to change their campaign among the comrades in jail and outside. Before long, these parties realised that father hadn't served the interests of the police in the real sense of the word 'surrender'. Their attitude changed with this realization and they let loose a world of terror and torture. Father's decision to continue with the struggle was not affected at all though he changed its settings as a result of the changed circumstances after the failure of Thalassery-Pulpally revolts.

I said so much about the response of the Marxist leadership. But what was the reaction of the Naxalbari movement?

We had got the news of father's expulsion from the Co-ordination Committee while we were busy with our preparations in Pulpally. But comrade Charu Majumdar glorified the Thalassery-Pulpally attacks. His greetings dated November 27, was published in the English magazine, *Liberation*. The revolts generated enthusiasm amongst numerous comrades who thought along the same lines.

There was a heart-warming incident during the days when I was out on bail. One fine morning, eleven comrades who were in Central Prison, Vishakapatanam, Andhra Pradesh scaled the boundary walls and escaped. Within a few days of their escape three of them came to visit us at our place — comrades Aadibhatla Kailasam, Nagabhushan Patnaik, and Shaik Hasinar, a Malayali. The first two were the Central Committee members of the Indian Communist Party (Marxist-Leninist). Comrade Kailasam was the leading light of the Adivasi movement in Srikakulam. This peasant comrade who believed fervently in the ideology of Naxalbari and worked valorously for it, was later captured and killed by the police along with another prominent peasant comrade, Vempadappu Satyanarayana. The police circulated the lie that they were killed in an encounter. The names of these two comrades used to spread dread among the local feudal lords. Nagabhushan was a famous advocate from Orissa. His devotion to the path of Naxalbari was famous. He was sentenced to capital punishment but never pleaded with the government to curb his sentence. But succumbing to the surge of public demand and pressure from the masses, the President had to commute Patnaik's death sentence to life imprisonment. He is still alive in the Vishakapatanam Central Prison afflicted with various ailments. Yet, he is not ready to forsake his beliefs. Hasinar was a Malayali who used to work in Orissa. The comrade, who played an important role in the Srikakulam movement of 1969, is still languishing in Vishakapatanam Central Prison. These comrades told us that they couldn't explain in words the extent of exuberance Thalassery-Pulpally events had evoked in the comrades of Srikakaulam, the peasants and the masses. The fact that Ma and I had taken part in this revolt had encouraged their women comrades to participate in armed struggles. They informed us that the party had sent them and according to the decision of the Central committee comrade Charu Majumdar would soon visit us.

Meanwhile, another significant historical event had taken place. The All India Co-ordination Committee of various revolutionary groups spread across the country had understood the need to establish a revolutionary party and founded the Communist Party of India (Marxist-Leninist) on April 22, 1969. Comrade Charu Majumdar was its chairman. The main organizers of the Naxalbari rising Kanu Sanyal and Jangal Santal were part of its Central Committee. Comrade Kanu Sanyal announced the formation of this revolutionary party taking up events that had led to its formation at a mass meeting at Calcutta on May 1, 1969. The Thalassery-Pulpally revolt found a place of pride along with Naxalbari in his speech.

At the international level, Peking radio applauded Thalassery-Pulpally within 24 hours of its execution. It gave information about these revolts on the following days of its transmission.

If this was how our actions were viewed outside Kerala, the reaction within was equally encouraging. From the moment we were out on bail numerous comrades and friends came visiting. They congratulated us and sought advice to prepare for further revolts on the lines of Thalassery-Pulpally. They told us that our actions had created a wave of fresh hope in people, particularly among the weaker sections of the society. They could feel a wave of self-confidence surging up among women too. These stories of new vigour and hopes of liberation among the peasant-worker sections of the hilly areas of Wayanad gave us the courage to go on despite many odds. It gave us strength to stay put in the path of Thalassery-Pulpally revolts and overcome our failures through a close study of political principles and an analysis of our practical experiences.

16

NAXALBARI AND THE PERVERSION CALLED ANNIHILATION

Was our decision to attack the wireless station and loot the landlords prompted by the unique situation in Pulpally? If so, why did we plan to attack the Thalassery police station as well? Most of the so-called Naxalite attacks that followed the Thirunelli incident (in February 1970 much after our initial strikes) were fashioned after the theory of annihilation of class enemies. What was the difference between Thalassery-Pulpally and the series of violent actions that ensued? Was the difference just in execution or were these the expressions of two fundamentally different lines of thought and perceptions?

These questions are significant for the revolutionary movement. It is important to know the right from the wrong for only then can the movement go on.

Some people don't even acknowledge Thalassery-Pulpally and Kuttiyadi in their list of historic events of armed struggle in Kerala. For some others, the history of the movement begins with Thirunelli. But could you possibly erase Thalassery-Pulpally from the history of our revolutionary movements? Was this disparity between Thalassery-Pulpally and the subsequent actions caused by natural differences that occur when Maoist precepts of the successful Chinese revolution based on Marxism were applied in a different country? To seek an answer for this question, we should first examine what Naxalbari means.

At the international level, the Chinese Communist Party under Mao had fought against the deceitful revisionist stand of the Soviet Communist Party leadership. Mao sought to safeguard the ideology of Marxism-Leninism by challenging Khrushchev who dared to rewrite them. This fierce ideological war had its impact on communists all over the world. As a result, the communist movement split into two. The struggle of the Chinese party based on ideology influenced the Indian communist movement too. The cadre became distraught. They began to express their frustration against the leadership that succumbed to pressure from the Government of Nehru, a colonialist crony, who cold-bloodedly crushed the heroic peasant revolts of Telengana and elsewhere during 1946-51. The frustration of the party workers against the leadership that withdrew the armed struggles soon erupted into a rebellion against the party's position upholding 'national pride' during the 1962 border issue with China. The party leadership split singling out the Dange section that supported the Soviet stand and the anti Chinese attitude of the Indian government. The leadership of the C.P.I. (Marxist) could deceive the cadre for some time that it was with the Chinese party. But this leadership, which accepted in principle the Chinese party's call for revolution in Afro-Asian countries, was plagued by parliamentarism. It had only one motive: Prevent the workers and peasants from following the path of Mao and the Chinese party, and thus, sabotage the Indian revolution. This was what imperialists like America and Britain, and revisionist, opportunist forces like Soviet Union wanted. After all, India, home to hundreds of millions was a lingering hope for colonisers and all imperialist powers. They couldn't exploit China after the 1949 revolution. So, the imperialist forces wanted to disrupt the Indian revolution, as liberation for India would end up threatening their interests. The 'pro-Chinese' party leadership served these vested interests. But the party workers didn't stop with the split of 1964. They looked for more and learnt more about the Chinese way and tried to gain practical experiences. That was when another revolutionary explosion happened in China — the great working class Cultural Revolution.

Mao had understood that war against opportunism and revisionism should not be limited to the party alone, it should go deeper into the masses. In the 17 years after the Revolution, class biases were gradually regaining ground in the Chinese cultural and educational fronts. Mao realized from his own experience that many of the leaders in positions of power within the Party were turning slaves to luxury and the corrupting influence of power. They were getting sucked into a conspiracy from within and outside China to overthrow the Revolution, for which an anti-communist clique was being formed as it had happened in Russia. Mao was aware that to contain this danger millions of Chinese people and party workers should have the courage to question the leadership and if necessary, topple it. He unleashed the Cultural Revolution with the slogan "Bomb the headquarters." The first rays of this historic revolution brightened up every nook and corner of the world.

This new revolution brought in changes in India too. Finally, some light was shed on the path of the communists of India and they could see their goals with greater clarity. They found that China, which had overthrown the brutal world of exploitation and oppression through a difficult, 22 year long armed struggle was now building up a new world for the working class. China should be India's model. One thing was clear about the present day India and the China before the revolution — these two had undergone similar imperialist exploitation and had an under-developed economic infrastructure. India's problems were worse because imperialism was far more rooted in India than in China along with a facade of independence. Indian revolutionaries understood this truth and Naxalbari was the first torch they lit, almost two decades after Telangana.

There was prompt praise for Naxalbari from Mao and the Chinese Party, which kept the interests of the world revolution above narrow Chinese nationalist considerations. They proclaimed their stand on Naxalbari in the Central Committee's important declaration "The thunder of spring on Indian horizon." The path of Indian revolution was the path of Naxalbari. But what had happened in Naxalbari?

The poverty-stricken landless farmers of Bengal, especially those from villages like Naxalbari, Kharibari and Fancideva in Darjeeling district, had fought many a lawful battle against feudal landlordism that was fostered by the colonizers. The workers who plucked the world famous, Darjeeling tea, were for centuries exploited by British tea estate owners. Charu Majumdar, Kanu Sanyal and Jangal Santal were the leaders of the kissan (agriculture workers) group of the C.P.I. (M) in that district. They were leading a struggle within the party favouring the Chinese path since 1964. The peasants got a shot in their arm when a coalition government came to power in West Bengal in 1967 with C.P.I. (M) politbureau member Jyoti Basu as deputy chief minister. They obviously thought that Basu would support them in their attempts to implement the Marxist slogan of "land for tillers." Basu was then the home minister as well. They hoisted the red flag in Naxalbari, Kharibari and Fancideva and declared the rule of the Communist party in these villages. Under the leadership of these revolutionary leaders the peasants and the masses seized grain, land and weapons from landlords and estate owners, and punished cruel local oppressors. Waging a guerilla war, they forced the police and the regressive army to retreat. Thus they established the power of the revolutionary armed struggle of the peasants. The imperialists, revisionists, corrupt officials, local oppressors, callous landlords, the regressive army and the police could not stop them. The radical section of the Indian Communist Party did the right thing, the right way...

This was what had happened in Naxalbari. The Telengana uprising of 1946-51 was very similar. This was what Punnapra Vayalar and Karivelloor in Kerala and the Tebhaga revolt of Bengal were all about. All these were armed uprisings of the peasants and the people under the leadership of communists against the prevalent oppressive social system. Naxalbari and the perception of the Indian revolution as envisaged by the Chinese party inspired Thalassery-Pulpally.

The Indian administrative system was a creation of the British imperialism. This system and the Indian state have been mere instruments of oppression; beneath the mask of an independent nation this so-called steel frame still exists with not so much as a scratch on it. With growing class contradictions, the police, the armed forces, the judiciary and the prison administration have only become more violently anti-people than they were in the days of the British rule. It is imperative to strengthen these pillars of the State for the continued economic exploitation of the imperialists. The feudalism that exists in India is one that had long ago surrendered to imperialism — a man-eater that had lost its teeth in its fight against the new masters who co-opted it. This ageing defeated feudalism is on a drip, sustained by imperialism. So, should this feeble feudalism be targeted? Or should we design our programmes to tackle the Indian State that is founded on the collective strength of feudalism and monopoly capitalists sustained all through by imperialism? This is the issue that led to attempts to mislead the cadre and also heated debates within the movement.

There is also related question: Would a few severed heads of landlords hoisted on spikes solve people's issues?

They, who convert the great revolutionary feat of the people of Naxalbari into a deed of annihilation of class enemies by a mysterious group, merely degrade the cause of revolution. In the face of criticism against the annihilation theory, some of its practitioners and theoreticians even uphold the 'Mangoorjaan' incident. Mangoorjaan happened when five-six masked persons seized guns from a group of policemen. By turning revolutionary activities into terrorist actions by a few people, they are actually misleading the revolutionary cadre and hence helping the enemy. Therefore they abhor the Thalassery-Pulpally comrades. Admitted, Thalassery-Pulapally had its shortcomings and they have to be seriously analysed and rectified. But why is Thalassery-Pulpally important? This is the first revolt in Kerala that struck like a lightning spreading the message of an armed struggle inspired by Naxalbari and guided by the Chinese Communist Party. No one could deny this fact. But our critics tried to obliterate Thalassery-Pulpally and tactfully used Mao and the Chinese party to legitimize their terrorist activities. They did not bother to assimilate the essence of Maoism drawn from the great leader's role in the Chinese Revolution. Mao, the indisputable leader of the Chinese revolution who transformed world history and unleashed the Cultural Revolution to ensure that China remained red, was just another referral point in their verbose arguments. Some times they averred that Mao had further expanded Marxism, but on other occasions some of them toed the Albanian Communist party's line that Marxism had not expanded at all. Then these supporters of the Albanian line shifted their stand when they realized that the cadre in Kerala would not brook anti-Maoism. They never cared to explain their changing points of view. When it comes to understanding the lessons of the Chinese Revolution they were no better than the Marxist party. For them, Charu Majumdar was the infallible leader, a cut above Mao.

Comrade Charu Majumdar who led the Naxalbari strike had one special quality — he had total faith in the ideal of armed revolt and worked for it selflessly. But he had internalized the style of working of the Marxist Party in which he had held important posts. This led him to commit serious mistakes. He did try to redeem himself after facing criticism from various quarters, but was soon brutally murdered. But our radicals do not want a leader who was willing to accept his mistakes; they adored the comrade who committed blunders. Their perception is based on his lapses. Their desire is to put comrade Majumdar above Mao, and then to place themselves along with Majumdar. Some of the accused of the Thalassery-Pulpally case, who decided not to argue their case in court now have acquired even more radical disciples. Though occasionally they too argued their case, their favourite slogan is "Boycott the bourgeois court!" In *"A Marxist-Leninist perspective of the Indian revolution"*, a book supposedly written by comrade Charu Majumdar and published in Malayalam, he sarcastically refers to Kunnikkal Narayanan fighting a legal battle. When Kunnikkal Narayanan fights his case in court it is termed as sacrifice of ideology and abject surrender to the enemy. But when some of these radicals move even the Supreme Court for bail arguing the case themselves, it is a matter of tactics. So the issue is not the correctness of fighting within the parameters set by the Indian legal system, it is all about who has taken the decision to do so. In the later editions of Comrade Majumdar's book, these radicals have made some changes on their own. Poor comrade Majumdar, how would he know about all these shadow fights? He was brutally murdered in police custody in 1972. After one's death anything can be done in his name. And that is what has happened to Mao too.

Mao Tse Tung, the loved and revered leader of the revolutionaries across the world died on September 9, 1976. A moment much awaited by the forces of the old world within China and elsewhere and by those lurking powers within and outside the international Communist movement. The regressive leaders who had been hurled into the depths of the Chinese society by the sky-high waves of the Cultural Revolution didn't miss this opportunity. The revolutionaries within the party who were implementing the bitter lessons of the Cultural Revolution were thrown into prison. A lot of their followers were murdered. Thus the colour of China changed, at least for the time being. Now we see Mao's line — giving importance to frontal struggles of ideas to create a communist who would keep the interests of the world revolution above all —being trampled everywhere. Instead, China is on its way to modernism, for which it has associated itself with the US and other military superpowers of the world. Now its model of socialism is the Titoism of Yugoslavia. The Chinese leaders are compelled to declare their devotion to Mao, but in real terms they are ardent admirers of Titoism, an ideology despised by communists all over the world.

17

THE POLITICAL RESOLUTION OF THE C.P.I (M.L)

With the defeat of Thalassery, the opportunists within the Naxalbari movement in Kerala got a fresh lease of life. The organized scandal-mongering of the Marxist leadership all over the state and the rumours they spread regarding my father's surrender became effective weapons in the hands of certain Naxal leaders who held official posts within the party. The propaganda of these critics confused the beedi workers who had on the appointed day come ready to take part in the Thalassery revolt and other comrades who sincerely desired a revolution. The group under K.P.R Kosalaramadas declared that Kunnikkal Narayanan was a C.I.A agent. The opportunistic Kanthalot Karunan went around saying: "Kunnikkal Narayanan is a betrayer, he has betrayed Thalassery revolt. A true revolutionary never surrenders; Kunnikkal is no revolutionary..." All these accusations had an impact on our comrades who only knew some of the facts or none at all. Once they were in jail, my father and comrade K.P confronted these strong allegations both from within and without the movement. The comrades in jail split into two groups — one, which upheld the failed Thalassery revolt and the other, comprising of those who condemned it.

I had earlier referred to my father's expulsion from the All India Co-ordination Committee, while we were preparing for the Pulpally revolt. In his place, Nagi Reddy from Andhra had become a member. He belittled the Thalassery-Pulpally attacks as C.I.A activities. Some comrades from Calcutta told us that even comrade Charu Majumdar had campaigned against Thalassery-Pulpally strikes in the first few days. But the Radio Peking broadcast which glorified these events within 24 hours of the attack forced comrade Majumdar to change his opinion. That was why he applauded Thalassery-Pulpally in an article dated November 27, 1968 published in Liberation magazine. But Nagi Reddy didn't change his stand. The revolutionaries who were organizing an uprising of scheduled castes in Srikakulam on the line of Naxalbari, protested against Nagi Reddy. They warned that Nagi Reddy should be expelled or they would resign from the party. Thus Nagi Reddy was sent out of the Co-ordination Committee. A declaration to this effect was published in *Liberation*. It was proclaimed that the prime reason to expel Nagi Reddy was that he was spreading rumours against the Thalassery-Pulpally revolts even while the international leadership (the Chinese party) approved of these incidents. We came to know about the fight between Nagi Reddy and the comrades of Srikakulam from those who came to visit us from the Vishakapatanam Central jail.

But later it became obvious that comrade Charu Majumdar had acknowledged Thalassery-Pulpally merely because of the support it had got from the international leadership and not out of sincerity.

A few days after comrades Kailasam and Nagabhushan went back comrade Charu Majumdar came to visit Kerala. This was in October 1969. He toured Kerala as Chairman of Communist Party of India (Marxist-Leninist). He had come on the special advice of the Central Committee to see Ma and me (as we were out on bail), to hold discussions with us and to invite us into the party. The comrade stayed in a lodge next to our house in Kozhikode and saw a few of the comrades who were opposed to us and toured south Kerala and Wayanad escorted by Ambady Sankarankutty Menon and Kosala Ramadas. He didn't meet us at all. He made these fake revolutionaries office bearers of the state organization committee of the Marxist-Leninist party. We came to know from his book "*A Marxist-Leninist perspective of the Indian revolution*" published in his name that he had attacked the Thalassery-Pulpally rebellions and my father while on this tour. The book, a compilation of Majumdar's speeches in Kerala, was made more colourful by Ambady's personal opinions. It said that my father "was bewildered and disappointed, and hence he surrendered", and that now "he was pleading his case". The book alleged that father was a petty bourgeoisie, and the Thalassery-Pulpally rebellion failed because it depended too much on the petty bourgeoisie, and that the experiences of these rebellions were destructive. Based on my father's surrender to the police and his decision to argue the case in court, comrade Majumdar alleged that the politics of Thalassery-Pulpally was flawed, and that father had ceased to be a revolutionary. Fake revolutionaries like Ambady and Kosalan, whose sole activity was making fiery public speeches and sucking the blood of labourers as officials in trade union organizations, were a bundle of nerves after the Thalassery-Pulpally attacks. Arayakkandi's experience taught them that even their revolutionary speeches could send them behind the bars. And so, they opposed these revolts publicly, at the top of their voices. These parasites could never forego the security of their homes to take up arms. Comrade Majumdar only got exposed by his own declarations, which were of much help to these people.

There were certain interesting developments after the formation of the Communist Party of India (Marxist-Leninist). Two months after the party was established, Radio Peking hailed it as the birth of, "the true revolutionary party to lead the Indian revolution." They also broadcast the political resolution of the new party. The conflict of ideologies that afflicted Kerala's Communist movement after Thalassery-

Pulpally reached its peaked with the contradicting perceptions of the contents of this political resolution.

Radio Peking, which relayed the resolution along with the news about C.P.I (M.L)'s formation, didn't refer to certain important aspects of the resolution. It deliberately omitted certain words and phrases here and there. It didn't include an important paragraph that dealt with the central contradiction in the Indian revolution. The resolution said that the victory of the Indian revolution lay in resolving the contradiction between landlords and peasants. The issue about the central contradiction is important regarding all revolutions. "Who are our foes? Who are our friends? This is the most important question regarding a revolution." Mao had pointed out. "The fundamental reason for the failure of earlier revolutions in China was that they all failed to ally with real friends against the real enemy." He continued. So, why did Radio Peking exclude the analysis of an issue that could affect the victory and failure of a revolution? Radio Peking was no ordinary radio station. We could listen to the authoritative voice of Mao and the Chinese Communist Party here. Ma and I marked in our copies of the resolution all those parts that were excluded from the broadcast. We listened to the hourly repeat bulletins to make sure that our markings were correct. We informed father, K.P and all the other comrades in jail about this. We interpreted this deliberate exclusion as a continued support and encouragement of the Chinese party towards the Naxalbari movement since the days of its inception. Even earlier we used to rely on articles published in People's Daily about the shortcomings of the various joint declarations of the All India Co-ordination Committee of the Naxalbari movement. These articles were read out on Radio Peking. The founding resolution of the Marxist-Leninist party too was analysed seriously for two and a half months by the Chinese Party before it was relayed on radio. With the broadcast of the edited resolution, the Chinese Party was indirectly asking the Indian revolutionaries to do a course correction. We felt that the new party was wrong in its analysis of the central contradiction. We also realized that it was our duty to let the people of Kerala know about the formation of Communist Party of India (Marxist-Leninist), and its resolution. We translated the announcement of the new party and the resolution to Malayalam and circulated it.

While I came out on bail, we had decided to renew our publishing programme. We began efforts to strengthen the fresh fervour and interest of the people after the Thalassery-Pulpally events. We kept getting monetary contributions as some sort of tokens of appreciation. Most of these were used to publish books, and we brought out books worth a few thousands of rupees. We concentrated more on Mao's military works. This was an attempt to overcome our earlier shortcomings in not attending to military details while planning the Thalassery-Pulpally revolts. Our publishing house was called China Publications. Government and its police, particularly the crime branch thought that all this was a result of me getting bail, so within a year they conspired to block my bail and sent me back to jail.

We took special care to make the people aware of those parts of the political resolution of the C.P.I (ML), which did not get approved by the Chinese party. We put in square brackets, the parts excluded by the Radio Peking broadcast. We explained that we opposed those parts in square brackets and hailed the rest of the edict. The issue was central to the idea of Indian revolution and hence it was important to let the people know about the shortcomings of the new party. Though the Chinese party praised the edict, it was clear that none of the issues that could sow seeds of destruction should be encouraged.

With this, the volcano that was smoldering within the communist movement in Kerala erupted. There was a final conflict between the opportunist, revisionist attitude and those who upheld the ideology. With the political resolution of the new party, the campaigners against

Thalassery-Pulpally had got an ideological and political ground to fix their feet on. This fight even divided the comrades in jail. K.P and Philip fell out with my father and other comrades. They glorified the declaration as a whole. They didn't find the Chinese party's advice acceptable. "Radio Peking must have omitted those portions because of lack of time. Comrade Ajitha may not have listened to it properly. Let's wait for the Peking Review (the official organ of the Chinese party in English). Till then, we should support the whole edict. The ideological conflicts within the party should not be made public. The best way is to mark the protest within the party." They criticized our deed of translating and publishing the resolution along with our reservations.

But I didn't have any doubt about the parts that I had marked. All the comrades who worked with me outside the jail subscribed to the views of my father and comrades Sankaran master and Krishnankutty. We couldn't turn a blind eye to the advice of the Chinese party, after growing up and flourishing under the bright sun of Maoism. Our stand, about making public the ideological-political conflicts within the party was contrary to the one held by K.P and Philip.

Millions of people — workers, farmers, petty bourgeois intellectuals, small time traders and students — have to come together for a revolution to happen in India. The duty of the revolutionary party of the working class is to lead them on the right path. It is only natural that the people would have a genuine interest in the position of such a party on important national and international issues. They also have to understand whether the party position is right or wrong. Only then could the people accept its leadership. In fact, in this context, the issue of the friends and foes of the revolution acquires greater significance. Hence, the argument that the cadre and the general public should be kept out of the debate on the most crucial issue regarding the party was unacceptable. That too, after the party was criticized by a sister party which had the experience of leading a victorious revolution. This was the lesson of China's Cultural Revolution. It insisted that the errors committed by party workers, even high officials within the party, should be crticised in public. It was absolutely essential to apply this rule to the Indian movement, which had an inherent handicap of growing up in a revisionist environment. Make the people active partners in the party building process; make them aware that they too are responsible for the rights and wrongs of the party; make ceaseless efforts to improve people's revolutionary spirit and knowledge of political philosophy so that they can distinguish right from wrong; take deliberate steps to bring the party under the supervision of the people. Only these steps could make the party and people inseparable. These were the fundamental lessons that we ought to have followed while building up a revolutionary party. Instead, attempts were made to veil the fierce disagreement amongst the leaders from the eyes of the people and give an impression that they were unanimous in their decisions. This was what the right wing and left wing parties had been doing all along — to consider the people as rivals and to keep them out of the core issues of the party. We believed that a revolutionary party, no different in character from opportunistic parties, would end up betraying the people sooner or later.

K.P and Philip argued that the only beneficiaries of a public debate on ideological conflicts within the party would be the enemy, who would get alerted. But we felt that the damage could only be minimal. Of course, the enemy could use the opportunity to cause further confusion. Eventually, good judgment had to prevail.

The Peking Review too did not publish those parts of the resolution, which Radio Peking had omitted (due to paucity of time?). The Indonesian Tribune, the mouthpiece of the Indonesian Communist Party, published from Peking too left out the contentious portion. This was ample proof that these portions were to be re-assessed. Comrade

Charu Majumdar came to Kerala a few days after we had published the declaration in its complete form. But when comrades asked him about the controversy over the resolution he replied without batting an eyelid that Radio Peking had not omitted even a single word in its broadcast.

We were determined to fight against the leadership's mistakes. That was what Mao and other Marxist teachers had taught us — never to compromise on ideals.

18

COMRADE CHANDY

While grave ideological conflicts plagued the Naxalite movement, the message of Thalassery-Pulpally was making a difference to people's lives. I salute another revolutionary who laid down his life for the new movement — comrade Chandy. The enemies of the people killed him in north Kerala. Not many know of this comrade who sacrificed his life within a few months of joining the movement. The ideological schism between those who preferred tactics of compromise and the others who sought open conflict was still widening within the movement. As the tactics of compromise gained the upper hand, comrade Chandy died a helpless man.

Comrade Chandy was a symbol of the fresh revolutionary spirit that Thalassery-Pulpally unleashed among the poor in the backward villages of the Malabar. The comrades who went into the midst of the poor with the message of Thalassery-Pulpally were warmly welcomed. The lives of the deprived settlers were a constant struggle against the prosperous landlords and officials of the police and forest departments. Elsewhere, in Kuttanad (the rice bowl in south Kerala) too a few days after Thalassery-Pulpally a big landlord was attacked. A group of armed peasants attacked the office of Murikkan, better known as the lagoon king. Apparently, the higher ups in the Marxist Party had to intervene to restrain the masses. Many similar localized uprisings have taken place! I know about only a few of them. One was the farmers' uprising in Nilambur forests (in what became Malappuram district later) in north Kerala or Malabar.

Comrade Chandy was from Pala, the Catholic bastion in central Kerala's Kottayam district. Chandy was unlike an ordinary Catholic and had turned against the orthodoxy of the revisionist Church very early in life. The Church and its leaders forced him out of his native village. This Communist was also at the receiving end of police brutalities, particularly for participating in the peasant revolts of 1946-48. The police beat him up so badly, that it was said that a piece of bone in his hand was crushed to pieces. Still, nothing could deter him from his political beliefs. Comrade Chandy was a prominent peasant-activist of Goodalloor and a member of the Nilagiri district committee of the Marxist party. His revolutionary zeal led him to resign from the Marxist party after the Thalassery-Pulpally incidents, to seek out the revolutionary movement. Chandy was no romantic youngster who wanted to make a leap into the unknown; he must have been around 50, and was settled in Manimoola near Nilamboor with his family. His son Francis was 17-18 years old. He too joined the movement along with his father. After a while, the comrade's wife and daughter returned to his native village, but his son stood by Chandy. Even after his father's death, Francis was active in the movement and was in jail for a very long time. He was a healthy young man when he went to jail, but was reduced to a zombie when released years later. The physical and mental torture and the medicines forced on him affected his mental health. After his release, he roamed around the countryside, a living testimony to the brutality of the enemies of the movement.

Comrade Chandy had got in touch with us in Kozhikode after shifting to Manimoola. We welcomed him. He had the key to open the doors of Nilambur to us. Two or three comrades were sent to Nilambur to help him in his mission.

Local struggles to capture excess land from landlords were going on in some parts of Nilambur under the leadership of Kunjali, a prominent Marxist leader. The Nilambur Palace owned several thousands of acres of forestland, where only the rule of brute force prevailed. The lords of the forest made the peasants who had toiled the land clearing the forests and tilling it, servile to them and had grabbed hundreds of acres. The peasants who had earlier grabbed some forestland and tilled it were now forced to be mere landless workers. The police and the Government did nothing to end the cruel reign of these jungle lords or their illegal occupation of the land. All political parties accepted liberal contributions from these rich masters and danced to their tunes.

Once the EMS government was sworn in, Kunjali, the local Marxist leader began executing his game plan. He knew that police, till then were working for the lords of the forest, would not intervene, if the peasants under his leadership grabbed land. He demanded a fixed contribution for the party from each farmer in lieu of the land that the farmer would be allowed to grab. Peasants, ever hungry for land, thus bought a right to grab land by paying the amount fixed by the party boss. But the story did not end with the peasants paying up to grab land. The rich landlords by then realized who the new masters were. Instead of the police, the landlords turned to the party boss. On being bribed with money and some land, the Marxist leader adopted new tactics. As the farmers were settling in after grabbing some land, the leader would take his team of peasant settlers to some other landlord's territory. Thus the leaders put the old slogan of "land for tillers" to new use. They got not just land, but money as well, that too from both the exploited and the exploiters. The only fear of these parasites was of the revolutionaries: they didn't want the poor landless peasants to join up with the revolutionaries, who came into their midst with the message of the armed revolt and peasant awakening. The revolutionaries were incorruptible and ready to lay down their lives for the cause of the peasants. Obviously, their entry into such a corrupt society would immediately expose the local Marxist leadership.

Kunjali who had instigated the peasants to grab land in Kathikkalanpoyili asked them to vacate when the illegal owner Gopalan appeased him. These families who had earlier occupied another piece of land were taken to Gopalan's fief by the same leader. Kunjali had lured them with the promise of better land elsewhere. The peasants were made to move around like vagabonds while they saw their leader growing rich day by day. Ithima, a spokesperson of the farmers met comrade Chandy and the comrades from Kozhikode at this critical point of time. Ithima, was a pillar of strength for the rest of the farmers. Earlier, she was closely associated with Kunjali. She had a dagger tucked to her waist all the time. She was the symbol of the working women of Malabar and was no less than any man in fighting for farmers' rights. She reminded one of those women who dared the British army during the peasant's revolt of 1921, which the British communalized and called the Moppila Rebellion (Muslims of Malabar are called Moppila). The double game of Kunjali gradually dawned upon Ithima and others. They realised that they were being cheated.

The new revolutionary ardour of Thalassery-Pulpally inspired the peasants to lift their heads and protest corruption and apathy. The peasants retold their woes to our comrades. They wanted our comrades to lead them. Kunjali had threatened them that if they didn't vacate Gopalan's land, they would be evicted forcibly. The comrades became active in Kathikkalanpoyili. They called upon the peasants to confront the jungle lord and the police and put up a resistance. Most of these peasants were Muslims. The peasants fought Gopalan, a Congressman and his minions who tried to disrupt the tilling of the land. There was a new vigour and self-confidence among the peasants after this incident.

Gopalan was a thorough scoundrel who would point his gun at the peasants at the slightest provocation. He bashed them up regularly and had even killed a few of the hapless lot. His defeat was a great victory for the peasants. The peasants in the neighbourhood who had to go through similar exploitation from cruel landlords secretly approached the comrades of Kathikkalanpoyili. They wanted to win back the land that they had lost. Thus, the comrades brought together around fifty of the landless peasant families and occupied some forestland fit for tilling in Poolappadam near Kathikkalanpoyili. The peasants knew that the landlord of Poolappadam had guns. They decided to confiscate those guns before they set up their huts in the forestland. A huge procession carrying spikes, sickles and rods marched to his house and demanded his guns. Even women and children joined the demonstration. They ransacked his house, but couldn't find any guns. He had hidden them somewhere. The peasants warned him that they were aware that he had guns and if he ever used those against the people, he would be killed. They declared that they were taking back the land that he had grabbed from them, except 10 acres, which they left for his use.

The incident at Poolappadam, where peasants led by comrade Chandy captured hundreds of acres of land threatened the Government led by the Marxists. The Government that boasted of radical reforms and laws to ensure "land for the tillers" didn't actually result in the distribution of land to landless peasants. Nor were the Marxist leaders interested in sincerely leading the peasants' protest for their rights.

Instead, the Government set up a new Malabar Special Police camp with 20 policemen to stop peasants from grabbing land. The day the camp was set up, the policemen razed four shacks near the camp. But the police got nervous when they saw the peasants preparing for a combat, and hence restrained from further provocative actions. They even feared an attack on the station. The peasants carried weapons with them wherever they went which brought back memories of Thalassery-Pulpally. The police had by now understood that the peasants who had the embers of revolution in them should be dealt with tactfully. So, they waited. It was at this critical stage that the old corrupting influences with the promptness of a time bomb took a toll on the comrades from Kozhikode. Despite joining the revolutionary movement, the comrades were not completely purged of the revisionism of the Marxist party and the class co-operation of trade unionism. These comrades were not sure who their enemy was. They saw the jungle lord as their main enemy, but failed to comprehend that he would not have survived without the support of the military force of the Government. They went in for a compromise with the police. They didn't have the basic understanding of the situation to attack the enemy before it began its campaign. They moved the court. Meanwhile, there arose from within an opinion that a law should be made to protect the rights of peasants on their land. The movement came to a standstill. Lack of experience and understanding led the leadership to make attempts to legalise the protest. Without wasting any time, the Marxist leadership conspired to take over the movement.

Meanwhile, Kunjali was murdered by Congressmen. He had turned into a rich and privileged man in Nilambur ever since the Marxist government had come to power. He had growing influence among the trade unions in some of the local rubber estates. This sent alarm bells ringing in the Congress camp. The fight to share the booty ended in Kunjali's murder.

Though Kunjali died, it didn't take long for the local Marxist leadership to exploit the inaction of the comrades from Kozhikode working in Poolappadam. It seems Rajan, the Marxist leader of Poolappadam was in touch with state leadership of the Marxist Party. Peasants like Ithima who were full of passion to fight for their land were anguished by the confusion of the comrades. The police party from Idakkara under orders from the Marxist party-led government arrested comrade Chandy, another comrade from Kozhikode and two local peasant comrades, Moosa and Chettiyar. This unexpected move distressed the comrades. Then they realized their mistake in striking a compromise with the police. Soon, five-six more comrades were arrested, and were remanded to the Manjeri sub jail. The comrades came out on bail within three days and were planning their next move. But on the second day of comrade Chandy's release on October 7, 1969 a group of rowdies led by the local Marxist leader Rajan brutally attacked comrade Chandy in a paddy field. He was shot on the leg and hit with an axe on the head and other parts of the body. The comrade did put up a fight, but his injuries turned fatal. This gang of goons rushed to Poolappadam and Kathikkalanpoyili to evict the peasants from their land. The police gave them all possible assistance. This was what they used to do earlier when the jungle lords grabbed land. The Marxist leadership, which nurtured the false dream of the government of the people, was actively helping the privileged class. It should not be forgotten that none of these farmers had even a single piece of land. The police did not listen to the peasants' demand that comrade Chandy's dying statement should be recorded and that he should be taken to a hospital immediately. The people forcibly stopped an estate jeep and carried him to a hospital in Nilambur. But he was brought dead. The police even rejected the demand of the peasants that the body of the comrade should be buried in Poolappadam. The police hurriedly buried the body depriving his son the right to organize a proper funeral.

Like Kisan Thomman in November 1968 in the deep forests of Thirunelli, Comrade Chandy happily laid down his life at the altar of the revolution, adding his name to the list of immortal revolutionaries.

19

KUTTIYADI AND THIRUNELLI

A pamphlet "One year of Thalassery-Pulpally" published to celebrate the first anniversary of the revolt says: "Thalassery-Pulpally failed temporarily in achieving its goal. But what invaluable thing did it gain? It spread a new ardour and message to every shack in each nook and corner of our state. It spread the message of Naxalbari far and wide based on comprehensive pragmatic actions by offering blood and flesh. The path cleared by our great respectable leader MaoTsetung has now been etched vividly in the minds of our toiling classes..."

There was a new hope, a new passion in the hearts of hundreds of poverty-stricken peasants who grabbed any weapon they could lay their hands on to proceed to the Thirunelli forests to join the revolutionaries of Pulpally. But they had to retrace their steps, when they realized that most of their comrades were arrested.

Koyippilli Velayudhan was one such peasant comrade who led a 50 strong group of peasants. He was killed in the Kuttiyadi police station attack.

The comrades who had been working in and around Kuttiyadi organizing revolutionary protests thought it was time to give a fitting reply to all those who bragged that the Naxalbari movement in Kerala had petered out with the defeat of Thalassery-Pulpally revolts. The valley of Kuttiyadi lies southwest to the mountains of Wayanad, a part of the Western Ghats that is thousands of feet above sea level. Poverty persisted like a debilitating disease here in this fertile stretch of land. Farmers were totally dependent on cash crops like black pepper and coconut and their lives were determined by the local and international market rates for their produce. This obviously favoured the rich farmers and traders who could hoard while the prices were low and sell when the market was looking up. But the market forces rendered the low and middle classes poor as they couldn't afford to wait to sell off their produce. And the prices of their produce could not match the rising cost of living. The fall of prices during the harvest was as commonplace as them shooting up after the season. So, in the course of years those who couldn't hoard their commodity slipped into a perennial cycle of debt and poverty. Even now, the situation hasn't changed much. Though the administrators boast of land reforms and green revolution the truth remains that all these have only added to intensify the discord in villages with poverty engrossing a large section of the society. Kuttiyadi's plight too was no different. On top of it were the caste conflicts. If it were tribals in Wayand, here the worst affected were the untouchables who belonged to the lowest strata of the society, socially and financially.

K.P and Philip could no longer argue in favour of the organizational activities of comrade Charu Majumdar as the Kerala unit of Majumdar's C.P.I (M.L) was being led by opportunists like Ambady Sankaran Kutty and Kosala Ramadas. Yet, K.P and Philip believed in Comrade Majumdar's idea of the destruction and eradication of the landlords. They encouraged some comrades in Kozhikode, Thrissur and Palakkad to organize activities on this line.

This bitter ideological fight spread to the field of action as well. A section of these comrades guessed that preparations were going on in full swing to organize attacks on the Thalassery-Pulpally line and tried to sabotage the attacks and demoralize the peasants who were ready to take on the State instruments of torture challenging the administration and the societal hierarchy. This in turn affected the peasant comrades and some of them found their revolutionary embers dying out. Most of them were plain confused. Some opportunists utilised this fluid situation to spread rumours in the countryside. But none of this was enough to dampen the ardour of valorous comrades like Velayudhan. These comrades, determined to keep the memory of Thalassery-Pulpally alive and to prove that the movement would not die down so easily decided to attack the Kuttiyadi police station and confiscate the weapons and to destroy the registrar's office. They also decided to loot a high caste landlord.

On the early hours of December 17, 1969 these peasant comrades marched to the Kuttiyadi police station armed with a variety of lethal weapons. In the attack that followed, the comrades blew up parts of the police station with hand grenades. They poured petrol and set the room where records were kept afire. Sub inspector Prabhakaran lost his left arm in the turmoil. The attempt to secure weapons saw a pitched battle for the next half an hour. The Government, terrified by the Thalassery-Pulpally revolts had given sentries permission to keep loaded guns. The sentry at the Kuttiyadi police station locked himself up in a room and aimed his bayonet-attached gun through a hole in the door. Comrade Velayudhan led the first-ever battle with the police from the front. He was shot dead. With this, the comrades began to retreat. They had run out of gun powder too. But before retreating, they scattered the pamphlet *One year of Thalassery-Pulpally* all around and announced who they were and what their motive was. It was hardly surprising that this daring incident shook all the parliamentary parties, whether in power, or in the Opposition. The torture that ensued in the Perambra police station near Kuttiyadi after this attack is by now well known. The attack was staged shortly after the fall of the C.P.I(M)-led E.M.S government. Achutha Menon of C.P.I was the new Chief Minister. The arrested comrades, according to newspaper reports, were forced to eat pieces of flesh that fell off from Inspector Prabhakaran's blown up hand, and drink urine. The police even beat up some Marxist activists who had nothing to do with the police station attack.

The Kuttiyadi incident met with stiff resistance within the Naxalbari movement. Though Radio Peking cheered the incident within 24 hours of its execution, Liberation, the party's mouthpiece was silent about it. Comrade Charu Majumdar who swore by the Chinese party and always reiterated that he would forever accept its guidance proved himself wrong by his reaction to the Kuttiyadi incident. His stand on Kuttiyadi as well as on Thalassery-Pulapally revolts confirmed that he adhered to the precepts of the left and right revisionist parties that supported any form of protest, provided it had the blessings of the Party leadership. It did not matter if such protests were based on wrong principles. He opposed even righteous struggles, which did not have the stamp of approval of the leadership. Even today the spokespersons of the annihilation theory don't add Thalassery-Pulpally and Kuttiyadi to their list of historic struggles.

It was on February 9, 1970, two months after the Kuttiyadi incident that comrade Varghese planned and executed a strike for the last time. This attack was an expression of the surging hatred of the tribals against the tyranny of the landlords in Thrissilery and Thirunelli villages. Comrade Varghese, who had resolutely led the Thalasssery-Pulpally action, was getting more and more impatient with his life in hiding after he had parted with the Pulpally comrades. Even while camping in the forests, the Pulpally comrades had decided to attack the landlords in Thirunelli. Comrade Varghese implemented that decision.

The attack on landlords left two killed in the Thrissilery-Thirunelli incident — Adiga, a landlord and Chekku, a Muslim who was taken for a police agent. Another landlord was looted. After the Kuttiyadi incident, comrade Varghese seems to have led these attacks determined to make his contribution to the movement. But his aim was a grand peasant revolution as envisaged by the Thalassery-Pulpally revolt, for which the tribals were his allies and the forest his cover. He was convinced that unless he fought and defeated the armed forces of the State, he could not continue his struggle.

But comrade Varghese and his companions parted ways since they realized that their determination alone was inadequate to confront the massive advance of the police force which exposed the true colours of the C.P.I leader Achutha Menon and his home minister C.H Muhammd Koya. It was the Central Reserve Police Force (CRPF) that led the manhunt in Thirunelli for comrade Varghese and his friends. It seems Achutha Menon wanted to rule out even a possibility of the local police harbouring any sympathy for the revolutionaries. So he brought in the beastly central force, which had nothing in common with the land or its people. The CRPF camped in the Thirunelli temple's *oottupura* or the dining hall for the upper castes. The torture unleashed by the CRPF on the poor tribals who had sheltered Varghese cannot be put into words. Men were beaten up and women were raped. The little that they had in their homes like earthen pots were destroyed and their animals and poultry stolen. The tribals fled the shanties with their women and children. The silence of the government legalized all these atrocities.

It was on one of those days comrade Varghese came out of the jungle. Hunted and tired of running around alone in the forests of Thirunelli, Varghese came out of hiding, probably for a day's rest. He reached Thirunelli in the dead of the night and took shelter in the house of a poor farmhand. He was on the run for some time then, days without food and a place to rest had taken a toll on him. He made the fatal mistake of not getting up the next day. He was still sleeping when the police discovered his hideout. The rest is etched deeply in the soil and soul of Wayanad. He still lives in the collective consciousness of the land like a leaf in its book that can never be erased.

20

THE BRUTAL MURDER OF COMRADE VARGHESE

Now we know how comrade Varghese was killed. How he was mercilessly beaten up, how he was made to stand in boiling water, how his eyes were gouged out... Yet, they couldn't break him. Then, orders came from above, clear instructions to take him to the Thirunelli forests and shoot him. A country made pistol was stuffed into his hand and journalists were called over to take photographs of the 'catch', who was killed in an 'encounter' with the police. This gruesome murder was the spiteful warning the government sent across to all brave hearts, who had designs to take on the hoary forces of a regressive society. It exposed to the world the true face of those who sat on the seats of power and the others who scrambled to replace them, plying liberally all the while the syrupy concoction of *ahimsa* and democracy.

By the dawn of February 18, 1970 the news of Varghese's capture spread like wild fire in and around Mananthavady in Wayanad. He was being tortured in the presence of God, within the divine precincts of the Thirunelli temple, even as thousands of people thronged outside to catch a glimpse of the revolutionary. But he was never taken out of the temple. By the evening the police let out a lie that the man in their custody was not comrade Varghese but someone else. No one believed the police. There were people who had seen the comrade being taken to the temple. When it grew dark and the crowd dispersed, the police took the comrade to a valley nearby. There, they tied him to a pole and shot him. They shot him because the comrade had not opened his mouth nor was he going to do their bidding. The next day morning, the people who had grown anxious about comrade Varghese were told that he was killed in an encounter with the police. People were shocked and Manathavady was in turmoil. For days, poor villagers all over Wayanad took to streets holding protest meetings and marches angrily defying the prohibitory orders, which were being enforced by the CRPF. The police did not dare open the wrapped up body of comrade Varghese, even to let his mother have a last look at her son. Probably, they feared that his missing eyes would tell a different story. The police dug a pit and buried Varghese near his house. When the villagers threatened to dig it out, the scared police guarded the grave round the clock for a month.

What was comrade Varghese to the people of Wayanad? He had grown up under the influence of Communist ideology challenging the regressive mores of the conservative church and the church-led Christian society. When the Communist party split in 1964, he became an active member of the Marxist party, which had pretensions of leading an armed revolution. He spearheaded the party activities in Kannur when almost all the leaders were in jail during the Indo-Pakistan war of 1965. He spent all his revolutionary ardour organising the Gopala Sena (literally Gopalan's army, the militant youth wing led by AK Gopalan) in Mananthavady block.

Kannur was the Marxist party's citadel in Kerala and comrade Varghese was the office secretary of CPI (M) in Kannur. But this top-rung leader was different. He hadn't slipped into the vicious circle that many leaders found themselves in. He hadn't surrendered his ideological commitment to the vested interests that had gradually taken over the party. The reason, of course, was this comrade's proximity to the toiling, subjugated classes of Wayanad, especially the tribals. A young man driven by compassion, he went into the midst of these miserable lives to understand more about their problems and to seek a solution. The tribals normally kept a distance from the settlers who grabbed their land and exploited their labour endlessly. The tribals knew only too well, the politicians who lured them with false dreams of liberation for votes to ascend the thrones of power. Yet, they adored comrade Varghese, a settler and a politician, who proved his sincere self through his actions, who had no inhibition in sharing their meagre food and their miserable roof. He was with them in mirth and misery, more often the latter. He brought the message of liberation and was one with them working for a new morrow.

The social liberation of the working classes of Wayanad was fast becoming a historical necessity. On the surface everything appeared peaceful and serene. But someone with deep social insight like Varghese knew that within these trampled lives was a seething volcano that could erupt one day, and like the deity of death, it could reduce the exploiter's world to ashes. The powers of the old world, that are blind to these truths would get crushed like paper tigers and flung into the dustbin of history. The tribals knew that the solution to their problems lay in the destruction of the social order that bound them in chains of landless labour and endless poverty. It was but natural for Varghese to seek the support of the Marxist party first, as it had all along championed armed revolution and ostensibly toed the line of the Chinese party. Gradually, Varghese realised his mistake and turned to Mao's teachings. It was a new dawn of ideology for him. He set out on the new path of Maoism along with millions of youngsters all over the world. Since then, his objective and his ideology were defined — the liberation of the Indian masses through armed revolution. Soon, he was busy organizing people, spreading the message of armed revolution without food, sleep or rest.

The tribals accepted his message without hesitation and this reinforced his belief. He hung on to the teachings of Mao even as he underwent acid tests of political commitment. But hardly a year after he was initiated into the path of Mao, his life, which to the tribals and the movement was so precious, was mercilessly snatched away. This happened when CPI was in power and the chief minister Achutha Menon, insisted that Naxalites should be dealt with compassion. And, the man in charge of the police, the then home minister was CH Muhammad Koya, who had written the preface to Janab Aalikunjisahib's great work *Malabar Revolt*.

There is nothing more fearsome to the rulers than the intimacy of a revolutionary with his people. It was hardly surprising that comrade Varghese who had gained the love and respect and moreover the trust of the tribals had struck terror in the hearts of those in power. But they were mere fools who dreamt of having destroyed Varghese. The day is not far when history would deliver undeniable justice to crucify his murderers. Comrade Varghese had laid down his life for the subjugated and he still lives in their minds. Their fire for revenge is still aflame.

I had the opportunity to know comrade Varghese personally by being part of the Pulpally revolt, which he led. It was his passion that saw us through those difficult days when we wandered the Thirunelli forests listlessly. I doubt whether the revolt would have been this successful, had it not been for his unwavering leadership. I am still proud that I was one of his comrades in arms.

Many national leaders like CPI chief SA Dange made a hue and cry about the accused of the Thalassery-Pulpally revolts being tortured by E.M.S's police and the slapping of conspiracy charges against us. They argued that the accused were revolutionaries and sincere youngsters who had gone astray. They professed undying love for these adventurous youngsters who had fallen out with the Marxist party and left the CPI(M). But their love subsided when they realized that these revolutionaries were not dimwitted enough to fall into the trap of those leaders who go about with a smile on their face and a dagger in their hearts. These CPI leaders saw the situation as a potent weapon against the Marxist party. Later developments proved that their aim was to get rid of the Marxist party from the seven-party coalition front in Kerala and to form another government led by the CPI. The police torture didn't come down a bit even as power shifted from the CPI(M) to the CPI. They too used the CRPF to their advantage. There were numerous instances of students being beaten up inside college campuses, hostels and on streets. The police went around the streets wagging their batons like wild dogs not sparing even the passers-by. This chain of events culminated in the government's order to capture Varghese, inflict all sorts of torture on him and shoot him down.

If this was the story of deceit of the new CPI-led Left front, the Marxist leadership was no different. Once out of power, they screeched louder than their opponents in the CPI about the need to deal with the revolutionaries politically. They cried themselves hoarse that the revolutionaries of Kuttiyadi-Thirunelli strikes should not be crushed using force. It was now their turn to shed crocodile tears for the victims of police torture. Their aim was also the same as that of Achutha Menon and Co. The police atrocities were a major issue in the campaign against the Government. The same people who saw the dark hands of intelligence agencies behind the attacks of Thalassery-Pulpally and declared it a mere 'adventure' far removed from the people's movement did not fail to turn the golden opportunity of comrade Varghese's death into votes. For them comrade Varghese, while he was alive, was a stumbling block as he had struggled relentlessly against the anti-revolutionary policy of the Marxist leadership and worked for the Thalassery-Pulpally revolts. But they were clever enough to pose as Varghese's friends when they realized the extent of support and love the people had for him. This same leadership was silent during the

Emergency when R.E.C student Rajan was killed in police custody. When Emergency was lifted and storms of protest raged over all walks of life, the Marxists were at the forefront beating their breasts and hollering about Rajan. Stories of torture in police custody became a money-making proposition for the Marxists as they wrote heartrending features in the party newspaper and books about Rajan and the Kakkayam camp where he was held in custody and killed. But there were no similar reports or biographies of comrade Varghese. Probably they knew that Varghese (who rejected the CPI(M) to lead Naxalite struggles against their government) was not saleable enough a commodity for them.

All the parties in the Opposition led by the Marxist party began smothering Achutha Menon Government. Among them were K.P.R Gopalan and Jose Abraham of the Revolutionary Communist Party who had come out of the Marxist party for the sake of revolution. Yet, they had sneered at Thalassery-Pulpally as C.I.A-sponsored activities. But they too raised a ruckus about comrade Varghese's murder. The issue was raised in the Assembly and the Opposition parties demanded a judicial probe into the matter. The pressure was becoming too much for Muhammad Koya to handle when help came in from the most unexpected quarters.

Liberation, the official mouthpiece of Kerala State Organisation Committee of C.P.I (M.L) came out with a report that comrade Varghese was actually killed in an encounter and not murdered in captivity, as it was popularly believed. They even tried to spread a perverted idea that a hero's valorous death was reserved only for those felled while fighting and that death in police custody amounted to cowardice. This treachery bailed out Achutha Menon Government from a seemingly hopeless political crisis.

During these chaotic days a development went almost unnoticed. One of my sureties, Kuttan Moosathu, was also made an accused in the Thirunelli case. On April 25, 1970 our case was committed to the Sessions court from Kozhikode District Magistrate court. The court had ordered the renewal of sureties, and each of them was required to present themselves in court that day. Since Kuttan Moosathu had become an accused in the Thirunelli case another surety had to be arranged for me. But somehow we didn't get anyone. We wrote to the other person to be present in court that day. But surprisingly, he didn't turn up. I was put right back in jail.

We came to know about the inside stories only much later. Balettan was supposed to start for Kozhikode on the night of April 24. But that evening the sub inspector went to his house and took him to the police station. He was forced to spend two nights in the lock up and let off on the 26th with a warning not to stand surety for me. Somebody from the high ranges (hills of Western Ghats) who read about my imprisonment came to Kozhikode jail the next day with an advocate. He had come with the registration papers of his property since the tahasildar had refused to sign on stamp paper worth Rs 10,000, 'if it were for Ajitha'. It seems special orders were issued to tahasildars from the government not to sign stamp papers worth Rs 10,000 if it were meant to bail me out.

The government and the crime branch doubted that I was running China Publications that brought out Malayalam translations of Chinese literature. As usual they had misconstrued that by putting me in jail the Chinese books would stop getting published in Malayalam. They also felt that since Ma did not know Malayalam well, it would not matter even if she remained out of jail. She was not in good health either. So, they didn't create problems for her bail because they also feared that she might not survive another jail term. Thus I was behind bars once again, after being out on bail for one year.

21

LIFE IN PRISON AT KOZHIKODE

Things had changed slightly for the better when I was put back in district jail on April 25, 1970. There was widespread anger against the police torture of the Thalassery-Pulpally accused among people at large and also among certain allies of the seven party coalition government of EMS led by the C.P.I (M). To blunt this stinging criticism and to get the vacillating sections of the accused back to the fold of Marxist party, the Government had recognized all of them as political prisoners, and treated them as special class convicts. This promotion happened in June 1969. Another obvious reason was to keep these prisoners away from the other convicts.

Thus on my return I was provided with 'first class' food and other amenities. There was no hitch in getting any number of books or newspapers. I was permitted to read Mao's works too. But something else began gnawing me.

We were not to be taken out to the court premises till our case came up for hearing in the Sessions court. Thus I lost the opportunity to meet my father and other comrades who were lodged in the male ward of the same jail at least once in two weeks. Ma used to visit us twice a week. That was when I met father. The discussions required to enlarge my political understanding were not possible within the short duration of the interview. My life in the women's cell was as good as solitary confinement.

Most of the inmates were, as I had said earlier, women from the streets. The women's cell was very narrow and congested. There were huge walls around it, which went up to touch the sky and the women's block was far away from the rest of the jail. I felt as if I was trapped in a deep well with unassailable walls on all sides. The women were lodged in a small block, which had two double rooms and two single rooms. At the other end of these rooms was a big pit covered with cement. This was intended for a flush-out latrine but the women had to defecate into the small hole in the middle of that cement slab. This they had to do in the open as the toilet was without any cover. The smell of faeces always filled the air. The double rooms had two bathrooms each, but they were useless. The women's cell didn't have tap water and hence male convicts brought in water for drinking and bathing. I was in one of the double rooms. The rest of the female convicts and their children were stuffed into the other double room and one single room. Women with terminal illnesses like leprosy and tuberculosis, and even others with infectious venereal diseases were not segregated. These helpless women were an oppressed lot and were shown no human considerations. In the other single room plates and mats were stacked for the use of the convicts. This doubled up as the rest room for the wardens. Compared to other inmates I lived a royal life. The plight of women wardens was pathetic too. They did this job to make two ends meet, but derived no pleasure out of it. At that time, there were two wardens in Kozhikode jail. They stayed in the jail quarters and therefore, had to report for duty any time they were called. Wardens could have their lunch only if those on night duty would come to relieve them for two hours. During nights, once the convicts were locked up, the warden was alone in her room. She could not step out of the jail premises without the permission of the head warden and senior officials. The key to the women's cell was always with a head warden. Thus the female wardens spent their lives locked up with us in jail. Their duty time could be changed according to the whims of the head wardens. Right in front of the women's cell was the Kozhikode Kasba police station. Though we couldn't see the station, often the stillness of the night was shattered by noises of policemen's baton and boots and the painful cries of the victims. This life severed me from the outside world, and threatened to break me from within.

As days withered away, loneliness began to eat into me. There were many provocations too, which declared aloud the authorities' attempt to weaken me. I realized that I had to break free to be sane. I had no friend there, who thought and lived like me to relieve me from this mind numbing confinement. When Ma came for one of her visits, I told my father and the other comrades about this. I convinced them that I had to have some time with father and other comrades and this was essential for my survival. I was even ready to go on a hunger strike to achieve this.

We had petitioned the Government on this issue earlier when we were shifted to Kannur central jail in April 1969. The petition then had resulted in the bashing up of the comrades including father and KP by the superintendent and eighty other officers. Shortly thereafter I was let off on bail and the issue was temporarily solved. Now the issue resurfaced with me returning to jail. The comrades convinced of my helplessness decided to give another petition to the government. We informed the Government that if I was not allowed to spend at least two hours with my father and other comrades to discuss Mao's thoughts we would go on an indefinite hunger strike from June 1, 1970.

There was little hope of our strike succeeding, as such privileges were not allowed in jail. But we took heart from precedents of special treatment for certain political prisoners during the 1965 Indo-Pak war.

The Government had given permission to Marxist leaders and couples like A.K Gopalan and Susheela Gopalan to stay together in jail during the war of 1965. If they could be allowed family life inside jail, why couldn't a daughter spend a few hours with her father? Since we were recognized as political prisoners, there shouldn't be any hitch in accepting my request. I know many couples who had been jail, but none of them was allowed to stay together. Rules are made to grill the poor and the needy, for the affluent and the power always have loopholes. Much after our strike, when A.K.G and Susheela Gopalan were arrested during the Emergency, they were brought together in jail within hours of being brought there. But couples serving life terms in jail were allowed to meet only once in six months, and that too after filing tomes and tomes of requests. They were not M.L.As or M.Ps but poor villagers, forced to commit murder for self defence or some such quirk or luck. Their longing for children or agony for dying parents or the misery of their spouses remains unseen and unheard by our courts and indifferent governments.

It was not surprising that our petition went unheeded. On June 1, I went on hunger strike. There was no other means to extract our rightful privileges and a fair deal from jail authorities. Only a few months had passed since comrade Varghese was tortured to death. Therefore, it was a time when the façade of Achutha Menon government was in rags and its anti-Naxalite face was exposed. But Mao's teachings drove me on and I was mentally prepared to face all odds. I gave up food on the 1st, father joined me on the second and Sankaran master joined us on 4 June. We got tired with each passing day. Water was our only source of relief. Sometimes we used to have water with salt. I had heard of numerous hunger strikes where people did not even drink water. We could at least have water. The officials used to bring in doctors every day and made certain that we didn't sneak in food. I grew weak after 4-5 days. Hunger was gnawing me and when at times it threatened to overwhelm me I found strength in Mao's words. Eighteen days elapsed without food. Ever since we began our strike we were not allowed to meet Ma. But she used to brief all newspapers about the strike inside the jail.

On June 19, I heard the gates to the women's cell being loudly opened. As I lay disoriented, within seconds, the jail I.G. and other officials of the district jail were in my room. He informed me that our request was granted and that during the day I could spend two hours in the block where my father and comrades were held. The Inspector General asked me to eat something immediately, but I insisted in meeting my father first. He accompanied me to my father's block. The long days of starvation no longer wore me down as I was overjoyed at the prospect of my liberation from the smothering solitude of the women's cell. I walked briskly. The I.G asked me to slow down and ordered the wardens to hold my hand. But they couldn't keep pace with me as I rushed to my father and the comrades and greeted them loudly with my raised clenched fist. Their happiness knew no bounds as they shouted slogans to greet me back with equal vigour. Thus my hunger strike drew to a close. The next day onwards I visited my father's block at 9.30 in the morning and spent two hours with him and other comrades.

22

TRIAL AND VERDICT

The trial began only in November 1970, that too six or seven months after the case was shifted to Kozhikode Sessions Court. Earlier the EMS government had dropped charges against 70 people implicated in the case, leaving 65 of us charged with conspiracy. Heated ideological debates went on amongst the accused whether to boycott the court proceedings or to defend themselves in court. A section of them insisted on not fighting the case at all and did everything possible to obstruct their co-accused who thought otherwise, and also to hinder a large group of sincere lawyers who had come forward to assist the accused. Most of the comrades, especially those involved in Pulpally revolt decided in favour of defending themselves.

Most of the Thalassery-Pulpally comrades were in police custody and it was a political necessity to rescue as many of them as we could. While opting to defend ourselves we didn't overlook the fact that the judiciary was one of the strongest pillars of the State. A large number of advocates across Kerala promised us all possible help and this was a reflection of the favourable responses that Thalassery-Pulpally evoked among people all over the country. We had also decided to give our brief to lawyers who sympathized with our cause and not to someone out to make money.

But for two, all those comrades who boycotted the court proceedings were involved in the Thalassery incident and not the Pulpally revolt. It was clear even when Thalassery event was considered a separate case that chances of getting punished in that case were remote. Any lawyer could easily demolish the conspiracy charges in the Thalassery case. Even the prosecution was not confident of proving conspiracy charges against the Thalassery comrades. If the conspiracy charge fell through there was nothing much left in the Thalassery case. All those who decided against arguing the case could also benefit from others' lawyers tearing into the conspiracy charges. And this assurance of legal help emboldened them to take a revolutionary stand of boycotting the bourgeois court.

But the Pulpally case was different. There was a real threat of capital punishment or life sentence to the accused in this case. It would have been outright stupid not to take the case seriously and bring the sentences down to the minimum, that too when so many efficient lawyers were ready to help us. To ignore legal loopholes and not to make attempts to lessen the sentence would have been a leftist position for the sake of appearances but surely rightwing in essence. The very fact that apart from eight of us accused in the Pulpally case, the court let off 60 comrades, is proof of our success in exploiting the paradoxes that existed between the administration and the judiciary. The Sessions Court gave the rest of us a sentence of five years each. The Government would never have got into this tight spot had we not argued the case in court, and had we allowed the prosecution to trample on us. It was this judgment given by Sessions Judge K.M Muhammadali that truly exposed the duplicity of chief minister Achutha Menon's CPI-led government. The day after the verdict, K Karunakaran, the then home minister reached Kozhikode and announced in a press conference that the Government would move the High Court in appeal against the verdict. The High Court, probably buckling under pressure, found 33 people guilty and 13 of us were sentenced to life imprisonment. So, one thing was clear. It was only because we had argued the case in the Sessions that the government was forced to go on appeal to put pressure and get the sentences enhanced. If we had not argued the case and the Sessions Judge had given us a severe verdict at the outset, the ugly face of the Government would not have got exposed.

I was drawing attention to the two contradictory positions of the accused of Thalassery-Pulappay over their own case. The sincere efforts of our lawyer-friends led to a genuine attempt to make the verdict as favourable as possible. And this in the end proved our stand on defending ourselves right.

When I went back to jail after the cancellation of bail, I felt as if I had almost got over the agony of my earlier stint in jail. I used to get books and newspapers and spent most of the time reading. That I could visit father was another boon, which helped me get over the helplessness of being locked up in a jail. I tried to learn more about my friends, my fellow prisoners.

As I noted earlier, most of the regular inmates of Kozhikode district jail were into prostitution. A good majority of them were victims of their circumstances. They were of all ages, fifty year olds to girls of fourteen. I heard their horrid stories that revealed the real, brutal face of the city. Most of these women were slaves of agents or pimps who got their commission even before a woman was sold off. They bashed up those women who didn't remain servile and left them in the lurch when they stopped fetching a good price. Flesh trade was not their only means of survival. The pimps alternated as pick pockets, thieves and even murderers. An instance that I came to know was particularly depressing.

One such pimp used to sell other women to provide for his youthful wife and two sons. In a brawl among pimps, he was stabbed to death. His wife was not a prostitute till then, but was suddenly forced into the trade. Soon she was arrested and brought to jail, along with her two sons aged five and three. The playful elder one soon charmed everybody in jail. But after two or three days the boy was down with fever and cold. The jail doctor dismissed him with a prescription of soda sulphate mixture. One day after returning from the doctor the boy's condition worsened. His body went cold and he was frothing at the mouth like an epileptic. The wardens got scared and immediately informed the head warden. After two three hours of impatient waiting, women cops came to take the mother and son to the general hospital at Kottaparambu. The next day we heard that the boy died. The jail authorities didn't want to take the blame of his death and passed the buck to the women wardens. But we all knew that the poor boy died because of the carelessness of the doctor and other officials. For a few days his memory lingered like a dull ache. His mother was released from jail and after about five months another bizarre thing happened. One night, she suddenly disappeared. She had left her younger son with an elderly woman in the neighbourhood before setting out for the night's work. After a week, her decomposed body was found in an unused well near the leprosy hospital in Chevayur in Kozhikode. It seemed many of her friends who were in and out of jail knew quite well who her killer was. But no one talked about it for fear of a similar fate. I gathered it was another casual act of a pimp. I never could know what came of the younger boy who was left alone at such a tender age.

These pimps had an unholy nexus with the police. The police ignored all their brutalities. The women were often arrested for immoral trafficking but the men who sold them and enjoyed the fruits of their labour always went scot-free. The police, who were on the payrolls of these brokers stepped in only to shield them from the ire of society. I have heard that even ministers served as watchdogs of these underworld pimps. Instances of politicians taking bribes from these lowly people to get them out of murder cases are numerous!

Another section of women, who ended up in jail was those involved in hooch cases. Most of them were elderly women who had no other means of livelihood. There was stiff competition from those who sold liquor with a government license and also from large-scale illicit hooch sellers. These unlicensed traders obtained implicit sanction to run their illegal trade from the excise department by bribing the whole department from petty staff right up to the top officials. These big-timers bribed the excise officials not just to ply their trade but to get the smaller fry arrested. Once they were caught, they were forced to cough up hundreds of rupees in various installments to escape litigation. Even they would still receive summons from the court. Then the prosecutors and court clerks had to be bribed. Despite all these efforts, they would still be punished. Thus, they lost the money that they might have raised pawning and selling off whatever valuables they had. The punishment would come like a bolt from the blue and the poor old women wouldn't know what to do. There would be no one to help and they would spend their days in jail shedding tears for their struggling children and hungry grandchildren. They even felt guilty about the food they had in jail. Many a time I have heard them saying, "My children would now be hungry. How can I eat this food?"

Who is responsible for these ruined lives? Even if their children want to work, they wouldn't get any work. Only a few lucky ones had regular jobs. These women turned to brewing liquor merely to ensure that their children didn't starve. But in turn they fell easy prey to the exploiters in the excise department of the Government.

During my second term in Kozhikode jail, which lasted for over a year and a half, I saw an entire family ending up in jail. The family, caught for forging currency notes was from Kalpatta in Wayanad. The woman had her twin daughters for company and her second husband, a son and a son-in-law were in the men's ward. The son-in-law was an expert in forging currency notes. There were similar cases against him in many south Indian courts. While he was using this family as a base for his operations, one of the twins fell for his charms and got married to him. At the time of arrest she was pregnant. The second husband of the woman had fallen out with the son-in-law over money and had informed the police about the counterfeit currency business. Finally, all of them including the woman's husband landed in jail. I don't know how the case ended. They were once petty landlords in Wayanad. The elderly Nair woman often reminisced loudly about her family's lost glory, about her coffee estates and paddy fields and the tribals who slaved there.

Also there were women involved in murder cases. I didn't get to know much about them since most of them used to get bail or were quickly shifted to the central prison in Kannur. Then there were those arrested for property disputes and still others for traveling without tickets in trains. There were women who used to buy rice from Palakkad to sell it illegally in Kozhikode. But all of them were let out on bail soon enough.

There was another totally different set of women — the mentally disturbed ones. If one such woman were brought in, whatever little peace of mind we had would be lost till she got shifted to a mental hospital. At times they were brought in when the jail was full and the jail authorities would lock them up with the rest of the inmates. Some of them were so ill that they would sing and howl and hurl abuses all through the night. The other inmates would spend the night in mortal fear till the person was shifted out, which normally happened in three-four days. But once the authorities continued to keep such a woman for a longer period, probably to provoke me. The woman had wreaked havoc in the block and I asked the authorities to shift her to the mental hospital. They deliberately dragged their feet for two more days just because I had made the request. I had to resort to protest. I refused to return to the women's ward from my father's block. The other comrades supported me. Finally, the authorities had to give their word that they would shift the woman the very next day.

Thus my life in jail taught me lessons, which society could never give me. The opportunity to experience the underbelly of the cities made me realize that I haven't yet seen much of the seamier side of life. My hatred for the societal forces deepened as I saw them trampling on human lives as if they were mere grains of sand. Life's school called jail gave me invaluable lessons about society's perception of woman. All this made me realize the significance of a cultural revolution. As a woman, I became more committed towards the Communist ideology and the movement, which I was sure would bring in changes in society. Jail life made me irrevocably one with the path of revolution, like steel I was being moulded in the fire of experiences.

It was during this one and a half year of my stay in jail that the annihilation of the elderly Krishnan Nambiar of Thavam in Kannur and Kongadu Narayanankutty Nair of Palakkad and Nagarur-Kummil and Kilimanoor incidents occurred. These incidents were a reflection of the annihilation line pursued by Charu Majumdar at the national level. This resulted in the destruction of the magnificent armed revolts, which were unleashed after the Naxalbari strike, among others by the tribals of the forests of Sreekakulam under the leadership of the revolutionary comrades. The police brutally murdered valorous comrades who were working with the tribals for years. It became a matter of routine for comrades who were arrested in public to be taken to the forests and shot dead to become statistics of those 'killed in encounter'.

If this was what was happening on the national scene, the global picture was exhilarating. The fire of revolution was spreading far and wide. America had turned the Vietnam War into an Indo-China one by attacking Cambodia. The national liberation movements of Vietnam, Laos and Cambodia joined forces against American imperialism, the common enemy. There were mass protests against American expansionism in almost all the nations of Europe and America and it shook the very roots of imperialism. Mao's insightful and guiding statement of May 20, 1970 about the Indo-China issue became the war cry of the revolutionaries all over the world. Thus under the leadership of People's China and Mao, the global community took great steps on the path of world revolution. In 1971, China became a member of the United Nations with the support of all nations except America and its cronies. America's attempts to isolate China thus came to naught. President Nixon sent Kissinger as a secret messenger to Peking to arrange a visit to China. China's status among world nations was on an all time high.

These international developments filled us with a passion that exuded the spirit of revolution all around us. We spent all the time available in jail in ideological studies. The comrades began to exhibit photos and red flag which they put up on the verandah in front of their block, wallpapers explaining our stand on contemporary political issues. This was a crowd-puller. The authorities panicked and commissioned their cronies among the inmates to beat up the comrades. But the wallpapers continued to make an appearance.

As our political discussions went on and our awareness increased, the case was drawing to a conclusion. The judge, the prosecution and all of us were convinced of the fresh energy that Thalassery-Pulpally had generated among the lower strata of the society and this was visible in the depositions before the court. The prosecution examined about 250 witnesses and accused from a list of 400. Yet the only prosecution witnesses were the policemen, the two approvers and the landlords who were attacked. My uncle Kunnikkal Purushothaman was called in first to establish that the conspiracy was hatched at our place. He had first testified against us in the District magistrate court, but later changed his statement. The prosecution was at a loss. The court was adjourned for some time. The special public prosecutor and the crime branch D.Y.S.P Muralikrishnadas insisted that my uncle should testify against us, but he said: "I know what I should say. How will I step out of the house after deposing in favour of the police? I have to face the people. I will do what I think is right." In the witness box, he repeated what he said in the morning. The prosecution declared that the witness had turned hostile and had teamed up with the accused. Almost all the examinations went this way. During the trial that went on for a year, almost half of the witnesses were declared to have turned hostile. Then in the end, as if they were ashamed of protesting, the prosecution kept quiet when somebody deposed in our favour.

The statement of the tribals of Chekadi village was what touched me most. The police had beaten up all the tribals whom the landlords had pointed out as our associates. We had seen an elderly woman lying paralysed after the police torture. She was a lean but healthy woman during the Pulpally strike. But when she was brought to the court, she had to drag herself into the witness box. She couldn't stand straight as if suffering from a spinal injury and was panting for breath even as the prosecutor attacked her with a volley of questions. We knew that we had caused all this agony, but couldn't do anything for her. Still, she said she knew nothing about the incident. The prosecution wanted to prove just one thing from the statements of the tribals — that there was a woman among the people who had attacked the houses of the landlords. But the tribals refused to commit this. The prosecution tried its best, but the tribals testified that the group had only men. They refused to identify any of us. The prosecution couldn't do anything when the tribals claimed that they remembered no faces. At last, the prosecutor pointed at me and asked the tribal woman: "Was this woman in the group?" "No." She said. This was just a reflection of the revolutionary ardour the event had sparked off in the minds of the tribals. This also proved their commitment and devotion to the revolution. This love was a blow to all the opportunists including those among us.

Our lawyer friends were optimistic about the outcome of the trial. The conspiracy charges failed to stick and it was getting clearer that the prosecution could not prove anything against my father, K.P or any other comrade involved in the Thalassery incident. The statement of Thettamala Gopi who had turned approver was going against us in the Pulpally case. Our lawyers hinted that the Pulpally case might end in conviction.

October 13, 1971. On the day of the verdict, we had only one desire. We wanted to appear in court holding aloft the photograph of Mao who had shed light on our political journey. We wanted to proclaim to the world once more that we were his foot soldiers. We also wore red badges with Mao's smiling face on them. I was supposed to hold a placard with the photograph on it. At 10 am sharp we walked towards the gate. The jail superintendent was at the gate to see us off. He was friendly towards some of us and ignored others. Some comrades had a bundle of books in their hands. When I reached the gate with the placard in hand, the sub inspector who had come to take us to the court whispered something to the jail superintendent and then told us that we couldn't take the placard along. We insisted that we wouldn't go without it. All the comrades in the Thalassery-Pulpally case became one forgetting their recent disagreements. This must have frightened the authorities. The Sessions judge sent in our advocate to inquire about the delay in producing us in court. A compromise was reached and we were allowed to take the photo inside the courtroom, but were advised to remove the rod of the placard. The authorities proved once again that they care two hoots for the judiciary. They contacted Thiruvanthapuram directly. Achutha Menon was the chief minister and Karunakaran, the home minister. We were told that we would be taken to court only after lunch and so we went to our respective blocks.

We were again called at four in the evening. As we reached the gate, the inspector snatched the photo from my hands. The policemen began to beat us. They beat us with rifle butts and kicked us with their boots. Then they hurled each of us into the van. Neelakantan, a poor peasant comrade of the Pulpally revolt was struck on the head with a bayonet. We shouted aloud: "Long live Mao! Long live C.P.I (M-L)! Victory to the armed peasant revolt, Naxalbari Lal Salaam!" Our voice rose to the heavens. The beatings became severe. They wanted to shut us up, but they couldn't succeed. There was a battalion of CRPF lined outside the gate. I couldn't control my anger. I spat at the CRPF. "We won't be suppressed by your torture. We will take revenge for every drop of blood that you have spilt." We shouted aloud glaring at the officials.

People had gathered on the streets outside the gate. They were worried when they didn't see us in the morning. People thronged the roads from the court premises to the jail gate. The police had filled the place with CRPF making it look like a military camp. The people were getting impatient not seeing us.

Our slogan shouting grew stronger as we reached the court. The large crowd filled us with more courage, but the police didn't stop their torture. We informed the judge about the tussle over Mao's photo. Comrade Neelakantan fell down unconscious before the judge. We warned that if the court were helpless on these issues, it would be better to remain so even when we struck back as and when we could. The judge sat in his chair mum, his face turning pale. He looked regretful for some reason. What could a judge possibly do to combat the highhandedness of the Government and its police! Could he express his dissent effectively within the confines of the existing system?

23

THE BANGLADESH WAR

The eight of us, who were convicted were taken back to the Kozhikode jail after the verdict was pronounced around 8 in the night. The next day was a Sunday and the police informed us that we would be sent to Kannur Central Jail only on November 1. The jail reminded us of a deserted battlefield. Inside the gate, the wardens were lined up with their batons in hand. Later we came to know that the superintendent had burned all the papers, books and clothes he could lay his hands on and beaten up the comrades involved in the Kuttiyadi case who were also locked up with us in the jail. These comrades and my co-accused of the Thalassery-Pulpally case were beaten up again the next day and the Kuttiyadi comrades were locked up in a separate cell. They tried to make up something that would let them torture me too. When we came back from the court, we understood that the special status given to the Thalassery-Pulpally accused during the trial was cancelled. Thus the Achutha Menon government actually withdrew even those small privileges granted by the E.M.S Government. The authorities even took away the saris and the books that I had left behind in jail when I went to the court. They didn't give it back even after repeated requests. I heard that the books were burned and the saris now belonged to the wardrobe of the superintendent or the jailer.

I set out wearing Mao's badge even when I was taken to the Kannur jail on November 1. The superintendent's supreme arrogance was on display that day. His face exuded beastly satisfaction of having tortured the comrades. He accompanied me to the gate taunting me all the while as if to test my morale. His words couldn't affect me. I kept on giving him instant replies. Then he took me to the block were the Kuttiyadi comrades were locked up and sneered at me: "Did you see the plight of your comrades?" The comrade who was lying down in the cell stood up seeing me and greeted me enthusiastically with a clenched fist. I greeted him back the same way. The superintendent was aghast. He shouted at the comrade and took me to the gate. Hundreds of prisoners were watching us through the iron grill doors of their cells. No one was let out during that time. As I reached the gate, the superintendent ordered the women cops to remove my badge. They dreaded and hated even the smiling picture of Mao! I had expected this attack. I shouted aloud: "Long live Mao, Victory to the Indian revolution!" They struck me down and snatched away the badge. I kept on shouting slogans. After a while, they asked me to leave. The expression of victory in the superintendent's face was clouded in anxiety. I looked at his despicable face and spat forcefully on the ground. Then I came out of the jail gate. The police beat me up in the van till we reached Kannur. I shouted slogans whenever I saw a small group of people. The police beatings couldn't douse my hurt pride. We reached Kannur Central jail after an eventful journey.

My parents came to see me within 10 days and I described to them all that happened in Kozhikode jail and on the way to Kannur. I was told that I was not allowed to read Mao's books. I informed my parents this, and they wrote a long letter to the Chief Minister. The authorities passed on books of Marx, Engels and Stalin, which my parents had deposited at the jail office. Thus I got an opportunity to go deep into the works of these great men. The fortlike stone wall around me gave me the concentration necessary for a comprehensive study.

Within a month of my getting shifted to Kannur, much had changed in the world outside. On December 4, 1971 another emergency was declared in India as part of its war against Pakistan. The Internal Security Law, which the Indira Government had passed in Parliament came to be enforced throughout the country. My father and mother had petitioned the Kozhikode district collector within a few days of their release from jail for permission to publish a magazine called *India-China Friendship*. They were arrested on December 8 under MISA and brought to Kannur. Kerala Amir of Jamaat Islamia was also arrested along with them. They were the only three arrested under MISA in Kozhikode. Seven more were arrested from Kannur district. Within 5-6 weeks most of them were released. Gopalan Vaidyar and KC Ayamutty who were acquitted in the Thalassery-Pulpally case were released first. They had joined the Marxist Party after their acquittal, and A.K.Gopalan's special recommendation saw to it that they were let off this time too. Now one thing was clear. The Marxist Party approved the pseudo-nationalism of the Indira Gandhi Government and the atrocities it committed for the sake of Hindu supremacy. There was a silent agreement between the two parties that none of the Marxist party workers would be arrested under MISA. The Kerala Government released the Amir of Jamaat based on a compromise it had with the leaders of the All India Jamaat Islamia in New Delhi. Thus after one month, my father and mother were the only MISA detainees in Kannur and soon after when others were released all over Kerala, they remained the only detainees under MISA in the entire state. They were in jail for more than a year.

They were denied Mao's works even though they were merely under preventive detention. The authorities used to deny them anything that had Mao's name on it. My father petitioned the high court challenging this attitude. It only proved the hatred of Achuthamenon Government for Mao and its real political disposition. The same Government had allowed us to read Lenin's *State and Revolution* and *How to organize a Guerilla War* by General Gap of Vietnam. The High Court decision was favourable, but before the order came they were released on December 22, 1972.

A few days after the Bangladesh war, a tragic incident took place in Thalassery, near Kannur. Some people with vested interests attacked Muslims in and around Thalassery on the pretext of a Hindu-Muslim riot. Houses, shops and mosques were burned down. Lots of Muslims were tortured. The police arrested a handful of Hindus and quite a few Muslims. In jail, the Muslims were subjected to third degree treatment. There was communal unrest all over India, and this was an attempt to incite communal feelings in Kerala too. The victory in the Bangladesh War propelled the Intelligence Bureau of the Central government and the Hindu communalists to go on a rampage. In Thalassery, Muslims were in a majority. C.H. Muhammad Koya was the minister in charge of prisons and still he couldn't do anything to prevent the torture of Muslims in jail. Such was the influence of the Hindu supremacists over the ruling class.

We were confined to the four walls of the jail. Still, all these developments in the state and the Indian subcontinent had a great impact on us. No one who was politically aware could distance oneself from these issues. The Bangladesh War saw my mother in jail, along with me. Both of us were in the women's cell and so, we could spend the days together. We used to read together during the day and separately at night. We could meet my father once in two weeks. Even during those short meetings, we discussed political developments and tried to get a clearer view of the situation. My father was alone in the vast eighth block once his MISA friends were all let off. He spent almost one year all by himself. Our meetings had their limitations. But father used this time effectively, going deep into the works of Marx and Lenin.

I was worried when I first came to Kannur. The sudden change from the Kozhikode jail, and restrictions on Mao's books upset me. When Ma joined me in jail after a month, I was happy and sad at the same time. I was sad because our activities had come to an end, albeit temporarily, but happy that at least for some time in my long jail term I wouldn't be alone. In Kannur I was not in solitary confinement, I was with other convicts. I gained further valuable lessons about life during this period.

24

THE INMATES OF KANNUR PRISON

The women's cell of Kannur Central jail was in a huge compound. There were three big blocks and one block of single rooms. The biggest blocks was reserved for those convicted for murder and other usual crimes. The other two blocks were empty most of the time. Only political convicts and those arrested under MISA were kept there. The women's cell was near the main road, a couple of hundred metres away from the prison's office and the men's block. It was less suffocating than the Kozhikode jail.

When I reached Kannur jail on November 1, 1971 I happened to see a 30-year-old convict whom I had met two years ago. I was drawn close to her during the 14 days I spent in Kannur before going out on bail. She was there when Ma was in jail too and took care of Ma when she fell ill. She was from the weaving Chaliya caste from Neeleshwaram. Her very emaciated appearance told the story of her poverty. She looked more than her age and her face wore marks of a wretched life. She was married and had a son. But soon her husband died of tuberculosis and she had to work as a maid in a landlord's house in the neighbourhood. The landlord's son chased her relentlessly and finally managed to have an affair with her. After a while, the youngster had enough of her and abandoned her. By then she was pregnant. She was in jail for having killed her newborn baby. She did it to hold on to an honourable life for herself and her son. But somebody betrayed her and she was arrested. The Sessions Court gave her life imprisonment. And the young landlord her partner in passion and crime, still went around without as much as a scratch. So much for our judiciary! The little boy who knew nothing about the right and the wrong dictated by the society also had to suffer the punishment. He was handed over to some distant relative. The Government had no system in place to protect these children who became orphans for no fault of theirs. The poor woman waited for her punishment to be eased and spent more than five years in jail.

There was a 17 year old girl in my block. She too was serving a life term and was from a poor family. She was a maid at a well-to-do relative's house. It was not clear what led her to commit the murder of her relative's child— whether it was hostility towards her relatives or her desire for gold. She had drowned a child of two in a nearby pond after robbing it of its ornaments. It was a horrid murder but the cause here again was poverty. She must have got frustrated with the affluence of her own relatives while she was reduced to menial work. She used to give vent to her hatred for the powerful even in jail. Her body language was that of a rebel. She was friendly towards Ma and me, still we had a few arguments. This was sparked off by the efforts of the jail authorities to turn her against us. She had to co-operate with them since she was serving a life term. They took the help of these convicts to make money and to suppress the other convicts. The convicts had to play along since their release depended a lot on the advisory board of the Government. The recommendation of the advisory board depended on the opinion of the jail authorities. So, the convicts knew that they could be saved only if they remain loyal to the jail officials. The jail authorities were told not to beat us, so they tried to use other inmates to provoke us and get us into a fight. This Muslim girl was chosen for this purpose. There were some silly arguments as well, which resulted from our lack of self-control. But still, when I was taken to Thiruvananthapuram Central prison she too joined in to give me a hearty farewell. She took care of my mother after I left and used to call her "Ma" as I did.

Sometimes women convicted in hooch cases were brought in too. A week after I reached Kannur jail, another friend of mine was brought there from Kozhikode jail. She was Pennoottiyamma, who belonged to the Cheruma caste and looked about 50 years. She was the sole breadwinner of her family and had two children from her first marriage. She married again when her first husband died but it became increasingly difficult to live with that man. Every night he would come to the hut dead drunk and beat up the poor woman and twice or thrice they had even decided to separate. Women belonging to poor families do not usually bear the man's torture like their middle class counterparts who depend on their men for sustenance. Middle class women never complain and consider wife-beating a normal routine of life. The role model of an average Indian woman is the mythical Sheelavati, who dutifully looked after her husband even when he frequented whorehouses to satisfy his libido. Any woman with a little self-respect should hang her head in shame when reminded of this queasy tale. Sheelavati is the symbol of the Indian woman's self-inflicted slavery. Pennoottiyamma couldn't take her husband's atrocities after a point. One night she hacked him to death and surrendered to the police. I respect this woman. She told us stories of her life and I was an avid listener. She sang folk songs for us, which told tales of oppression of her caste through generations. They were stories of tears, of never ending pain, and of revenge born out of misery. These folk songs were the medium to convey their protest against the society. When she sang, it was as if she forgot herself. Everything about her was different, there was a basic candour and simplicity about whatever she said and did. The authorities couldn't digest my friendship with Pennoottiyamma, who was almost of my mother's age. The women wardens and the superintendent were sure to ill treat those who became close to us. Pennoottiyamma's sentence was for three years. She was warned not to become friendly with us, but still our relationship was not affected.

Mentally challenged women were brought in at times as well. The intensity of their disease varied, but all were victims of circumstances. Some of them were in jail for murder or for attempting to murder some close relative in a fit of madness. Some of them spent their days and nights in laughter, songs and dance; others were abnormally still and silent. Sometimes some of them turned violent and then even four-five people could not match their strength. These women were mostly put in the single room block. The authorities in Kannur jail were even more lackadaisical than the Kozhikode jail authorities in shifting these patients to mental hospitals.

Sometimes we got a break from all this agony when followers of some political party would get arrested en masse and brought to jail. Once a few peasant women who had participated in the 'surplus land distribution' struggle organized by the Marxist party, and two-three girls from middle class families who led these women were brought to the Kannur jail. Usually women who participated in this struggle were let off that day itself, but these women were sentenced to a month's jail term. The leaders had told the women that they would not be arrested and even if they were, they would be let off by the evening. Some of them had left behind babies who had to be breast-fed trusting the words of the leaders. We tried to pacify them and to an extent we succeeded. Softly we explained to them about the hollowness of the Marxist Party's struggle, and the horrifying betrayal involved with it.

But this life didn't last long. I had mentioned how the Muslims who were arrested for the Hindu-Muslim riots in Thalassery were tortured in police custody, under the direct order from the collector. Subramanyam was the jail superintendent then and the investigation turned against him. He was a pain in the neck to all the higher officials including the I.G and D.I.G in the prisons department. They wanted to get him out of their way and didn't let go of the golden opportunity. Subramanyam was suspended. George, who was the superintendent of Kozhikode jail was transferred to Kannur. George was the villain in most of the fights we had in Kozhikode jail. The day he took charge, trouble started afresh. Since I was a sentenced convict, he had many opportunities to seek revenge on me. One such argument resulted in George ordering that I be sent for solitary confinement. I realized that these vengeful measures had the blessings of the Achutha Menon government only when I got shifted to Thiruvananthapuram soon. The authorities understood that I would not give in meekly. They wanted me to apologise to the superintendent, but I refused to do that even if it meant spending the rest of my life in solitary confinement. The authorities couldn't do much as Ma was there to give me moral support and so did many other inmates. The authorities calculated that I could be cowed down only if I was plucked away from my land, northern Kerala where I always won sympathy, and away from the loving gaze of my parents. This would prove to be a punishment to them too. They sent me away claiming that there was lack of security in Kannur women's cell. Later, Ma was to give me another interesting bit of news. The day I was shifted to Kannur, six wardens were brought in and put up in a shed in the jail garden, to keep guard. The day I was sent to Thiruvanathapuram these temporary employees were dismissed and the shed was removed.

On November 2, 1972 I was taken to the Thiruvannathpuram Central Prison. I felt like a sacrificial lamb being led to the altar. I was being uprooted from a place where I had lived all my life, to be transplanted on totally strange and oafish environs. Their aim was to put out the spark in me, which still gave me the courage to stand tall and look the world straight in the face. A new life of fresh tribulations awaited me.

25

THIRUVANATHAPURAM CENTRAL PRISON

While walking into the Central Prison, one would get the impression of entering a well-guarded fort. The women's cell was a part of the main building. The prison was built by the Travancore kings and its structure and everything else about it was different from that of the Kannur central jail.

As a police van took me to Thiruvananthapuram on November 23, the jail authorities welcomed me contempt writ all over their faces. Sukumaran Nair, the superintendent, warned me: "Better behave yourself. Or, we will have to use force." I was not surprised. I knew exactly what this transfer meant. My revolutionary ideas didn't permit me to live a life of subjugation even inside a prison. So, I told him that I wouldn't create trouble without provocation from his side. He didn't like my reply. But he didn't react, and asked a woman warden to take me to the women's cell.

The women's cell was a long block of 18 single rooms. The first room near the gate was a sort of waiting room for the wardens. I was allotted a small cell next to it, with a tiny window covered by a wire mesh. Anyone who entered that eight feet by six feet room would feel like a caged animal. That suffocating cell, so different from the vast blocks of the Kannur Central jail was to be my home for the next four and a half years. There was no facility even to relieve oneself in the night. One of the wardens told me that it was here that the valorous comrades of the historic Punnapra-Vayalar struggle of 1948 were locked up by Diwan Sir C.P. Ramaswamy Iyer's police. There were no separate female wards then. The faint sketches of 'sickle and hammer' on the walls bore testimony to the legacy of the cells. The 'facility' of a ventilator came much later in these cells when the E.M.S government of 1957 implemented jail reforms.

Opposite my cell was a big block. This was meant for A-class convicts — political leaders who landed up in jail. This had a full-fledged toilet fitted with a flush and faucets. The government had made arrangements for a fan too for these special guests. But during my stay this block was used for a different purpose. The female convicts were made to clean wheat and rice there. Women convicted for murder, who did weaving for nominal wages were forced to stop weaving and do this job. The murder convicts got into weaving for the meagre wages and more to get their sentences reduced. No law permitted jail officials to take them out of this job. But in jail, the word of the officials or worse their whim was law. Anyone who dared to speak against it would be silenced most brutally.

About six furlongs away from the big block was a small building. Its second room was the pantry for A class prisoners. The first room had normal doors. Gauriamma, Marxist leader and minister, was kept here when she was arrested the first time. The elevated portion of the women's cell ended with this building. The first nine rooms of the women's block were in this elevated section. The other nine rooms were at a lower level. One had to climb down about three feet to reach those rooms. The weaving room was on the other side of these nine rooms below. It had eight or nine looms. The women who were sentenced for longer terms used to sit there daily and weave cloth. There was a woman instructor who taught the inmates how to weave. Thus six wardens and one weaving instructor were the government employees who controlled the female convicts.

These two lines of buildings, which faced each other ended in a triangular corner marked out for laundry. There was also a row of flush toilets adjacent to the block. These crowded buildings were surrounded by huge walls and one had to come out of the buildings and stand in the verandah to get a small glimpse of the sky. In Kannur jail, gardens in the women's block and green trees all around gave relief to the eyes. But here I felt as if I was lost in a desert. There were no trees as far as the eyes could see. One could watch the tip of the branches of tamarind and mango trees of the jail farm, which extended beyond the high walls. Sometimes the rustling leaves of a gigantic peepul near the jail office brought in a cool breeze during scorching summer days.

It seemed the men's block too had no trees. This prison complex must have been built during the reign of some cruel administrator. Even now conditions were almost the same, despite continuing talks of jail reforms. The authorities looked at the prisoners as if they were some wild animals, which ought to be kept under strict vigil. The officials' routines came as a shock even to me, who was mentally prepared. The attitude of the authorities from wardens to the superintendent was absolutely different from that of the two major jails in Malabar where I had spent three years. Of course, there were no basic differences. All of them were part of the same blood sucking officialdom.

I was a part of the new revolutionary politics and in the last few years the Government, or rather my main foe, didn't get an opportunity to tackle me all alone. The Government had no option but to deal with us carefully since the people of Kerala at large and Malabar in particular were sympathetic towards our cause. They knew that I couldn't be broken down in northern Kerala or Malabar. The annihilation attacks in Travancore and the hilly tracts of the high ranges that followed Thalassery-Pulpally events snuffed out that spark in the people and brought down the movement to a level where it was even derisively termed 'head-chopper's movement'. Therefore, in those areas where these annihilations happened even the petty bourgeoisie came to fear and despise the movement. Indiscriminate killings led to the murder of poor workers, who at times unknowingly came to the rescue of their masters. The police used this opportunity to the maximum and hunted down each and every one whom they thought were associated with the movement. There were even instances when comrades who took part in annihilation strikes were bashed up by the people in court. Then, who was to stop the police? The capital city saw the scientific experimentation of torture by police officers like Jayaram Padikkal. Thus, as the first phase of the Naxalbari movement in Kerala directed the spearhead of attack towards the armed forces of the enemy through Thalassery-Pulpally, Kuttiyadi and Thirunelli revolts, the annihilation strikes that followed aimed at individuals belonging to various sections of society. They didn't even realize that without the support of the peasants and workers, they couldn't withstand the counter attack of the armed forces of the enemy, which would come searching for the perpetrators of such annihilations. All this led to counterproductive reaction to annihilation politics from almost all sections of the society.

It was inevitable that this mood would get reflected in the attitude of the officials inside the jail too. The incidents outside surely resulted in the jail officials getting more and more brutalised.

The day after I reached Thiruvananthapuram, the deputy jailer called me in to say: "You are not supposed to leave your room and the verandah. If at all you have to go out for something, you should take a warden along with you. You must not talk to any other woman here. And, better remain in your room." What if I didn't carry out his order of being confined day and night to the smothering little cell? If at all I tried to talk to any other woman, the wardens would not punish me, but her. That woman might have been counting her days, trying hard to get into the good books of the wardens so that her sentence would get reduced and she could get out of this accursed place. I didn't want to bring more agony into such a person's life by prolonging her stay there. So, voluntarily I restrained myself.

There was only one way of overcoming this killing loneliness and depression. I went deep into the books of great masters of Marxism. I tried hard from the day I reached Thiruvananthapuram to get more books. I had brought a few books from Kannur, which were with the officials. I pestered them daily to get the books out of the jail office. They were hesitant to censor those books and pass it on to me and that led to some tensions as well. But I tried to concentrate on whatever books I managed to get. *The Class Struggles in France, The Eighteenth Brumaire of Louis Bonaparte, The Civil War in France*, that dealt with the Paris Commune that extended from March 1871 to May and *Critique of Gotha Programme* were some of the great works by Marx that I read during this time. I tried to read *Das Kapital* too, but had to stop since I stumbled on certain issues, which required ideological clarification. I also read *The Origin of the Family, Private Property and the State* by Engels. I could read Lenin's *The State and Revolution, Left-Wing Communism - an Infantile Disorder, Imperialism — the Highest Stage of Capitalism.* Besides these Marxist works I also read Franz Mehring's *Karl Marx: The Story of His Life.* Initially I couldn't get Mao's works. But later they too were given to me. This was something different from the attitude of the Kannur jail officers. But later I found out that it was a result of my father's appeal in the high court and its favourable decision. I knew that Achutha Menon government had not only refused books of Mao, but even works of Lenin and Marx to the comrades in the men's block.

The Naxalbari movement was facing disintegration. It became essential for each responsible revolutionary to learn from the failures of the past and analyse their activities. Though a few of them let go of the path of revolution and went their separate ways to pursue their individual lives, those who remained in the movement grew stronger like tempered steel. For this, they needed the guidance of revolutionary ideology.

Here lay my profit in being able to read Communism. I made good use of the most difficult phase of my life, my solitary confinement in the Thiruvannthapuram prison.

26

THE HIGH COURT VERDICT

On December 22, 1972 my father and mother were released from jail. They began sending me letters once they reached home. I was happy. I knew very well that they would do their best to take the movement forward as long as they were out of jail. Their letters filled with revolutionary optimism gave me a lot of courage.

Two months went by. Then I got a letter saying that my father would be coming to meet me in prison. The train journey from Kozhikode to Thiruvananthapuram was tedious and Ma was not feeling up to it. So my father decided to come alone and the letter told me that he would bring with him all the books I needed. He was supposed to reach the jail on March 15, 1973.

This was a time when harassment by the crime branch was at its peak. At least five policemen from the crime branch stood guard on the streets outside our house. They followed my father and mother wherever they went. I had a similar experience when I was out on bail in 1969. There was another police ploy those days. People were openly kidnapped from crowded public places and were kept in secret custody for months together, and later they were implicated in Naxalite cases. A young man called Lakshmanan who was an employee in a bakery was taken from his workplace and later convicted for a crime in

Vijayawada in Andhra Pradesh. Muhammad Koya, who used to work in a sweet shop was also taken away and after a few weeks the police claimed in news reports that he was arrested from Nagercoil and was later implicated in Nagrur-Kummil case. He was kept in remand for five years. Kuttappan, a tailor, was also arrested and charged in the same case and put in prison. There were several instances in North Malabar too, where people were whisked away and kept in secret custody for days before they were presented before the court. If this was the treatment meted out to Naxalite sympathizers, it was not much better for others. Nawab Rajendran, editor of a newspaper published from Thrissur was taken into illegal custody for days under special orders from Karunakaran, the then home minister. Rajendran was neither a Naxalite nor a sympathizer of the movement. His crime was that he had the gumption to publish the photostat copy of a letter, which proved that Karunakaran had received lakhs of rupees of bribe from somebody. For this "crime" he was subjected to third degree torture in police custody. So, it was a period in time when Karunakaran's police reigned supreme and that was when my father intimated me that he would visit me. And then he went into hiding.

In the last letter my father wrote he was not sure about the visit. He had expressed his doubts of getting kidnapped by the crime branch, which was waiting for an opportunity. It was a ploy to dupe the Government and a warning for me. He didn't turn up on the 15th, the day he was supposed to come. I was confused. I didn't have an inkling that my parents had decided to pay back the Government and the police in the same coin. I believed that the police had really taken father away. Ma's press release after two days and the letter she sent, accentuated my fear. On the 14th before my father boarded the train for Thiruvananthapuram he had posted a card in my mother's name in which he told her that two policemen in plain clothes were following him. All this went according to a plan my parents had worked out together, but I remained in the dark for quite some time.

I kept on writing to Ma about my fears regarding father's disappearance. Ma was in a dilemma now. Many of her letters didn't reach me either. She came to know of it only when I wrote to her complaining about her not writing to me. After a while, she began to send me registered letters. Mother wanted to tell me the truth about my father's disappearance. She took the help of my uncle, who in spite of his bad health agreed to visit me in jail. He was a heart patient, who panted for breath after every few steps. Yet, he travelled all the way to meet me. The jail authorities were particularly rude to him. This was my first interview after I had come to Thiruvanthapuram. Still, they gave us only five minutes to talk to each other. I had numerous questions to ask him, and much of it was left unasked.

I gathered from the wardens that the condition of the Naxalite comrades in the men's block was even worse. They were subjected to third degree torture even though jail laws didn't allow it. They were locked up in dark cells day and night and beaten up mercilessly.

I continued my ideological study amidst all these. Then, in September 1973, I was summoned to the high court. I requested the jail authorities to sent a telegram to my mother informing her about this so that I could meet her there. But they didn't do it. I concluded that the Government didn't want me to meet my mother anywhere other than the jail premises.

I was given dinner at four in the evening and handed over to the police to be taken to the High court. I was put in a huge police van and had for escort, two women constables, one sub inspector, one crime branch sub inspector, two gun-toting reserve policemen and the van driver, who too was a police constable. I was asked to be present for the hearing of the Government's appeal against the Sessions's court judgement of the Thalassery-Pulpally case. It seemed, earlier, the comrades from Kannur too were summoned. We started from jail on the previous evening. The jail authorities had given just two rupees to the police for my food for the next day, since they had already served me dinner in the evening and hence, my ration for that day was over. I was supposed to fend for myself with this two-rupee note till I reached back jail at 10 the next night. Food was dear those days, as India was going through a difficult phase after the Bangladesh War and globally the oil shock was pushing up petroleum prices sky high. A normal meal cost two rupees those days. The people's representatives who passed bills that increased their allowances in the name of inflation whenever the Assembly met, never found about the two rupees travel allowance given to low class prisoners! I requested the authorities to grant some money from my personal funds kept in jail, but that too was turned down. What could I do? We reached Kochi that night. I was lodged at Thevara police station lock up. In one of the high walls of that building was written 'Model police station, Thevara.' Indeed, it was a classic example of a terrible police station. Wherever my body touched the walls, it was smeared with dirt. The room was covered with cobwebs. The stench of urine of the miserable beings who had to be there before me came in from the small verandah in a corner. There were mosquitoes all over. I voiced my protest and the policemen arranged a bench for me to lie down. I spread a newspaper on it and lay down, but couldn't sleep. During the night three-four young men were brought in and I could see the policemen bashing them up, with pleasure. I was reminded of the torture the Pulpally comrades had to undergo. Were these policemen some bloodthirsty beasts? I couldn't help wonder. What would they gain from bashing up these men? Did they have no twinge of guilt at all, or had they overcome it and started deriving enjoyment from their daily routine? The night at Thevara police station still festers in my memory like a sore wound.

The next day morning I was taken to the high court. The judges asked me if I had anything to tell them. I requested them to send me back to the Kannur jail and brought to their attention the absurdity of the travel allowance of Rs.2. They asked me to give my requests in writing, but nothing happened. Advocate Kunjirama Menon who had appeared on our behalf requested the court to meet me and talk to me personally about the case. He told me that the situation was bad and that our sentence could be increased. He warned me that the government was very particular about it. I bid him farewell and returned to Thiruvanathapuram.

The judgement came in November 1973. Thirteen of the accused in the Pulpally revolt including me were sentenced to life imprisonment. The five-year term of some comrades was upheld by the High Court. Among the comrades who got life term were Thomas master, Kunjupanicker and Keshavan who had nothing whatsoever to do with the Pulpally strike. Philip M. Prasad who was let off by the Sessions court, probably due to some conspiracy got a life term this time. Some others who were involved in the Thalassery attack but who were not punished earlier were given a sentence of three-four years by the high court. My father too was sentenced for three years rigorous imprisonment. Thus the Government emerged victorious.

It is a fact that in no other case involving Naxalites was maximum punishment given by the high court, that too enhancing the sentences given by the sessions court. Home minister Karunakaran had felt that the verdict of the sessions court was very mild and had announced in a press conference that his Government would move the High Court in appeal. No other case had evoked such a public outburst from the Kerala home minister.

I had first thought of not defending myself against the State's appeal in high court. I didn't underestimate the Government's ability to manipulate and pressurize the decision of the lower court. We also couldn't reproduce the same favourable atmosphere of the sessions court in the high court. First, we had to force our lawyer friends to travel to Kochi just for this case, knowing well that it wasn't going to help either. The Government was hell-bent on getting us the maximum punishment. In fact, I was even prepared to face death penalty. But the others decided to appeal and advocate Kunjirama Menon persuaded me to sign the petition along with the others. I didn't want to cause problems and did as the lawyer asked me. But I told him we wouldn't do anything more than this to fight the case.

It was obvious that the case was not decided in the high court. It was made elsewhere by somebody more powerful and that too much earlier. This was clear from the fact that the case was heard by a division bench, which was completely submissive to the Government. Apparently, one of the judges had told a common friend that they would be forced to enhance the sentence and that they could do nothing about it.

The sentence proved how scared those who wield power were of anyone, even the weakest, who tried to defy their dictates. But then when I see certain "notorious" Naxal cases getting dismissed, and the Government not challenging the acquittals, I could only wonder about a conspiracy behind all this.

The Government has its agents even amongst the radicals. They know who to rely on and who to suspect. History stands testimony to the fact that often those who mouth revolutionary slogans the loudest turn out to be the most dangerous for the movement. It was Judas who was the most vocal about the powers of Jesus Christ. Lin Biao, who posed as Mao's comrade in struggle and managed to get into the Ninth party congress leadership as his heir later plotted to get Mao murdered. History is full of such instances.

Now I was sure of one thing. My hope of getting out of jail was but a dream. For the rest of my life, I was fated to live in that tiny cell in the Thiruvananthpuram prison. They wouldn't even send me back to Kannur. But I was determined to fight it out to the last. My revolutionary fervour couldn't get subdued this fast. Once again I found solace in the teachings of the great masters to tell myself that nothing could break the spirit of a true Communist.

27

THE WOMEN'S CELL OF THIRUVANANTHAPURAM PRISON

In November 1973, after the high court judgment my mother visited me in jail to lend me moral support. She brought me books and other things that I needed.

I was beside myself with joy. It was one year since we last met in Kannur Central Prison. I wanted to tell her that the sentence had not affected me in any way and that I would always stick to the path of revolution all through my life. I met her at the jailer's office. Her face bloomed in joy when she saw me. She warned me to be prepared to be in jail for many more years to come, and advised me not to stop my ideological studies. She told me that the Achutha Menon Government wanted to break me from within and asked me to find solace in the combined study of Marxism, Leninism and Mao's teachings. She reminded me not to forget the multitude of people hurled into poverty every passing day. She asked me about my life in jail. I told her that it was different from Kannur. I couldn't say all that I wanted, still I was allowed to speak to her for half an hour. The jail authorities accepted the books and other things that mother had brought with her.

In the oppressive lonely life in jail these meetings were like shining rays of light. They faded away fast, but the effect lingered on, making my life bearable for many more days. The authorities were rude, they never hid their political prejudices. But what pained me more was the ill treatment of the other inmates.

The women were made to thresh paddy and clean wheat. The jail laws insist that women under trial should not be assigned any work against their wish. And, that women convicts should be paid, however meagre it might be, for the work they do in prison. But I found that the prisoners were forced to do all sorts of work. None of them was paid anything. Even if a woman was too ill to work she was beaten up and forced to work. Sometimes a new inmate was bashed up at her arrival in prison without any provocation. If they were prostitutes, the unfortunate souls were in for more trouble. Murder convicts too invited similar treatment. Sometimes I felt that this gave the wardens immense pleasure. There was a woman called Sarasamma who was convicted for drowning her baby fearing societal snub. The moment she came in, a warden whom I had nicknamed Idippees (the boxer) aimed not less than 50 blows on her back. How could a woman be so cruel to another woman? All the women were shocked into silence hearing the loud thumps. I was moved to tears when I saw that woman, her eyes popped out with horror and pain, walking back to the cell in a daze. The women wardens vied with each other in torturing the inmates. The young wardens especially took pride in bashing up the convicts mercilessly at the slightest provocation. They had special instructions from the officials to deal quite harshly with the convicts. That way, the older ones were better.

I was not allowed to be friendly even with little children. The jailers used to threaten the mothers if they doubted that I was growing close to their children. Chellamma, a murder convict had a two-year-old daughter called Sujatha. The little girl was a ray of brightness in the lives of all the inmates, including mine. But how could she know the difference between the other convicts and me? She used to run up to my verandah, and I would pet her. The officials didn't take this demonstration of love too kindly. One day she had come into her room. I was trying to send her out when a warden rushed in. She gave the child a tight slap. I put her down, and she ran away with silent tears in her eyes. I felt a sudden surge of pain. I couldn't bear it. That day I had a terrible fight with the warden. I still wince when I think of the little girl's frightened tearful face.

The meals provided in the prison told the story of unabashed corruption. If meals were given according to the jail laws with no fraud or sleaze, 'C' class food was not all that intolerable. But the prisoners got what remained of the quota of the contractor, the jail superintendent and the jailer. The Government had made provisions for meat and fish. But what we got was nothing more than rotten, dried fish and fat and bones in the name of mutton and chicken. Fresh fish is readily available in Kerala, but the officials insisted that the prisoners should be given only dried fish prescribed by the British. It was the same with the clothes, soap and oil given to us. The wardens took two litres of coconut oil for every cake of lifebuoy soap because bath soap was not part of the ration, though we got two small cakes of soap for washing clothes. Whatever be the supplies, the wardens took the lion's share. Every Monday top officials had a farce called the parade, just to listen to the complaints of the convicts. But if at all an inmate dared to speak out about the corruption in jail, the top officials themselves would order her to be bashed up.

The jail doctors too were an irresponsible lot. The wardens didn't want to accompany a sick inmate to hospital. So even if someone was seriously ill, they tried not to inform the authorities. The contempt with which they treated pregnant women often forced me to wonder if these women wardens were really mothers and wives. Once, a woman went into labour at midnight. The wardens were informed, but they rained such abuses on that the poor woman that she got scared out of her wits. Her baby had come out partially even before the wardens decided to take a look at her. She sat in a corner pushing the baby back. After a while the baby died. The inmates told the details to the jail doctor and other officials but to no avail. After all, who gives a damn about a prostitute and her bastard? No court would want to punish those jailers who killed the infant. These are but regular events in our jails and all I have attempted is to tell those tales, which would give reveal the real face of some hopeless lives.

I had read Mary Tyler's "My Years in an Indian Prison." She spent five years of tortuous life in Hazaribagh and Jamshedpur jails in Bihar. I know how authentic her description of life in an Indian jail is. There could be minor variations in the apparent atmosphere of jails in different states under different political circumstances. But essentially it's all the same. There was a campaign that the E.M.S Government had brought about substantial jail reforms after it came to power in 1957 and that the prisoners had a comfortable life thereafter. But this was just another brazen lie to win over a few votes. Inspection tours and reforms wouldn't mean anything if the basic instinct to crush the prisoners doesn't change. I hope that sincere well-wishers of the society would realize that this problem too would be solved only when the larger issue got addressed — the issue of the oppressed and the oppressor.

I was isolated from the other inmates. The government refused to give me a job, which was the privilege, if I can say so, of every convict serving a life sentence. That way I would have got a chance to step out of my suffocating cell. But they didn't want to relieve my misery in any manner. Now, when I look back I see uncanny designs of the government to make me a lunatic.

The books that my mother brought were censored and given to me only after months of pestering. Some books were not given to me at all and were not returned to Ma either. Still, I continued my studies. Those days I read some books on China by some foreign writers. I used to buy newspapers with my own money, but in the name of censorship some news reports were torn off. It only meant that they thought I could pose problems for them if I read certain news reports about what was happening in the outside world.

The inmates of the jail, however, were quite friendly despite all the restrictions. When I fought with the wardens or other authorities they always supported me and encouraged me, though not openly. They believed that they would find a voice in me and that their humiliations and agonies would be avenged one day. They kept the sparks of self respect lit in their hearts. The affection they showered on me was like dazzling flames, warming my otherwise cold and dark life.

My life went on like a small boat sailing against hostile currents. But the strong waves of adversity could not shake my ideas and beliefs.

When Ma came for an interview the second time, another officer was present in the room along with the jailer. We came to know that he was a crime branch officer. We protested that this was highly provocative, but it didn't make any difference. The next time, my uncle accompanied Ma. That time too, an officer was present and he even tried to manage our meeting. Immediately after meeting me Ma gave a press release protesting against this and once she reached Kozhikode, wrote a letter to the Chief Minister. That had its effect, the crime branch left us alone in the subsequent three-four meetings.

The authorities tried another means to check out if I had a change of heart. The high court had convicted Philip M. Prasad along with the thirteen of us. He pleaded that he be given B grade privileges in jail and his wish was granted soon enough. The jailer told me that I too could make a request for better treatment in jail. I saw through their plan. They wanted me to be obliged to the Government forever for better food, clothes and other facilities. During the trial all the accused of the Thalassery-Pulpally case were given B-class treatment. That time I had accepted it. May be that had prompted them to bribe me. They might have felt that if I accepted their offer I would lose my revolutionary spirit in course of time and soon could be tamed like a dog. But I refused their offer downright.

The year 1974 went on in suffocating solitude and in struggles against the Government, yet firmly footed in ideological beliefs and studies. I got another friend in October — Thankamma, a 50-year-old from a wealthy family arrested under COFEPOSA. The room next to mine was given to her. Later, she was to make my life more miserable.

28

THE DECLARATION OF EMERGENCY

I read in the papers the next day that my father was arrested from home on June 7, 1975. The news was unexpected still there was nothing to worry; after all he was arrested from home. Actually, my father had only the high court's sentence against him. Though he was sentenced for three years, they could have put him in jail for just one or two days. The Supreme Court had recently ordered that the period in prison during the trial should be deducted from the total sentence. My father had already spent his sentence of three years in jail during our trial.

So he was being held in jail illegally. The superintendent told him that the order to release him should come from the top. He was arrested for the Thalassery-Pulpally case, but he was not allowed to go anywhere near the other comrades' block. He was locked up in a solitary cell meant for those awaiting hanging. He was released from jail on July 1 after a bout of diarrhoea and weakness. This was 23 days after his arrest. Indira Gandhi declared Emergency on June 26. My parents were again arrested under MISA on July 3, just three days after his release. The first day they were provided a little food. The second day they were blindfolded and taken to some unknown police station and locked up. They weren't even given water. The third day they were taken to Kannur Central jail. This ended a phase of our political life.

So, the three of us were among thousands of comrades who were arrested and thrown behind bars along with numerous leaders from the ruling class like Morarji Desai, Jayaprakash Narayanan and others. The C.P.I (M.L) was banned. Atrocities and arrests during the Emergency are well documented now. But let me try and explain, as I know, the reasons that led Indira Gandhi to declare the Emergency.

Probably because of the censorship imposed on English and regional papers, the reason cited by the media for the declaration of the Emergency was the Allahabad High Court order that made Indira's election to the Lok Sabha invalid. Even after the Emergency, it was argued that the Emergency was the result of autocratic tendencies of Indira as a person and the caucus that surrounded her. But the most pathetic was the political understanding of those revolutionaries who, using Marxian tools are supposed to know the real friends and foes of revolution and show the way to the rest of the society. They got duped by empty socialist slogans of "bank nationalization" and "government take over of private industries" and the revolutionaries claimed that she was now rid of American influence and that she had declared the Emergency in the interests of the Soviet Union against the fascist forces led by Jayprakash-Morarji combine.

The "stabilization programme" in India was part of a mega game plan of US imperialism, which involved a recovery from an economic crisis, an attempt to increase its influence in other Asian countries and thereby square the losses in Vietnam and also ensure that another similar situation did not prevail. This programme was designed to put down the numerous people's struggles in India and intensify the colonial exploitation. The Emergency was the declaration of war against the people as a whole including the opposition in the Parliament. The US obviously had wherewithal to destroy any leader who opposed these plans devised by the World Bank and the IMF. Chile's Allende and

Sihanouk of Cambodia are examples. The US had deliberately created the myth that Indira and her Congress were closer to the Soviet Union than Morarji was with the US. The Indian newspapers repeated this lie under the influence of the US and the Soviet Union so much that even our revolutionaries bought this argument. But it is getting clearer that both Indira and Morarji were loyal servants of the US imperialism, one played the pro-Soviet role, while the other sought total revolution, pure democracy and the rule of law.

29

TORTURES DURING EMERGENCY

I lost my last point of contact with the movement when my parents were arrested. I seemed to slip into a world of darkness. I was not allowed to have any sort of relationship with my fellow prisoners, and so, mother's letters and interviews were like badly needed fresh air. Every bit of news about the movement made me more resolute. I often pondered about the consequences of the Emergency. I felt that it would backfire at the ruling classes who had vested interests in perpetuating it. History testifies to the fact that the most horrifying oppressions come up against the most powerful resistance.

I could gather from newspapers the atrocities being committed all over the country. Since there was censorship on press, I could imagine that the real picture would be much worse. Yet, everybody knew of the arrests of Indira's political rivals on charges of smuggling, money laundering and black marketing. Lots of comrades from our cadre, middle rung leaders of the Jan Sangh and the Marxist party were arrested. But all top leaders like E.M.S and A.K.G were spared. These points to the extreme trust Indira had in these leaders. The Naxalites bore the brunt of it all. Numerous people were put behind bars and tortured as they were suspected to be sympathizers of the movement.

People arrested under MISA belonged to this group. Lots of people were even murdered. Many youngsters were sent to the Thiruvananthapuram prison under MISA. All this, along with solitary confinement began eating into me.

Man is a social being. What could I do to get over this suffocating atmosphere? I didn't do any work and this had a debilitating impact on my health. One day I asked the jailer to give me some work. Every prisoner, whether under trial or convicted was made to work in jail. But I was made to sit idle for four years. Since I was sentenced for life I was entitled to a job and wages. But it was the government's policy that no Naxalite would be allowed to work inside the jail. But when I asked the second time the superintendent ordered the weaving instructor to employ me. A warden was to accompany me and stay with me till I got back to my cell. They didn't want to take a chance. What if I tried to be friendly with the others, what if I influenced them!

I was happy at this opportunity to exert myself physically. I would learn a new occupation too. Anyway, it was better than spending a whole day in a cell.

Initially it was a little difficult for me. But within two months I gained an over-all knowledge of weaving. I used to weave *tumkri*, a narrow, inexpensive cloth. More experienced people used to weave the towels, which were supposed to be distributed among the inmates once in four months. The only instruments we had were eight looms and one *raat* to spin the thread. The looms should have been thrown away long ago, but they were considered fit for convicts. No amount of complaints brought new looms. The convicts competed among themselves to get hold of the better ones because a good loom could spin more cloth. That would mean more wages. The weaving shed had a thatched roof and the walls didn't reach above half its height. So, during the monsoon with a strong wind blowing the rain came in from all four sides the looms and yarn got wet. Weaving then became a difficult task. As we weaved, the yarns would keep snapping. We would tie it again and at the end of it our fingers and hearts would be left frozen.

The wages given for weaving was an excellent example of exploitation. One was supposed to weave 18 metres of *tumkri* a day. A little wider *thorthu* (native towel) had to be 16 metres. Later, another cloth wider than the *thorthu* was brought there, and it was called *cambric*. One had to spin ten metres of *cambric* a day. The wages varied a little according to the breadth of the cloth. One roll of *tumkri* which came to 100 metres fetched a little over Rs. 3. If a convict could meet a day's target she was given the wages. But not meeting the target would mean no wages at all for that day's work. Could this happen anywhere else but in prison? The prisoners didn't have the right to question any injustice meted out to them. Any faint voice of protest was mercilessly stifled.

The meagre wages didn't reach the hands of the prisoners either. It would get accumulated at the jail office. A part of it was meant for buying stuff from the prisoners' canteen. Some amount would be given away to the prisoners when they were finally released. The third portion of the wages was really special. The prisoners could use this to get their number of days in jail reduced. Thus a part of their minimal wages went back to the government. It was termed as "scoring marks". This great reform had been brought in during the E.M.S rule of 1957. Till then, however hard you worked there were absolutely no wages. But these wages of slavery only helped to nurture false hopes in the hearts of prisoners. This was a terrific means of exploitation too. Earlier, the prisoners wouldn't work too hard for there was nothing to be gained in return. Those who worked more and less were treated the same way then. In fact, the wardens had to use all their might to get the prisoners to work. There were no fights to work more and earn more. And, they were united in their protest against the authorities. But today, the situation is just the opposite. The miserable wages has helped to divide the prisoners and reinstate the authorities' supremacy. Now, the prisoners worked hard without even caring for their health. They fought to get the better looms to weave more. In brief, this reform measure only helped to degrade the prisoners both mentally and physically. One little act of disobedience could at one stroke cancel all the marks they had scored and the days they had managed to deduct from their term of punishment. Only if they behaved extremely well to the satisfaction of the wardens would the prisoners get the good conduct certificate. So, this was just another inhuman method the authorities had invented to keep the prisoners under control.

I had grasped these things before I started weaving. I had decided that I wouldn't get my days in jail reduced bribing the authorities. And whether they would give me any wages at all was doubtful. I had decided not to overwork for my own sake. For me, it was just an opportunity to be with other inmates and get some exercise. I knew that I wouldn't be released from jail until the Emergency was over. And I knew quite well that it was just a false hope that I would be released when I still stuck to the path of revolution. If there are no false hopes there are no disappointments either. The day the high court enhanced my sentence I lost all hopes of freedom. But I was firm that I didn't need freedom at the cost of forsaking my ideology.

I can't help but think of those hundreds of youngsters whose bones were shattered during the Emergency just because they believed in a cause. It's when you see the change of attitude of the authorities towards a "reformed" revolutionary that you actually realize the depth of their hatred and fear of that political ideology.

Still, I began to lose my balance with the news of sudden unexpected atrocities and the peculiar situation in jail where restrictions were imposed one after another. I used to read Marx and Mao. I continued with it even after I started weaving. I had begun to lose weight with regular work. My parents' letters reached me once in four or five months. They used to send me letters every week, but I never got them. I had to send at least four petitions to the I.G to get these letters. My letters seldom reached the Kannur Central Prison. Once they had received one of my letters after eight months. This was a major upsetting factor for all the three of us. Once, after my parents were arrested my uncle, who had a heart condition, came to meet me from Kozhikode. He came in December 1975. He had to wait four days for the interview. The authorities sent him back twice saying that it was a holiday. He was so harassed that after that incident no one ever came to meet me in jail. My uncle had brought some books with him, but I had to pester the authorities for days together to censor them and gain access to them. I was crushed by these tortures rather than the physical exertion of doing an unfamiliar work. Gradually, I became just skin and bones. None of my acquaintances would have recognized me then. After a while, it became difficult even to get up from the mat I was lying on. The moment I started weaving I would get drenched in sweat. Once the jail authorities brought in a female doctor and she prescribed some vitamin tablets. I was given milk and eggs on the superintendent's order. They must have thought that I would die soon if left untended.

The heart wrenching condition of the other inmates made me more depressed since I could do nothing to alleviate their pain. I couldn't decide which of them had the most pathetic life story. They had landed up in jail convicted for theft, murder, country liquor trade and prostitution.

Lucy Chechi was the first woman sentenced to death after the Kerala state was reorganized in 1956. Since the Kerala Government decided not to award death for women, her sentence was later reduced to a life term. Lucy Chechi was born into a middle class Christian family and was mentally disturbed even at a young age. She underwent treatment whenever she grew sick. It would be assuaged temporarily. Still, it was not treated completely so that she could lead a normal life. But no marriage proposals came her way. So, she was forced to become the second wife of the headmaster of her own school. His first wife was no more. He had four grown up children from the earlier marriage. She might not have been happy with this marriage. Later, she too had four children. Fights broke out between the husband and wife over money and Lucy Chechi returned to her parental home. It was said that the headmaster used to get drunk and beat her up during the night.

Apparently, a month before the incident Lucy Chechi's younger brother was beaten up by her husband and her brother-in-law. All this might have distressed her disturbed mind. One morning she hacked to death her husband, his two children from the first marriage, and two of her own children. Then she stuffed the body of her eight-month-old baby in her handbag and went to the priest for confession. Horrified, the priest informed the police. The police thrashed her up, and arrested her younger brother too. These murders were heinous and most incredible. I believe that the killings of her own children only proved that she was out of her mind. No mother in her senses would kill her own children whom she had brought to this world. She used to sit alone, laugh and mutter to herself in jail, and sometimes fought with others whom she didn't like. She never did any work. The female wardens used to bash her up for no rhyme or reason knowing very well that her complaints would never be taken seriously. One day at dawn, before the cells of others were even opened, two female wardens came in with a group of other life timers and two-three other healthy prisoners. They beat up Lucy Chechi mercilessly. We could hear her shrieks of pain, and after a while the cries stopped and she collapsed. For weeks she walked with great difficulty, dragging her swollen legs. We could do nothing, but shed silent tears. A priest came every Sunday to hear the confessions of Christian prisoners. Lucy Chechi used to tell him her sorrows. But he had made it plain that he could only help her with his advice and nothing more. This was one incident that agonized and infuriated me.

Another couple had ended up in jail for killing a goon, who lived in their neighbourhood. The couple wasn't rich but they somehow had managed to save money and buy some land and build a small house there. They had two girls aged 12 and 8, and one boy of 10. The local thug had been bothering them for long before they ended up killing him while defending themselves. They sold their land, and worked day and night to raise the lawyer's fee. Law stated that murders committed for self-defence would not be punished. The same applied here. But it had to be proved in court. An eminent lawyer can make murders look like mistakes and vice versa. The husband and the wife were given life terms. One could only imagine the plight of their young children. The Government had no responsibility towards them. When you are punishing both the parents aren't you punishing the innocent children as well?

Another couple was convicted for murdering a man over a property dispute. The husband had killed the man in a fit of rage. But someone advised the wife that women had better chances of getting acquitted. So she owned up the crime along with her husband. Though they spent a considerable amount of money on the case, both of them were sentenced to life. They had three daughters. No one did anything to support these children. The couple spent their days in jail counting every second.

I had seen several women who had killed their children before they tried to commit suicide. These women would have taken this extreme step because of abject poverty, humiliation or familial discord. They wanted their children to die with them since they felt that there would be no one to look after them once they were gone. But as fate would have it, mostly the children died and the women were saved. The mother would be left alive to lead a life of guilt and remorse. But they too are the victims of our rotten social order. Some of the girls in jail were teenagers of 15 and 18. They ought to be sent to juvenile homes. But since there was no such institution for girls in Kerala they remained in jail.

The Government claims that the prisoners are sent to jail to get reformed. But from what I saw, the result was just the opposite. A person convicted for a petty theft would leave the prison as a master smuggler. He would meet experts in jail capable of imparting the 'right' kind of training. The same was true for girls caught for prostitution. An innocent girl tricked by her lover and betrayed would find a whole new world of opportunities opening before her as she entered the jail. She would come out as a full-fledged prostitute. There is nothing left in our culture and society to lead these young minds away from such perilous paths. Eight years of prison life reiterated my belief that along with a political revolution that would overthrow the economic foundation of the present social set up, a revolution was vital the cultural front too, one that could stop the venomous influences over our youth.

I had referred to the story of Thankamma earlier, she was arrested under MISA just before the Emergency was imposed. Her husband was in Singapore, who according to Thankamma was a tailor. The case against her was that of money laundering along with her husband. Since the police couldn't get hold of her husband, they arrested Thankamma. She had a son and a daughter. She was over 50, and diabetic. She was given C-grade food and forced to sleep on the floor. I had great sympathy for her then. The wardens looked at her with utter contempt. But gradually all this changed. She was given better food, and a bed to sleep. She was even permitted to go on parole. She too was under severe restrictions and not allowed to speak to anyone. But after a while she used to spend hours talking to other inmates and the wardens turned a blind eye to it. Thankamma proved to be a pain, when she stared spying on me, informing the wardens about anyone who tried to talk to me. This led to endless fights between her and me. Thankamma had bought the friendship of the wardens. And, money mattered a lot in prison.

The female wardens were a frustrated lot like all other government employees. They were neglected most of the times. So, they tried to supplement their meagre income by grabbing the ration meant for prisoners. They also fought among themselves for the ration. They gave vent to all their frustrations and hostilities against their senior officials and colleagues by bashing up the prisoners. The senior wardens were a little softer, but they never went out of their way to express their humane side.

These atrocities took a toll on me. Gradually, I lost interest in weaving. Almost every day, I somehow finished my work, and went back to my cell to sleep. I would even forget to read the papers. On September 9, 1976, I heard the news of Mao's death on the radio. It was as if a sinking boat was suddenly tossed into a tumultuous sea.

30

THE DEATH OF MAO AND THE MARCH ELECTIONS

Mao was dead. The brilliant sun that lit up our world and led us through the path of righteousness had set. Would the world be the same ever again? His death was a great blow to me. I wore a black badge on September 11 challenging the authorities. They asked me to remove it, but I told them that I was ready to die for it. It was my birthright to join the mourners all over world for we had lost Mao's life, which was heavier than the Tai mountains. Let them beat me up, kill me. But I wouldn't remove the badge, I decided. I wore the badge till the time the cells were locked. On October 6, I came to know that Mao's wife comrade Chiang Ching, and three other revolutionaries who were called the sons of the Cultural Revolution — Chang Chunchio, Yavo Ven Yuvan, Wang Hung Wen — were all arrested. This news shocked me and I got even more depressed. Never had Mao arrested any party members, even after the victory of the revolution in 1949 or before it. Even during the Cultural Revolution no leader was arrested. But all this happened the moment Mao closed his eyes. I lost all interest in life.

On October 25, I refused food. I informed the superintendent about my decision. He asked for an explanation, but I refused to give him any. He was furious, but he left without uttering a word. He asked me to be locked up in my cell. He ordered that I should be escorted by the head warden even while going to the toilet. I was not worried. To be frank, I myself didn't know why I was refusing food. The next day morning even before the head warden came to take the count of prisoners I threw up five-six times. What was the use of not eating? They told me that they would force food in through the nose. Years before in Kozhikode and Kannur jail we had fasted for a cause and had attained success in spite of the government's efforts to spoil it. Mao's words had given us strength then. But this fasting had no meaning. There was nothing to gain from it either. I made up a story that the fast was meant to get a transfer to Kannur jail Anyway, the next day I resumed my meals.

I was locked up again for five days. After that I was never asked to go for weaving and I discontinued it altogether. But that didn't improve my health. I never ever left my cell. I was mentally broken. Still I didn't think of signing a deal with the Government to escape prison. I never had any doubt about the ideology of revolution. I was only worried that the movement had lost its vigour and that the revolution as we had envisaged it would not be a reality in the near future.

In January 1977, Indira Gandhi declared elections in March, and released Morarji, Jaya Prakash and other leaders from jail. I considered this as just another of her ploys. We had heard enough stories about rigging of elections by the Government to believe that something similar would not happen again. But the election result stunned everybody. The Marxist party and its allies were pathetically defeated in Kerala where they were expected to win with a comfortable majority. But all over the northern states Janata Party was leading. The Marxist party's performance in other states was better than what it expected. The Congress swept all the states south of the Vindhyas, but was completely routed in the Gangetic plains. Congress was defeated in all those constituencies, which it had maintained since the transfer of power in August 15, 1947.

A commission of enquiry constituted by the Janata government had later found that Congress had rigged the election held in West Bengal in 1971. The Marxist leaders had shed tears in 1971 itself about this rigging. In 1977, elections to the assembly and Parliament were held together in Kerala. The Marxist leaders who had blamed their defeat on rigging during the Kerala Assembly elections held in the shadow of Emergency in 1977 were simultaneously delighted about their increased number of seats in Parliament. Even revolutionary leaders behaved as if their politics was nothing but a means for acquiring Parliamentary and Assembly seats. They could have exposed the fraud involved in this election, but were satisfied by the crumbs of power that came their way, and remained silent. They too became part of a larger game that hoodwinked the world and the people of India into believing that revolution happened through votes.

But what had happened behind the scenes? In March 1976, a branch of the World Bank called Aid India Consortium met at a conference in Tokyo to decide on the extent of financial aid to India. It is relevant to mention a discussion that took place there. The newspapers reported that some member nations had voiced their protest against giving financial aid to countries ruled by autocrats where elections were not held at all. McNamara, the then president of the World Bank came to visit India just after that conference. This was the time when Sanjay Gandhi was enforcing the brutal family planning scheme as advised by McNamara.

The people who had at first relented without much protest to the Emergency declaration were slowly gathering power. The Turkman Gate incident in Delhi, where people put up a resistance to the bulldozers of Sanjay Gandhi, sent to knock down their huts is now famous. The imperial powers were worried that their exploits would come up against a wall of people's protest. Though Indira had enforced a police Raj in India, messages from countries like Vietnam prodded her on to view issues differently.

The members of the Aid India Consortium felt it was better to put on a mask of Parliamentary democracy and put pressure on Indira Gandhi through McNamara. It was just two weeks after his visit that Indira Gandhi ordered fresh elections. No one had any doubts about the outcome of the elections. Indira Gandhi had in her control all devices of the Constitution. The leaders of Parliamentary parties were released from jail. They went out to the fields with the promises of a total revolution and democratic rule. These leaders vouched to repeal the Emergency and internal security laws, to release from jail all political prisoners, especially the Naxalites, and to re-establish democratic rights. The imperial powers knew that it was impossible for Indira now to carry on the role of a democratic ruler. So, they used these leaders who had the halo of sacrifice around them, for their selfish ends. Thus Janata Party won a majority much to the surprise of the nation. A stunned Indira talked of handing over the rule to the army. The army refused as if everything had been planned. There was no other instance in the history of India when the army turned down orders from its rulers. What did all this mean? If we think about it, isn't it clear that the masters realized that Indira and her cronies had done their bit and now the need was for a new set of servants to create a new wave of dreams for the people. They have done this many a time in other nations too. Once their need is over they get rid of their dependents. America had pulled a fast one to defeat their devoted man Godin Diem in South Vietnam. C.I.A's role in his defeat is well known now. The truth behind Indira Gandhi's defeat might take many more years to reveal itself. But it did create a false hope in the minds of people, and even among those who believed in revolution.

Indira revoked the Emergency before she lost power. The ban on certain organizations including the C.P.I (M.L) was revoked. Thousands of prisoners who were arrested under MISA and COFEPOSA were released. Lots of Naxalites too were set free. But even after Morarji assumed power on March 24, there were comrades arrested under MISA who languished in various jails all over India. My parents were set free along with hundreds of other comrades. That was when stories of brutality came to light. The shocking facts about police atrocities after the Kayanna police station attack, and heinous crimes of Kakkayam camp were brought out. It was here Rajan, a Regional Engineering College student was brutally murdered. The stories of how its youth was snuffed out marred the very soul of Kerala. No one could speak about these things during the Emergency. People were happy that democracy was restored.

Another interesting incident opened the eyes of those who believed that Indira was serving the interest of the Soviet Union. From the very day Indira stepped down and Morarji ascended to power, the Soviet Union began praising Morarji. It had always applauded the policies of Indira Gandhi, even the Emergency. But suddenly the Soviet Union did a somersault. They too found Indira a wooden doll, who lisped and laughed according to America's orders. Too often Indira had wailed that a foreign power had pulled the strings of her defeat. She could never reveal its name, because she had been at their service all the while she was in power.

Something happened in our women's block before the Emergency was revoked. Thankamma was taken to the Velloor women's jail in Tamil Nadu. The government had decided to proceed with the cases of those arrested under COFEPOSA. So, there were cases against Thankamma and these were for crimes committed in Madras (now Chennai). So, she had to be taken to Velloor for trial. This transfer was very painful for her. Till then, she had led a relatively easy life in jail. Her relatives used to come for interview often, and she was even sent out on parole. Though she had tried her best to make my life intolerable, I was upset with this callous attitude of the government. It was cruel to kick an old woman around. But, she was released once the Emergency was revoked.

All of us were happy when the Emergency and Indira's brutal rule finally ended. I was joyous that my parents were out of jail. They sent me a telegram informing me that they would soon come to Thiruvananthapuram. All this had a positive impact on me. I was saved before I reached the bottom of the abyss of despair from where there would have been no return.

31

PERSUASION

One of the most important poll promises of the Janata Party and its allies was the unconditional release of political prisoners. The majority of these prisoners put in jail all over the country were thousands of revolutionaries. Some of them were arrested and put behind bars without as much as a sham of a trial, some were given death penalty, and still others had nothing to look forward to, but only a long uncertain wait. There were numerous comrades under pre-emptive custody. Most of them had a miserable existence in jail, locked up in one-room cells, their hands and feet chained. The callous treatment of the comrades by the Government was nothing less than what the Shah of Iran did to his prisoners or what American prisoners suffered in South Vietnam prisons that became notorious as "the dens." All over North India, especially in West Bengal and Bihar the comrades who were suspected to be Naxalites went through hell. This was not due to the Emergency. Even in 1967, at the time of the Naxalbari Movement the comrades had undergone similar horrifying experiences.

I feel that even the British, prior to the transfer of power in 1947, did not treat the Communists the way our Government brutalized the Naxalites. Why did the central and state governments, whatever their ideologies were, consider the revolutionaries their common enemy? The answer is only this:

Lenin had once said that if revolution succeeded in countries like India and China the existing economic order of the world would be left to rot. The majority of the world's population is concentrated in these countries and revolution in these countries would put an end to imperialism since its very existence is based on exploitation of colonial and semi colonial countries. Therefore, the imperialists had to put down these threatening forces with an iron hand. Even the minutest awakening could gather force in course of time. The imperialists could not stop the Revolution in Russia and China. It is evident from the temporary backlashes of the Revolution in these countries that even a successful revolution would only make the anti-revolutionary forces stronger, and their counter attacks more bitter. The imperialists have learned their essential lessons from these revolutions. In a way, that comes easy to them than to the forces of revolution. Since they are in the cockpit of the world order they get information faster, and through analysis take further steps to anticipate and defeat the attempts of the revolutionary forces. They even resort to menial ways for this. They crawl into the folds of the party and try to ruin or divide the movement. Their slogans would be more high-pitched than that of the real revolutionary. The real revolutionary party should fight against and defeat these forces that try to weaken the party from within.

In India too, things were not different. On one side were the brutal attempts of the enemy to suppress the Revolution and on the other side were the clandestine moves to lead the movement astray from within the party under the cover of fiery slogans.

Once the Janata Government came to power they forgot their promise to release the revolutionaries unconditionally. There were talks of conditional release. A section of the revolutionaries were party to the government's deception. Satyanarayan Singh and some other party members of the Marxist-Leninist party were involved in negotiations with Home Minister Charan Singh regarding the release of the revolutionaries. Satyanarayan Singh urged the revolutionaries to sign a pact with the Government, which said that they don't believe in armed revolutions anymore and that they would never again engage in armed conflict. Could there be anything more disdainful to suggest to the comrades who were languishing in jail? Most of the comrades rejected his appeal outright. There was nothing more humiliating than to bargain their ideology to end their sufferings in jail.

Two *sarvodaya* members came to Thiruvananthapuram Prison as part of a campaign for converting us. The Government had asked them to find out how many comrades in jail were ready to forgo the path of revolution for their release. Most of the comrades were not willing to surrender to the government except Philip. M. Prasad who was also serving a life sentence for his participation in the Thalassery-Pulpally case. He was ready to pay any price for his freedom from jail. But that was least surprising since he had already showed his true colours and was treated as a B class prisoner with all facilities while the others faced immense torture for the sake of their ideology.

In June 1977, after surveying the comrades, two *sarvodaya* workers — M.P. Manmadan and Ramachandran Potty came to me. They sat on chairs in the big hall in the women's block and I sat on a chair opposite to them. I could guess why they were here. From the days of the Telengana uprising till date whenever the peasants rose up for their rights, Gandhians toured those places with their *sarvodaya* mantras.

They started off with the preface that they had come to check out if there was any change in my stand since they had heard that there has been a change in attitude among Naxalites. They promised that they would keep the conversation a secret. I asked them again if they would tell the Government about my opinion and they said, "No, we would never reveal this to anyone." I knew that this was just another *sarvodaya* lie. I told them that I didn't care if anyone has changed his mind. As for me, I still believed in the ideology of Marxism-Leninism. At the end of my eight years in jail I still considered that only an armed revolution would help solve the basic problems of the exploited classes in India. Thirty years of peaceful agitations had only worsened the situation. Gandhi's disciples were a little taken aback. People should take up weapons for their rights and only that would provide a lasting solution, I said with determination and their faces fell. They argued again to confuse me, but I was firm. Finally, they folded their chairs and withdrew.

After some days, another important visitor came to see me. I was called to the office of the jail superintendent. The visitor was N.E. Balaram, the state secretary of LDF. I could guess his intention. My parents had told me that Philip M. Prasad was out on a long parole then and that in all possibility the parole would get extended. Balaram told me that Philip had been to him several times and that he wanted to be active in politics once he was out of jail. It was on his insistence that Balaram was visiting me. I was quite firm with him. Thalassery-Pulpally case was under the jurisdiction of Kozhikode Sessions Court and so the convicts should normally be sent to Kannur jail. Still, the Government had transferred Philip to Thiruvananthapuram to facilitate easy access to his family. And, they had sent me 400 miles away from my family stating security reasons. The charges against us were the same, and still the government had singled me out. "How could I trust you when your Government had treated me with such hostility just because I had stuck to my ideology?" I asked him. I was prepared to be in jail for any number of years. I wanted no sympathizers. He decided not to waste his time, and went back promising me to send some Soviet publications, which quite expectedly, he never did.

I understood that the Government was keen on setting Philip free. It was time for chief minister A.K. Anthony to seek votes for his by-elections to the assembly. He had taken over the reins of Government after Chief Minister K Karunakaran had to resign over police brutalities during the Emergency, particularly against Naxalites. Karunakaran had to step down because as the then Home Minister he was held responsible for the murder of a Naxalite Rajan, a student of the Regional Engineering College. All over India, the Janata Government kept on releasing small groups of political prisoners. They had to do it if they had to maintain their veneer of decency. Anthony too needed some sort of a political stunt to win his Kazhakkoottam by-poll seat. Anthony became Chief Minister only because of popular anger and judicial intervention in cases of Karunakaran's brutalities against Naxalites and in such a surcharged atmosphere he had to contest elections too. But there was a problem in releasing Philip and a few others who had lost their revolutionary fervour. Some of the convicts of the Thalassery-Pulpally case were in jail for the last nine years. I was in jail for eight years, whereas Philip had spent hardly four and a half years in jail. To set Philip free when others were still in jail would do only more harm than good to Anthony. I had become a pain in the neck for them, and this predicament prolonged the Government's decision.

On July 15, a letter to the editor from Philip was published in the *Mathrubhumi* with a prominent headline. It said that Philip had written it from the prison, though he was actually out on parole those days. In that letter Philip had expressed his decadent views on the similarity between Gandhism and Marxism. His acceptance of Jaya Prakash Narayanan in a way demeaned the whole revolutionary movement. He had set the stage for his release. He stooped to such levels to get his release and worse, he even dragged down his comrades along with him. He lied that the majority of the comrades were ready to move away from the path of revolution. Philip was a torturer who had never lost an opportunity to harass his comrades by manipulating the authorities. But an ordinary reader of the *Mathrubhumi* daily would never know all this. This letter proved to be what Anthony was looking for. The Government now had a way out of its dilemma. So, it was decided that 20 of the Naxalites including me would be released from jail.

32

FREEDOM

I had mentioned earlier that my parents were released from prison along with other MISA detainees on March 24, 1977. After their first visit to the Thiruvananthapuram Prison they sent a petition to the then Chief Minister A.K. Anthony. This was after the Janata Party government took over, when there was a lot of public proclamations by politicians about the basic necessity to change the attitude towards political prisoners. My parents requested in the petition that they were not keeping well and had severe financial crisis and therefore either to transfer me to Kannur jail or to allot them transport passes to visit me in Thiruvananthapuram Jail. It was said that Anthony was not a bloodsucker like Karunakaran. He was known to be a man of principles with a kind heart to match. My parents were hopeful about the outcome. They got a message from the Chief Minister's office that he had received the petition and that it was under consideration. But nothing happened for months.

We lost all hopes about a transfer. On July 19, an old family friend, who was also a renowned journalist working in Thiruvananthapuram called on my parents in Kozhikode. He wanted to talk about their petition to the C.M. He explained to them that it would not be a problem to shift me back to Kannur, but providing them pass could give rise to controversy. He advised them that still it was better to request for parole, and it wouldn't be a difficult process. My parents rejected that idea. Two people had to stand surety if one had to get parole. More than that, after the parole you have to go back to the jail again. Once you were out of jail, you wouldn't want to go back in there again. That would create a dilemma for me too, and I might even think of saving myself from the sufferings of incarceration, even it meant signing on whatever papers the Government offered me. The offer of parole was a trap, and we didn't want to walk into it.

On July 20, somebody called up my mother. The phone call was made to my uncle's radio repair shop. That person left a message and a phone number saying that the call was from the *Deshabhimani*, the mouthpiece of the Marxist Party. The caller wanted to convey a message about Ajitha's release from jail, and so, my mother was to return the call immediately. My parents found out that that the number was not that of *Deshabhimani* and they didn't return the call. Half an hour later, someone called up again. My father then called back on the number, and realized that it was from the LDF office in Kozhikode. He said that he doubted that my parents might not call back if it was revealed the call was from LDF's office. They were told that I would be released at 10 a.m. the next day (July 21) and that N.E. Balaram would receive me at the gate. My parents went mad. Who was N.E. Balaram to pick me up at the gate? He was not even an acquaintance, and far from a family friend or a political companion. My father told the L.D.F secretary: "Just inform N.E. Balaram right away that Ajitha's parents are still alive and they would receive their daughter at the gate."

I was unaware of all these developments. I never expected the government to release me from jail because I was not ready for a quid pro quo. The radio news bulletin had announced the Government's decision to free 20 Naxalites, but that evening, the jail radio was silent.

I came to know about it from the head warden who came with my breakfast. Philip got his parole cancelled and was back in jail on the 20th evening.

The Janata governments that came to power in various north Indian states, though they went back on their promise of unconditional release, continued to release groups of political prisoners with much hype. Even then, the man of principles at the helm of the Kerala government didn't budge. The L.D.F had led a crusade for the release of the revolutionaries, but that didn't make any difference, despite the fact that CPI and others were part of the ruling Government. After months of deliberation the Government released just 20 of us! Even now 55 comrades are still languishing in jail labeled as Naxalites. This release was merely for the sake of Kazhakkoottam by-election. Later, the government re-iterated that it would never set free any other Naxalite.

On the morning of July 21 my father and mother reached the Central Prison. They were relieved to know that I was still inside. The jail superintendent told them that I would be released by the evening. The jail authorities were yet to get the order of release from the secretariat. My parents requested for an interview with me. I was briefed on what had happened in the past days. Now, I looked forward to my freedom from jail. The other inmates were happy for me. They asked me not to forget them and to tell the world outside about their sufferings in jail. How could I forget those poor souls who were counting every second of their lives in jail? My relief was that I had suffered for my ideology, and that actually had become my strength while they had no such consolation.

At 4.30 in the evening I heard the gates being opened with a bang. The wardens told that the I.G had come. Two men convicts set a table and two chairs in the hall. The I.G. cam in, escorted by the superintendent and seeing me holding a bundle of belongings asked me: "What is all this?"

"I heard that I am being released."

"What is the hurry? Shouldn't we get the order?" He asked me. I didn't understand what he meant.

Later, he called me to the hall. We sat across the table. He told me that the cabinet had decided to release some prisoners, but that would take some more time. I asked him whether there were any conditions for the release.

"Nothing that I heard of. Of course, you might need to sign on the usual papers of release. But, that's not any government paper. It's for our official records." He said softly.

The prisoners who were released for good conduct after the advisory board's recommendation were required to sign on a paper, and that was what he was hinting to me. "It's just a formality. Nothing political about it." He added again.

For a second, I was confused. Should I sign on the paper? The Government seemed hell-bent on getting me to sign some paper or the other. I was naturally looking forward to my freedom from jail. It was easier at this moment to think that a perfunctory signature on their official records wouldn't do any harm, and I had a world out there waiting for me. But I restrained myself. I oughtn't do anything against what I had already decided.

"I won't sign on any paper. I don't care even if I have to be in jail for the rest of my life for this reason," I told him.

He didn't like my reply, but didn't demonstrate any signs of anger or disappointment, and continued with his friendly conversation. These officials, well versed in diplomacy are so adept at hiding their emotions that, he even talked about politics. He wanted to brainwash me out of my ideology. He didn't forget to give me a piece of advice before he left — 'don't make any more trouble.' I knew for sure that the Government was scared of letting me free.

There was no sign of my release all through the 22nd morning. At 5.30 in the evening the jailer came to the women's cell and informed me: "Get ready to leave. We will get the order now." At 7.30 p.m. I crossed the gate of the women's cell to go to the office. My father and my mother were waiting for me. As I reached the jailer's room, I could hear him talking to the Home Secretary over the phone: "Sir, we are releasing her, hope there wouldn't be any problem." After a second he turned towards me and said: "You are released." I collected the money that I was to get from the office and went to meet my parents. I could see Philip and the others being taken to the office while I walked out of the gate. We went to our friend's place in Thiruvananthapuram. It was late, and we decided to stay the night there.

The next morning we started our journey. Somehow people at the Thiruvananthapuram transport bus stand got to know about our presence, and there soon was a crowd around the bus. But, the bus started within ten minutes. At 8.30 we reached Adoor, where the bus had a breakdown. We had to wait for two hours before resuming the journey.

People gathered around the bus in Adoor too. We didn't get down from the bus. They asked us all sorts of questions, whether we were coming from jail, how many others were released with me, how many others were still in jail, and most importantly whether I signed a pact with the Government. I told them that I had not signed on any papers. That got me their appreciation. The place looked like some festive ground with people from the town and the nearby villages streaming in to see us. Traffic was blocked. A woman from the L.D.F office nearby came to invite us to their office, which we politely turned down. Two constables arrived to control the crowd. I was taken aback by this show of camaraderie and love. I wouldn't have been able to face them had I signed on the dotted lines of the government conditions. Those two hours in Adoor proved that revolutionary politics always succeeded to strike a chord in the hearts of the downtrodden.

After that, wherever the bus stopped people greeted us warmly. In Thrissur a group of labourers gave me a handful of sweets. "This is our humble gift. Please accept it," they said. Even the co-travellers seemed to get affected by these expressions of love and respect. The bus journey lasted for about 12 hours, and it inspired me further to stick to the path of armed revolution. The people pining for revolution reminded me of my duty again, to uphold Mao's thoughts all through my life.

33

LOOKING BACK

A phase of my life, which was an inseparable part of a turbulent decade in the history of India and the world when the great revolutionary movement inspired millions of people to sacrifice themselves for a greater human cause, ended with my release from jail.

Still, the question remains, what is my motive for these reminiscences? I wanted to reiterate my commitment to my ideology through an open declaration, and also to make known to the public many hitherto unknown facets of the movement, things that others had always tried to hide or cover up. What I have attempted is to project the images deeply imprinted on my mind. Naturally, there could be errors. Some things have slipped out of my mind; some others may not be accurate. I have not written this to hurt or offend anyone. Still, if I have hurt anyone in the process of describing an event or anybody's role in it I ask for forgiveness. I thank all those well-wishers who read the memoirs when it was serialized in a periodical, and encouraged and supported me.

Some people have asked me: "What did these ten years of your life earn you? Isn't Communism done with even in China?"

The enemies of Revolution argue that that the onward march of the working class' Revolution since the Paris Commune of 1871 has ended with the beginning of a process of re-establishment of capitalism in China. Both international and local forces campaign that the changes that have been taking over China after the death of Mao prove that Communism is just a utopian dream. Let's see how far these arguments are true.

These forces had celebrated the brutal suppression of the Paris Commune too, and thought that Communism would never raise its head again. But they panicked when Russian working class revolution marking the end of the First World War became a success. All attempts made by the western countries to suppress the Russian Revolution through external attacks failed. Then they decided to weaken it from within. When all doors of victory are firmly fastened in the time of socialist reforms, the enemy strikes at the leadership trying to demoralize the movement. That's what Mao, the great had observed in Yugoslavia regarding Tito's experience. The vanquished bourgeoisie would never admit defeat even for a second, and the resistance would gather force with every defeat, Lenin had pointed out. We can spot the power of this class in the small entrepreneurial linkages across the nation and in the resilient feudal mores and prejudices. The attempts to overthrow the working class government from within began to show signs of success with the assumption of power by Khrushchev in 1956. It was the top leadership of Communism, which initiated the rebuilding of capitalism in Russia. The communist party of China and Mao who were trying to set up socialism in their country after the victory of the revolution in 1949 studied the reasons behind the Russian coup. They didn't want a re-establishment of communism in China, and pondered how to steer clear of it. Mao analysed the events that took place from the setting up of the Paris Commune in 1871 in the light of Marxism-Leninism, and arrived upon a strategy to stop the re-establishment of Capitalism — that was the beginning of the great Cultural Revolution of the working class which went down straight to the soul of the common people.

It aimed at making the people aware of the changing hues of the Communist Party leadership and its attempts at establishing the bourgeoisie clout instead of the supremacy of the working class. He wanted to further ignite the spirit of revolution through struggles against corrupt leadership and a greater study of ideology. The public had the right and responsibility to supervise leaders and criticize and evaluate them. Leadership is inevitable for any movement or class. But history teaches us that disloyal and selfish leaders lead to severe setbacks to the movement. Mao unleashed the Cultural Revolution for the first time in the history of the working class to solve this paradoxical nature of the leadership. The essence of the Cultural Revolution was its slogan: "Bomb the headquarters!" But Mao never believed that the Cultural Revolution would forever wipe off re-establishment of capitalism. He had reiterated that all through the years of socialist reform, classes, class paradoxes and class struggles would remain and hence, the importance of a continued working class Cultural Revolution in all walks of life. He had pointed out the need for at least 20 to 30 revolutions before the world could achieve the communist order. So, he had asked each Chinese working for the good of the working class to give priority to ushering in a World Revolution than to the modernization of his own country.

The tide of revolution did create in the mind of revolutionaries an illusion of ultimate triumph. They believed that capitalism would never be restored in China, where the first Cultural Revolution had taken place. I too thought the same. The military coup that took place in China immediately after Mao's death was a severe shock to all revolutionaries including me. How was such a coup possible in the Chinese party, rendered pure by the flames of the Cultural Revolution? It was unbelievable and it hurt. I watched the despicable resurrection of Deng Xiao Ping in horror. Still, aren't there enough events in the world today to prove that the victory of these regressive powers is only momentary?

In 1848, Marx and Engels declared to the world in the Communist Manifesto: "The Communists disdain to conceal their views and aims. They openly declare that their ends can be attained only by the forcible overthrow of all existing social conditions. Let the ruling classes tremble at a Communistic revolution. The proletarians have nothing to lose but their chains. They have a world to win. Working men of all countries, unite!"

For the last 130 years, till 1979 how many working class revolutions have gripped the world! 130 years is a very short span in the history of human civilization. The conversion of the world order from primitive communism to slavery to feudalism and then to capitalism has involved centuries of class struggles. No ruling class can be toppled in the first attempt. Any revolution will have to face several set backs and restorations before the final victory. But there is a fundamental difference in the revolution of the working class. Earlier, all revolutions were aimed at pulling down an exploiting class to enthrone another class of exploiters. But the working class revolutions aim at obliterating the very system of exploitation. So, all exploiting classes have to come together to oppose their common enemy. Therefore, the path forward is particularly difficult for the revolutionaries. The revolutionary fervour of the Paris Commune of 1871 was not enough for the Russian revolutionaries of 1917. The bourgeoisie learns its lessons faster than the revolutionaries, and does its homework well. The revolutionaries of China had to absorb new knowledge in the light of the Russian Revolution to lead their mission to success. The revolutionary spirit of the working class of 1949 was not sufficient to take on Khrushchev's reformism. The Revolution movement ought to have analysed the negative impact of Russia's socialism and continued its struggles for working class supremacy throughout the period of socialist reformation. Today, the working class should learn its lessons from the temporary setbacks in China after Mao's death. Only such a working class could consummate any sort of revolution in the future.

In our homeland, there has never been a situation more conducive to revolution. The political parties, which are part of the established order and the country's economic order, have all begun to rot. The mask of Parliamentarism has fallen off, revealing what it really is. I conclude quoting Marx: "Proleterian revolution, like those of the 19th century, constantly criticize themselves, constantly interrupt themselves in their course, return to the apparently accomplished, in order to begin anew; they deride with cruel thoroughness the half measures, weaknesses, and paltriness of their first attempts, seem to throw down their opponents only so the latter may draw new strength from the earth and rise before them again more gigantic than ever, recoil constantly from the indefinite colossalness of their goals – until a situation is created which makes all turning back impossible, and the conditions themselves call out: hic rhodus, hic salta (here is the rose, here is (your) jump)".

APPENDIX
WE HAVE RISEN IN REVOLT!

We, the workers of Ganesh, Bharat beedi factories, weavers, estate labour, farm workers, students and teachers, have lost all hope in peaceful protests and set out on a path of armed revolt against the beastly system of exploitation that exists today. We have declared a class war against the Government propped up by forces of feudalism and big capital.

We know that Prime Minister Indira Gandhi and Chief Minister EMS Namputhiripad have millions of soldiers, the most modern weaponry of the imperialist forces and the Soviet reactionary clique behind them. We raise the blood red flag of armed revolt fully aware of what we are confronting.

Our great leader Mao had said in 1946, "All reactionaries are mere paper tigers. They appear to be giants, but they are not all that strong. If we look at them from a distance, we can make out that real strength lies not with reactionaries but with the people."

It is this understanding that gives us confidence for such a venture. We depend on the crores of our people for our success, particularly the peasant masses of our villages. We are completely dependent on our allies, the ninety per cent of the country's population, whom we know are longing to destroy the semi-colonial, semi-feudal system that has made their lives miserable. We have now revolted, after all means of our lives' sustenance were barred.

Our people have a tradition of innumerable worker-peasant struggles. This is the land that turned red with the martyrdom of innumerable peasant comrades. We once again raise the glorious red banner made deep crimson by the warm blood of those comrades. This is not to repeat 1948, nor Telengana, nor Punnapra-Vayalar. Then, we have set forth to learn the lessons of the defeats of those valiant struggles, and to launch a long and tortuous 'people's war' under the leadership of the working class and through a peasant's revolution to demolish the imperial-feudal-comprador capitalist system and to replace that gradually with a new democratic system based on the alliance of workers and peasants. The great people of China have shown us the way; the historic armed revolt of the people of Vietnam against the imperialist and reactionary forces, and the struggles of crores of people of Asia, Africa and Latin America only prove this path right. The brave Nagas and Mizos of our country and the revolutionaries of Naxalbari lead us in this direction. The reactionary ruling class has left us with no other option.

There would be some who doubt our apparent lack of strength; others might unleash a campaign to label us adventurers, but we will soon prove them all wrong. Our real strength lies in the crores of our allies in the villages. We are leaving our home and hearth for villages to seek that great force, carrying openly the banner of armed revolt. We will join forces with our peasant allies and together we will fight a life and death battle against our enemies, and gaining strength we will return. No one should have any doubt about it. All our class siblings, friends and relatives, whom we bid adieu today, can surely expect our return. Our pathfinder in this great venture is Maoism; the great Mao is with us. Let all reactionaries including those who have adorned the masks of coordinating revolutionaries, revisionist leaders and class betrayers like Dange take this as their last warning! Their death toll has begun. The winds of revolution have begun blowing in our land.

Worker comrades, peasant comrades, students, revolutionary intellectuals, small traders, toiling women, pick up a stick, an axe, sickle, hammer or whatever else, in your hands that you have for years used only to vote; march on for the last battle with the oppressive government; lie low and snatch the enemy's guns and all his other weapons. We have become an armed force now; a force that belongs to you, join up in thousands and ten thousands with this "people's army"! Let the flames of revolution spread all over! These flames will burn down the enemy to ashes.

Victory is only ours!

— Revolutionaries of the Indian Communist Party

(The declaration made just before the revolts of Thalassery and Pulpally on November 22 and 23, 1968)

35

EPILOGUE

It was as if my father was waiting to edit the last page of my memoirs. He didn't wait even a single day; he developed severe chest pain and cold and was admitted to the cardiology ward of Kozhikode Medical College. He had suffered a severe blow on his chest during one of the many strikes in jail, which left him a heart patient ever after. Our financial condition didn't permit us to seek any specialist treatment and father could not even think of accepting favours from anyone. We were so poor that even food was scarce.

Á month earlier MA had left for Mumbai to be with my critically ill grandmother, whom I called 'Ba'. Ma's presence made a difference and Ba was recuperating fast. Father didn't let me inform Ma of his illness. We will tell her once we get back home from hospital, he insisted. But later, as his condition worsened I called Ma back urgently. Father was taken to hospital on August 16, 1979 and he breathed his last on August 25. Ma and I were at his deathbed. My father's death was my life's biggest setback. His love, guidance and assurance had played a big role in shaping my perception of life.

Father had discouraged all talks and thoughts of marriage while I was involved in the movement. His attitude was: If my marriage meant harm to the movement, it was better that I remained unmarried. I was in love with comrade Varghese and wanted to marry him. Of course, we had never spoken about love, but both somehow understood that the feeling was mutual. Other comrades had confronted him with slanderous allegations of an affair. I came to know that though he had never admitted those charges of an affair, he had also not denied our friendship. We were together for just 10 days of the Pulpally action and the perilous retreat through the forest, thereafter. That was when I met him and was awestruck by his personality, commitment and his leadership. There was no opportunity to exchange any sentiments other than our revolutionary ardour. Twice he had come to meet me when I was out on bail; that was the time when he was underground, hiding from the police. Ma was with me on those two occasions. I had let Ma know of what I thought of comrade Varghese and she in turn had sounded it out with father. He was dead against the idea. "You'll not only ruin yourself, but also comrade Varghese, who is very important for the cause", were his exact words. For me, those words had the ring of finality. Later, comrade Varghese was captured and killed, that ended a short-lived dream.

I had stuck to father's decision all my life, but now after his death I felt insecure. Ma too was not keeping well. A friend had told me that mother's doctor had given her just five more years to live. They wouldn't have known about her zest for life and inner strength. She lived for many more years providing me all the support and courage. She passed away on 16 December 2006. But at that point in time I was in despair. I couldn't imagine living all alone in this big world with the whole society and even our relatives having turned hostile to our activities. That was when all the comrades including Yakoob decided to search for a life partner for me. But I couldn't accept their advice. I was against arranged marriages whether arranged by families or the party. Then one day I asked Yakoob if he would marry me. He was eight years younger to me. Moreover, he came from a Muslim family. He had many doubts and anxieties. But I was adamant. Finally, we got married with the help of comrades, friends and relatives. No garlands were exchanged, but we were declared man and wife. Later we registered our marriage under Special Marriage Act. This was on November 25, 1981.

After marriage we tried to get on with the activities of the group led by father. Gradually, the bond with the other members slackened. Still, we tried hard to bring out a magazine called 'The Red Guards'. After six issues that too stopped. On October 19,1982, Gargi was born. Our family, including Mother, Yakoob and me had moved out of my father's ancestral Kunnikkal house once we got our share of the property. We moved into comrade Vasu Ettan's house in Pottammal. Later, with his help we bought 20 cents of land at Thondayadu, and built a house. We moved in here when Gargi was around a year old. All this time, my mainstay was Kala Kaumudi magazine, which serialized my Memoirs, and later the royalty from D.C Books, the publishers who brought out the book. Also, my uncles in Mumbai used to sent us a small but sure amount every month. Those days Yakoob didn't have a regular job; he still devoted all his time for the movement.

Meanwhile, the world was changing. After Mao's death, China under the leadership of Deng Xiao Ping was hurtling towards capitalism. The Soviet Union had begun to shed even its communist-socialist mask. All the proclaimed socialist countries saw rebellions for democracy that were backed by the U.S.A. The nations of the world were slowly getting re-conditioned to a unipolar world under the US control. Globalization and the GAAT treaty were thrust upon the third world nations. Things were no different in India with Narasimha Rao at the helm of the Government.

After Gargi's birth, Yakoob's parents and family began to accept our marriage. His brother, Muhammad Ali who was working in Saudi Arabia was one person who had not opposed the marriage at all. Yakoob began to help his father in his business. I had nothing much to do. Ma brought up Gargi, literally. I was disturbed leading a placid life of a housewife, tending to my household chores and looking after the child. I did value that life, and my child gave me much contentment, still I could find myself asking this question to myself time and again: Is this really enough? Am I doing justice to my father who had wanted me to give my life to the society and revolution?

In 1985, I conceived again. Around that time I happened to read about the second national conference of feminist organizations that was to be held in Mumbai in December 1985, in a Malayalam magazine called "Padabhedam". I was eight months pregnant then, but with some friends prodding me on, I left for Mumbai and took part in that conference. This was a turning point in my life.

Our activities in the Marxist-Leninist movement had died a natural death. Yakoob was busy earning a livelihood. We were anyway against the activities of the group led by K. Venu, especially the pursuit of the annihilation theory of Charu Majumdar. But we identified to an extent with movements like People's Cultural Forum. The public trial of Dr. K.G. George, which was a protest against corrupt doctors of Kozhikode Medical College made us think differently. We came to the conclusion that such events had brought a change in the attitude of the people towards the M.L movement. But soon the murder of a landlord, Kenichira Mathai of Wayanad re-directed the course of the M.L movement; again declaring to the world that it held fast on to the annihilation doctrine. We could never be at peace with this political stream of thought.

I knew very well how the movement regarded its women. Those days I couldn't have related with feminist ideas, though in my memoirs I had pointed out many instances when I felt discriminated against for being a woman. The male comrades considered women as slaves and sex objects. Women were never involved in the decision making process. Usually, their opinions were scoffed at and rejected. Yet, those days I considered feminist movements as a means for sexual promiscuity for vain women. But my experience at the Mumbai conference changed my perception of feminism. All the fiery feminist leaders like Vibhuti Patel and Veena Shatrugna were actively involved in left movement for years. The oppression of women in families and society, the hierarchical power equations in man-woman relationships, the male dominated system and the attacks against women were the points of discussion there. Male domination has deep roots even in left movements. The need for autonomous women's liberation movements that could handle gender discrimination, exploitation and oppression without vested interests of any political factions or groups was re-iterated. Therefore even while generally accepting class struggles, there was a need to move away from left movements that totally ignored gender paradoxes.

I came back from Mumbai with the firm belief in changing the negative attitude of society towards women's issues in Kerala. I had decided to work for women's liberation movement from then on. But this didn't happen immediately. On February 14, 1986 Clint was born. I had to devote one whole year for him. I did attend The All India Women's Studies Conference in Chandigarh once. There I got an opportunity to meet and grow closer to Vibhuti Patel, the activists of Women's Centre of Mumbai, Forum For Oppression Against Women, and Vimochana of Bangalore. Slowly, I started looking at the world from a woman's point of view and started getting involved with their issues.

That was how 'Bhodhana' was formed in 1987. It was a small group that reacted dynamically to atrocities against women in families and outside, to dowry-deaths and suicides. We were just four or five of us, but we upheld the slogan 'Personal is Political' and got strongly involved in women's issues. We treated atrocities against women at all levels as political and questioned the male dominated system that ignored these issues as too trivial to be considered at societal or political spheres. The lock up murder of Kunjibi, the problems of the starving workers of Gwalior Rayons of Mavoor when it was locked out for three years, the societal boycott and humiliation of PT Usha after her disappointing performance in the Asian Games were all issues that Bhodhana took up. We could bring in a feminist dimension to all these issues.

Meanwhile there were many other women's organizations that had taken shape —— Manushi led by the celebrated writer Sarah Joseph, Prachodhana at Thiruvananthapuram, Chetana at Thrissur, Prabuddhatha at Payyannur were a few. This new wakening among women encouraged us to organize the fourth national Conference of Women's Liberation Movements at Kozhikode. Bhodhana took the initiative to form a co-ordination committee and hosted this conference. Almost three thousand women from all over India took part in the meeting that took place at Kozhikode Devagiri St. Joseph's college ground. It really was a grant success. But after that all the groups in Kerala lost its vigour. The same was the fate of Bhodhana too.

Later, in 1993 Anweshi Women's Counselling Centre was established. We began working from an office in 1995, where counselling was the main concern, though facilities were limited and for a while we had to struggle hard to remain afloat. But the U.N Population Fund grants that we received through the Central Government in 2000 did make things easier. Our activities widened to include legal aid cell, community work, legal literacy classes, awareness seminars, workshops, library, documentation centers and so on. After three years, once that grant was over, we received another from the Dorabji Trust in Mumbai. With this we were also able to open a short stay home for women and children who were victims of family violence.

Anweshi was a major factor in the Kerala Sthree Vedi, a forum of autonomous women's organizations in Kerala, formed in 1996. Sthree Vedi had dynamically pursued the Suryanelli case in which a prominent Congress leader, MP and former Union minister P.J. Kurien is alleged to be involved and also the infamous Ice Cream Parlour case, both of which were initially taken up by Anweshi. The political impact of these cases was much in display during the April-May Assembly elections of 2006. Muslim League's undisputed general secretary, former minister and the number two in the UDF government P K Kunjalikutty lost a seat which the League had never lost. Though the courts exonerated him, the people's court seemed to have punished him for his alleged involvement in the Ice Cream Parlour case.

Sthree Vedi was formed with the intention of upholding women's political rights at the state level and to organize agitations if need be and thus to bring women into mainstream politics. I was one of the founder members of Sthree Vedi.

Even while I am totally involved with Sthree Vedi and Anweshi, I do take part in all issues that affect people. The Muthanga revolt under the leadership of Gothramaha Sabha, the protests against the Coca-Cola company in Plachimada, struggles against the so-called mega developmental programs which are actually mired in corruption like the Express Highway, Smart City and of course, movements against the exploitation and oppression of tribals in Attappadi... I had the opportunity to participate in all these people's agitations, contributing in my own small way to usher in a new better world without gender, social or economic exploitation and discrimination.

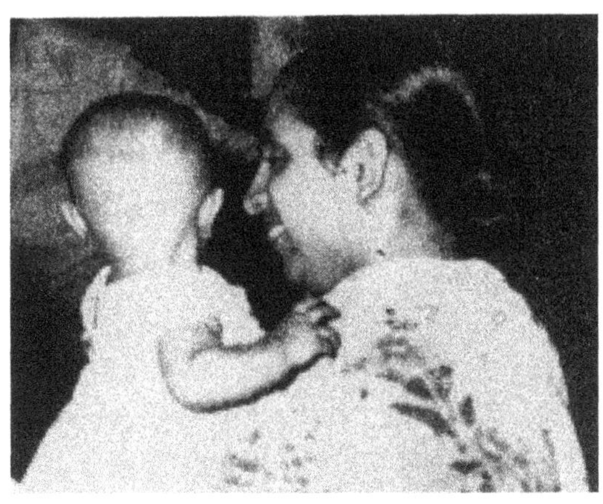

The firebrand revolutionary turns a doting mother; with Gargi

From a Maoist to a feminist — Ajitha now heads 'Anweshi', an NGO working for oppressed women.

www.ingramcontent.com/pod-product-compliance
Ingram Content Group UK Ltd.
Pitfield, Milton Keynes, MK11 3LW, UK
UKHW021706190726
13853UKWH00001B/449

9 788188 575633